Romantic Cities Series

ROMANTIC

DAYS AND NIGHTS™ IN

SAN FRANCISCO

INTIMATE ESCAPES IN THE CITY BY THE BAY

Second Edition

by Donna Peck

The
Globe
Pequot
Press

OLD SAYBROOK, CONNECTICUT

Romantic Days and Nights is a trademark of The Globe Pequot Press
Cover design, text design, and illustrations by Mullen & Katz
Cover photo copyright © Michael J. Howell/New England Stock Photo

The quote on page 49 is from *Heart Beat: My Life with Jack and Neal,* by Carolyn Cassady. Copyright © by Carolyn Cassady. Reprinted with permission of Creative Arts Book Company.

Library of Congress Cataloging-in-Publication Data

Peck, Donna.
    Romantic days and nights in San Francisco : intimate escapes in the city by the bay /
        by Donna Peck.—2nd ed.
        p.   cm. — (Romantic cities series)
    Includes indexes.
    ISBN 0-7627-0290-7
    1. San Francisco (Calif.)—Guidebooks.   2. San Francisco Bay Area (Calif.)—Guidebooks.
  I. Title. II. Series.
  F869.S33P43   1998
  917.94'610453—dc21   98-29740
                            CIP

Manufactured in the United States of America
Second Edition/First Printing

This book is dedicated with love and gratitude
to Noelle Peck-Daly, Michael Daly, and my parents Ralph and Alberta.

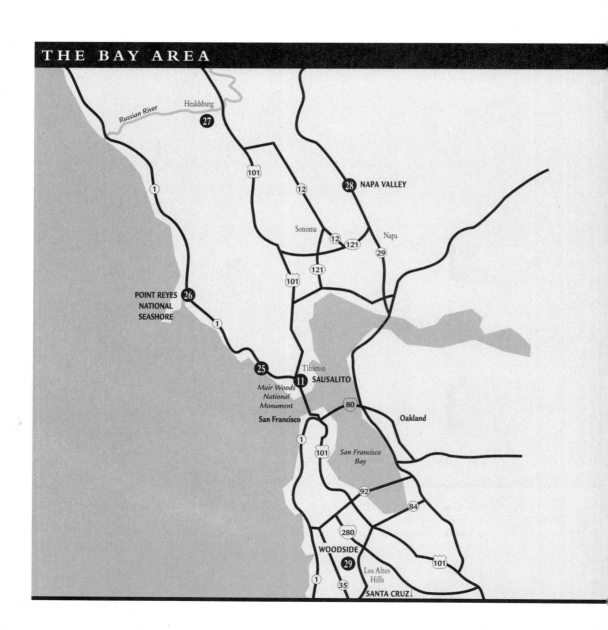

DOWNTOWN SAN FRANCISCO

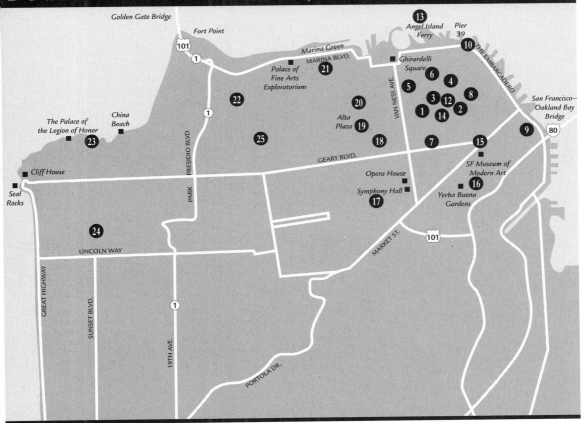

Golden Gate Bridge

Fort Point

101

1

Marina Green

MARINA BLVD.

Palace of
Fine Arts
Exploratorium

21

22

The Palace of
the Legion of Honor

China
Beach

23

Cliff House

Seal
Rocks

1

Angel Island
Ferry

13

Pier
39

10

Ghirardelli
Square

THE EMBARCADERO

San Francisco–
Oakland Bay
Bridge

VAN NESS AVE.

5

6

4

3

12

8

1

14

2

Alta
Plaza

20

19

7

9

80

18

25

GEARY BLVD.

15

SF Museum of
Modern Art

PRESIDIO BLVD.

16

Opera House

Symphony Hall

Yerba Buena
Gardens

PARK

17

24

LINCOLN WAY

101

MARKET ST.

GREAT HIGHWAY

SUNSET BLVD.

19TH AVE.

1

PORTOLA DR.

1. Nob Hill
2. The Financial District
3. Chinatown
4. Telegraph Hill
5. Russian Hill
6. North Beach
7. Union Square

8. Jackson Square
9. Cityfront District
10. Northern Waterfront
11. Sausalito Waterfront
12. Paris of the West
13. On San Francisco Bay
14. An Aerial Fantasy

15. Historic Market
    Street
16. South of Market
17. Hayes Valley
18. Japantown
19. Upper Fillmore
20. Pacific Heights

21. The Marina
22. The Presidio
23. Golden Gate Bridge
    to Ocean Beach
24. Golden Gate Park
25. Tamalpais to
    Muir Woods

26. Point Reyes National
    Seashore
27. Russian River
28. Napa Valley
29. Santa Cruz
    Mountains

CONTENTS

[*Contents*]

ACKNOWLEDGMENTS

Thanks to Jeff Nead, Helen Chung, Diane Shields, Louise Hanford, Sam Folsom, Samara Zuwaylif, Stan Schilz, Bob Licht, Christine Berlin, Doe Boyle, Landry Kimbrough, Eleanor Bertino, Pam Hunter, Angela Jackson, Marsha Monro, Meridith Post, Ann Byington, Catherine Boire, Sandie Wernick, and Laura Strom.

*D*ylan Thomas wrote to his wife, "You wouldn't think that such a place as San Francisco could exist. The wonderful sunlight there, the hills, the great bridges, the Pacific at your shoes. Beautiful Chinatown. Every race in the world."

You can trust what you've heard about San Francisco. It's a sensory experience on par with none. And not only poets and songwriters take note.

Many people have passed through the Golden Gate and gotten hooked. Gold seekers abandoned ship and camped on the hills around Yerba Buena Cove. World War II soldiers found partners at USO dances and kept the Venetian Room swinging past midnight. Hippies wore flowers and patchouli oil during the Summer of Love in Golden Gate Park.

Some of their stories are inscribed in the cityscape: in Mission Dolores cemetery, in the freesia-lined promontory above Seal Rocks, in the salons of Pacific Heights mansions. Others left their tales in books. Writers from Robert Louis Stevenson to Jack London to Dylan Thomas scaled Mount Tamalpais at dawn to kiss melon sunrises. And at noon they unfurled sails to ride the wind across San Francisco Bay.

As you get ready to follow in their footsteps, keep in mind these notes and suggestions. Always request an early check-in. It's a lot more convenient to check in at 9:00 A.M. than at 3:00 P.M. Ask for special packages, seasonal rates, and the romantic getaway rate. Discount rates are subject to availability and are offered at various times throughout the year. Downtown hotels discount rooms as much as 30 percent on weekends, while hotels outside the city lower prices in winter. The Huntington Hotel, for example, offers a luxury room for $198 per couple, per night throughout the year for rooms that normally cost $240. Madrona Manor in Healdsburg, on the other hand, offers its antique-filled rooms at half-price from January through March.

Once you arrive, most of the activities included in each itinerary are within walking distance of your hotel. The most unromantic thing you can do in San Francisco is look for a parking space. Museums and stores open at 9:00 or 10:00 A.M. and close at 5:00 or 6:00 P.M. Museums charge a nominal admission of $7.

The price ranges quoted for dining out are per person, including one drink, tax, and tip. Expensive means $80 per person. Moderate is $50. Inexpensive is $30 (35 percent less for lunch). This does not include extra charges added in for dancing, entertainment, or a cruise on the bay.

Consider this guidebook an invitation to unfetter your romantic soul. You are holding not a catalog of information but a miniature of the city encased in a prism. Strike it with a beam of light and the city refracts into dozens of romantic adventures. Some itineraries are elegant on-the-town celebrations, others fulfill a long-time fantasy. Following twenty-four city itineraries are five countryside itineraries. You'll recognize the perfect match for you and your lover. Do you fancy yourselves connoisseurs of European pleasures? Of the avant-garde scene? Do you thirst for fresh air and exercise? Do you seek serenity and escape from frenetic schedules? Whichever itinerary you choose, it will pluck you out of everyday life and set you down in a city synonymous with romance. With someone special by your side, your days and nights become an intimate adventure. Count yourselves among the romantics, adventurers, and dreamers who claim the city as their own.

Ten Romantic Things to Do in and around San Francisco

1. Enjoy a picnic at one of Angel Island's secluded beaches.

2. Attend opening night at the opera.

3. Cruise through Raccoon Straits on a moonlit night.

4. View a springtime sunset from the summit of Mount Tamalpais.

5. Ride the ferry to Sausalito and check into the Inn Above Tide.

6. Feast at Fleur de Lys under a canopy of Provencal fabric.

7. Wander through Muir Woods on a foggy morning.

8. Survey the city from cloud nine while seated in the Carnelian Room, one of the city's famous skyroom cocktail lounges.

9. Ride the California Street cable car "halfway to the stars."

10. After nightfall, rendezvous in the back seat of a limousine on a tour of the Golden Gate Bridge and other romantic viewpoints.

The prices and rates listed in this guidebook were confirmed at press time. We recommend, however, that you call establishments before traveling to obtain the most current information.

HEART OF THE CITY

ITINERARY 1
Two days and one night

THE COUPLE WHO LIVED HIGH
NOB HILL

*S*ince the gold rush era, the hill bound by California, Sacramento, Jones, and Mason Streets has been a fashionable residential district for wealthy citizens. Who else but millionaires could hire servants to haul groceries and supplies up the hills? With the advent of the cable car in 1873, nineteenth-century railroad and silver barons claimed this small summit as their own. Resplendent residential palaces cropped up on every corner. Nob Hill is San Francisco's elite, old-money enclave, over which the millionaires and their wives presided until the 1906 earthquake reduced the great mansions to smoking ruins.

The current neighborhood is populated by the twentieth-century successors of the wealthy "nabobs" of Nob Hill. Today's nabobs live in elite apartment buildings and luxury condos. They walk their dogs in Huntington Park, and many attend services at Grace Cathedral. Because of its exclusive hotels, the elegant area also draws couples with a special occasion to celebrate. In this itenerary you stroll hand in hand around Nob Hill, exploring its parks, its cathedral, and the grand lobbies, dining rooms, and cocktail lounges of four hotels.

Practical Notes: Headliners often appear at the stately **Nob Hill Masonic Auditorium** (1111 California Street at Taylor; 415–776–4702), which greets patrons with a marble facade, tall pillars, and two-story stained glass history of Masonry. Tickets (510–762–BASS) are available to enjoy diverse entertainment that in the past has included poet Maya Angelou, sitarist Ravi Shankar, comic Steven Wright, and Celtic singer Loreena McKennitt. For innovative entertainment don't overlook **Grace Cathedral** (call for concert tickets at 415–749–6350). Ask for a schedule of events. Recently Anne-Lise Bernsten of Norway sang cuts from her best-selling CD *Engleskyts* (songs from Angels); and the London Brass performed Mozart's Coronation Mass. Organist John Fenstermaker plays the cathedral's 7,400-pipe organ to accompany the screening of silent movies. The Grace Cathedral Christmas concerts are the best-attended holiday performances in the city.

Romance at a Glance

♥ *Stay in a Jacuzzi suite at the Mark Hopkins Inter-Continental (415–392–3434 or 800–327–0200).*

♥ *Dine at the Big Four Restaurant inside the Huntington Hotel (415–474–5400).*

♥ *Ride the California Street cable car and visit the Cable Car Barn and Museum.*

♥ *Hear show tunes in the New Orleans Room at the Fairmont Hotel.*

♥ *Tour Grace Cathedral, a soaring Gothic masterpiece.*

DAY ONE: AFTERNOON

For a day and a night, live like nabobs atop Nob Hill. Check into the **Mark Hopkins Inter-Continental** (1 Nob Hill, California Street and Mason; 415–392–3434 or 800–327–0200; $200–$750). The Jacuzzi suite number 1609 has a terrace facing north and a glass-enclosed solarium furnished in white wicker. If you are going to splurge, why not do so on a hotel right at the crest? That's what Mary Hopkins thought when she built her home on this site. Mary had free rein in the mansion's design, while her husband, Central Pacific Railroad founder Mark Hopkins, lived in a simple cottage on Sutter Street. He tended his vegetable garden, occasionally raising a disapproving eye to what his wife was erecting uphill. By the time Robert Louis Stevenson visited this "hill of palaces" in 1882, Mark Hopkins's widow was residing on this site in a forty-room Gothic Victorian mansion.

True to the "romantic period," as the first quarter of the twentieth century was known, the hotel's elaborate terra-cotta facade evokes the style of French Chateau and Spanish Renaissance. Photos of the lobby, Peacock Court, and Room of the Dons helped designers return the hotel to its original look.

In the twenties, thirties, and forties, **Peacock Court** hosted top dance bands such as Benny Goodman, Tommy Dorsey, Glenn Miller, and supper club entertainers like Betty Grable and Dorothy Lamour. Compare that to the images of conquistadors and Indians, trappers and traders in the **Room of the Dons,** which holds a treasure of nine luminous panels painted by California artists Frank Van Sloun (former teacher at the Mark Hopkins Institute of Art) and Maynard Dixon. The rich medley of blue, turquoise, melon, and persimmon paints is on a background of gold leaf. Find the panel of Calafia. The allegorical virgin queen of an Amazon tribe, she symbolizes an untamed and bountiful California before European settlement.

DAY ONE: EVENING

The cable car bell clangs the signal for "all aboard," so you slip into a seat. Since 1926 the cable car has been stopping at the Mark Hopkins's front door. The underground cable clickety-clacks at a steady 9½ miles per hour. The grip man latches onto the running cable and hitches a ride downhill. To stop, he releases the grip from the cable and sets the brake. Get off at the **Ritz-Carlton Hotel** (600 Stockton Street at California; 415–296–7465). The plush chairs, crystal chandeliers, high coffered ceiling, rich marble, and wood paneling make the Ritz-Carlton Lobby Lounge the most civilized cocktail lounge in the city, perhaps the universe. What are you in the mood for? Happy-hour hors d'oeuvres include a sushi bar and a caviar bar. The dessert cart, laden with fruit tarts, truffles, and fresh strawberries, is positioned at the entrance beneath a flower-filled urn. Sink into a high-backed chair, watch the light-and-shadow dance of the fireplace, listen to a piano or the soft voice of a soloist. Remy Martin Luis XIII cognac is offered at $95 a glass for those with deep pockets.

Dinner

Step aboard a cable car and ascend the summit of Nob Hill for dinner at the **Big Four Restaurant** (Huntington Hotel, 1075 California Street at Taylor; 415–474–5400; expensive). Go through the lobby of the hotel, which is hung in red and gold damask with a carved Italian table holding an arrangement of lilies and roses. Constructed in 1924 as a luxury apartment building, the hotel has been under the stewardship of three generations of the Copes family, who also collect art. Two masterpieces hang in the lobby. In Charles Austin Needham's *Union Square at Early Candlelight*, figures scurry through Union Square on a foggy, drizzly night. In another alcove a sunset washes the flanks and valley of *Yosemite* by J. E. Stuart.

The Big Four restaurant has an Edward Muybridge panoramic photograph that includes Nob Hill. In the photograph, you can't miss the spite fence Charles Crocker put up. He erected a three-story fence around a small house belonging to a long-time resident, a retired city caretaker who ignored Crocker's attempts to oust him. Unable to have the block to himself, Crocker got even by building the fence. The block now belongs to Grace Cathedral.

The Big Four perpetuates 1880s restaurant decor with rich oak paneling, high-backed leather banquettes, ram-horn wall sconces, a polished copper bar, and railroad memorabilia. One of the city's preeminent restaurants, the Big Four offers attentive service and creative cuisine. You may start with smoked salmon and Nantucket scallops, smoked in applewood, with a potato-scallion puff and spicy mustard sauce; or Dungeness crab cake with red pepper rouille. Entrees include rack of lamb with green mango–fig chutney and zinfandel sauce; and Silver Oaks organic ostrich steak in a chive crust with Portobello pot pie and port sauce. Also recommended is the tea-smoked duck breast with sesame-ginger glaze, shrimp wontons, jasmine rice and roasted shiitake mushrooms. Entrees range from $18 to $28.

❧❧❧

End the meal with dessert and after-dinner drinks in the nineteenth-century bar, warmed by a glowing fire and the show tunes of pianist Michael Parsons. The Big Four lounge evokes

the city's glory days, from the gold rush to the heyday of the railroad barons in whose honor it is named. Sit beside a crackling fire, brandy glasses in hand, and contemplate the lives and times of four Sacramento merchants and prominent railroad men: Leland Stanford, Charles Crocker, Mark Hopkins, and Collis P. Huntington.

After dinner, cross the street to **Huntington Park** at the heart of the hill. Created by Collis Huntington's heirs, the park has a central fountain that is a replica of Rome's sixteenth-century Tartarughe Fountain. If you decide to play chase around the sea-cherub fountain and kick your heels back on high-flying swings, don't be embarrassed. Others before you have raced to see who can swing to the Big Dipper.

You'll have to come back to earth to see the stars at the **New Orleans Room** (Fairmont Hotel, 950 Mason Street; 415–772–5259). Squeeze into a booth at the city's most intimate club. If jazz piano and show tunes don't suit you, perhaps a concert at **Grace Cathedral** will. This is the city's consummate accoustical space for Renaissance brass, sacred, and classical music. By midnight, your Jacuzzi suite will be calling you back. Not long ago, a couple had reserved a Jacuzzi suite to celebrate a special occasion. At the gentleman's request, the concierge filled the tub and floated gardenias as an after-dinner surprise.

DAY TWO: MORNING

Breakfast

Wake up to the pealing of Grace Cathedral's carillon. Put on your terry-cloth bathrobes and go out onto the terrace for a morning stretch. Have breakfast at the **Ritz-Carlton Terrace** (Ritz-Carlton Hotel, 600 Stockton Street at California; 415–296–7465; moderate). Considered by many San Franciscans to be the city's best Sunday brunch, the Terrace serves an excellent American breakfast other mornings. Having a leisurely breakfast in the courtyard is the thing to do on a fine sunny morning with the roses blooming, the fountain singing, and doves cooing. You can linger over French toast, eggs Benedict, or lobster and eggs. menu items range from $10 to $16. Continental buffet is $19 per person and Sunday brunch is $42 per person.

ತಿಂಧಿ

The Cable Car Museum is nearby. Walk down Taylor Street and turn right at Washington. At the **Cable Car Museum, Barn & Powerhouse** (1201 Mason Street at Washington; 415–474–1887; open daily), you watch the wheel that pulls the little cars halfway to the stars. The Cable Car Barn, a three-tiered 1907 red brick barn, is the control center for today's fleet. More than a decade ago, a $60 million overhaul included new tracks, cables, turntables, and winding gear. Overhaul notwithstanding, cable cars operate today in much the same way they did when Andrew Hallidie guided the first car down steep Clay Street in 1873. In the glass-enclosed room, you observe the huge sheaves of cable that guide the cars from under the street. Among the collection of cable cars is an 1873 car with a metal roof.

DAY TWO: AFTERNOON

On the return walk go through the park to **Grace Cathedral** (1100 California at Taylor; 415–749–6330) to view the soaring nave and roseate stained glass window.

To appreciate one of the finest examples of Gothic architecture in the United States and the country's third-largest Episcopal cathedral, take a tour from 1:00 to 3:00 P.M. A virtual gallery of

The northwest window of the Top of the Mark is called "weepers corner." During World War II teary-eyed women gathered by the window to watch their GI boyfriends sail under the Golden Gate Bridge.

religious art, this neoclassical cathedral took fifty-three years to complete, opening in 1964. The doors at the east entrance are replicas of the Ghiberti originals in the Florence Baptistry.

Walk down California Street, passing the Pacific Union Club, a private men's club (1000 California Street at Mason) and the only Nob Hill residence to survive the 1906 quake and fire. This baroque Italianate brownstone was built in 1886 at a cost of $1.5 million for tycoon James C. Flood, who, like James Fair, made his fortune in the silver mines.

The decor of the **Fairmont Hotel** (950 Mason Street at California; 415–772–5000) recalls the glory days of Nevada silver baron James G. "Bonanza Jim" Fair. He started building the hotel in 1902, but it was destroyed by the 1906 earthquake before completion. You walk into a lobby of marble columns, rococo friezes, gilt-edge mirrors, dark wood paneling and coffered ceilings, and plush carpets. Opened in 1907, the hotel has hosted several presidents and foreign leaders, and the penthouse was the site of the drafting of the United Nations charter in 1945. For the occasion, Maude Flood—the daughter of James C. Flood and a long-time hotel resident—was persuaded to move out temporarily. She had pledged the only way she would leave the penthouse would be "feet first." She kept her promise. The most expensive hotel suite in the United States, the penthouse, which became available for rent after Maude's death has appeared in fifty films—from Alfred Hitchcock's 1957 classic *Vertigo* to the 1996 *The Rock* with

Sean Connery and Nicholas Cage. After touring the lobby and roof garden you can drop onto a plush banquette in the lobby and order **afternoon tea**.

Stop by the **Top of the Mark** for a farewell cocktail. The Top of the Mark, on the nineteenth floor of the Mark Hopkins Hotel, is the city's oldest skyroom, dating from 1939. Soon after its opening, lovers discovered the spot as a fine viewpoint for enjoying the fading light of sunset. It became a tradition for GIs to spend their last evening of liberty here with their sweethearts before shipping out. When they came back, the bartender reached under the bar for the "squadron bottle." Once the serviceman signed his name on the label, he could drink from the bottle for free. Whoever took the last drink replaced the bottle.

FOR MORE ROMANCE

To whet the appetite for Nob Hill–style dining, stroll the quaint side streets and charming alleyways of Leavenworth and Sacramento on the way to dinner. You'll be rewarded with the fresh evening air and distant views of bay, skyline, and hills at intersections. Walk down California Street, passing Grace Cathedral, to Leavenworth. Walk north or right on Leavenworth and turn left onto Acorn Alley, one of San Francisco's most colorful, verdant alleys. The green walkway invites you to view the raised beds of flowers tended many years by residents.

Start wandering over to the intersection of Jones and Clay Streets. At **Charles Nob Hill** (1250) Jones Street at Clay; 415–771–5400; expensive) you are seated in a private dining room and attended by a phalanx of tuxedoed waiters. Chefs Michael Mina and Ron Siegel, formerly of Yountville's French Laundry, have created remarkable dishes. If price is no object, splurge on the sample tasting menu, which may include puree of wild mushroom soup with scallops, roasted lobster with potato ravioli, chilled pear soup and warm bittersweet chocolate torte with ice cream. The tasting menu costs $65 per person (prix fixe dinners $45; entrees range from $22 to $28).

ROMANCE FOR MODERN TIMES

THE FINANCIAL DISTRICT

If heights make you woozy, read no further. Even the food in the financial district can be dramatically vertical. But for those couples moved by urban vistas, this itinerary is a match made in heaven. Back in the early sixties, real estate developers scoffed at San Francisco's provincial skyline and pushed to make it more like that of Manhattan. When Ben Swig said, "You've got to live modern; you've got to think big to be big," people listened. Raised twice as an instant city, once in 1849 during the gold rush and again in 1906 after the earthquake, the financial district has emerged as a modern metropolis.

In the 1980s, city planners got after architects for making the skyline blocklike and boring. Since then, asymmetrical setbacks and whimsical, sometimes comical touches enhance office tower summits. Don't bother craning your neck looking for them. For a rotating, sky-high view of some of the most interesting examples of city architecture, visit the Exinox at the Hyatt Regency. Back on ground level, you'll also be delighted by the museums tucked away in banks and scores of vest-pocket parks and urban oases meticulously maintained for public enjoyment. Architecture, the key word in this itinerary, applies to food as well. At Vertigo, home of towering lobster salad, the food fits right in with the neighborhood.

Practical Notes: Since most museums and some rooftop parks require bank access, you cannot visit outside banking hours. Even the gate to the redwood grove adjacent to the Transamerica Pyramid locks at 5:00 P.M. On Friday, though, most banks are open until 6:00 P.M. The Park Hyatt also has early check-ins on Friday. Don't plan to shop on Sunday morning. Embarcadero Center shops open at noon on Sunday. Other days they open at 10:00 A.M. The SkyDeck is open 12:30 P.M. to 9:00 P.M. except in summer, when it opens at 9:00 A.M. or 10:00 A.M. The financial district is bounded by the Embarcadero and Market Street, Kearny and Washington Streets. The main thoroughfare, once a muddy shore, is now the Montgomery Street canyon of concrete, glass, and granite. Skidmore, Owings & Merrill is credited with many high-rises built from 1959 to 1990, including the First Interstate Center, 353 Sacramento Street, Bank of Canton, and 505 Montgomery Street.

Romance at a Glance

♥ *Stay at Park Hyatt (415–392–1234 or 800–233–1234).*

♥ *Enjoy cocktails at the Carnelian Room (Bank of America, 415–433–7500).*

♥ *Dine at Vertigo (415–433–7250) in the base of the Transamerica Pyramid.*

♥ *Visit the SkyDeck, One Embarcadero Center (1EC, street level, 415–772–0585 or 888–737–5933).*

♥ *Shop at Embarcadero Center's 125 shops.*

♥ *View the finest examples of twentieth century urban architecture.*

DAY ONE: AFTERNOON

Check into one of the most sophisticated places to stay in the city. At 360 rooms, the **Park Hyatt** (333 Battery Street at Clay, 415–392–1234, or 800–233–1234; $169–$250), is more intimate than its behemoth cousin, the Hyatt Regency, at the opposite end of Embarcadero Center. If you opt for afternoon tea and caviar in the lobby lounge, you are surrounded by rich lacewood paneling and polished granite. Sophisticated, neoclassical in decor and tone, the rooms at the Park Hyatt all have views. You can relax in a club chair in the formal library over a chess game or with the Hong Kong daily *South China Morning Post*. A Mercedes awaits to shuttle you through the downtown area. In a word, this is the perfect private club for financial district aficionados.

The better part of the day includes a tour of the city's most fascinating architecture. Begin next door the Park Hyatt at **Old Federal Reserve Bank** (400 Sansome Street at Sacramento), now part of the Embarcadero Center complex. Sierra-white marble covers three sides of this 1924 building, which has been renovated for law offices and retail space. The interior features both real and hand-painted faux marble. By crossing Sansome Street you can see the eight eagles perched above its entrance. Walk toward Market Street. **Bank of California** (400 California Street at Sansome; 415-765-0400) is a Corinthian temple where the devout concern themselves with matters of money. Built in 1908, the banking hall has a soaring 50-foot high ceiling. Downstairs is the Museum of Money of the American West, tracing the financial rise of San Francisco. In the early days of the gold rush, the city had no money. A pinch of gold substituted for a dollar, and a dollar's length of gold wire, divided into eight parts, served as smaller coins, referred to as two bits, four bits and so on. Then bankers converted the miners' raw gold dust to gold ingots stamped with their value. A ledger page lists the largest nugget as weighing 195 pounds, a solid mass of native gold.

Royal Globe Insurance Building (201 Sansome Street at Pine) is a 1909 white marble building with an ornate British crest bearing the unicorn and lion flanking a clock. **Pacific Coast Stock Exchange** (301 Pine Street at Sansome) is a 1930 building that combines classical columns and 21-foot-tall Art Deco statues of a family group by Ralph Stackpole. At **235 Pine Street** (between Sansome and Battery) is a twenty-five-story limestone-clad high-rise designed by Skidmore, Owings & Merrill in 1990. Look above the entrance at the bronze bas-relief, *Called to Rise*, of Juan Bautista de Anza, Phoebe Apperson Hearst, A. P. Giannini, and Timothy Pflueger. A legend on the right identifies their contributions to the city.

The marble conservatory of the **Citicorp Center** (1 Sansome Street) sports the country flags of the United Nations' charter members beneath its skylights. Cafe tables amid fountains and trees make this an ideal resting spot. You can order light refreshments from the Conservatory

Café at one end of the plaza. The Star Girl figure in the corner dates from the 1915 Panama-Pacific Exposition.

Walk down Market Street toward the Ferry Building, and you'll see **101 California** (between Front and Davis), an eye-catching addition to the skyline. Clouds, blue sky, and sunsets are reflected on its circular glass surface. Walk left at Davis Street to the California Street plaza. Noontime entertainment draws office workers to the spillover fountain with tiers of comfortable cushions. Join them if a concert is taking place.

Walk up two blocks to Montgomery Street (passing Battery and Sansome), the grandest concrete canyon in the metropolis. Office towers soar together to make a skyline many consider America's most romantic. Viewed from the street, these buildings possess interesting features. The 1927 **Russ Building** (235 Montgomery Street) fills the entire block between Pine and Bush, an exceptional skyscraper in its day and the first to incorporate a parking facility within its structure. Inspired by Eli Saarinen's Chicago Tribune Tower, it remained the tallest in the city until 1964. **Mills Building & Tower** (220 Montgomery Street at Bush) is modeled after the Chicago School of Architecture's winning design. This ten-story edifice was the earliest steel-frame building in San Francisco. Built in 1892, it suffered only interior damage in the 1906 fire. Visitors are invited to view the lobby exhibits.

The **Hunter-Dulin Building** (111 Sutter Street at Montgomery) was built in 1926 by the same architects as New York's Waldorf-Astoria Hotel and the Biltmore in Los Angeles, a blend of Romanesque and French-Chateau. Its setback is crowned by a copper-crested, red-tile mansard roof. To get a better view, slip into the Wells Fargo Bank lobby (Montgomery and Post Streets) and take the elevator to the roof garden (press *R*). Beautifully landscaped, this garden allows closer appreciation of the chateau-style Hunter-Dulin Building. Look at the "skin" of more modern buildings designed to mirror blue skies and roiling white clouds often streaked with pink at this hour. Seek out the alcove with the metal sphere whose arrow points east. I followed it with my eyes one March afternoon and saw the faint outline of a three-quarter moon.

DAY ONE: EARLY EVENING

Wander the streets until 5:00 P.M., when building doors open and it seems all humanity has taken to the streets. Escape to the city's second-tallest building, the **Bank of America Headquarters** (Carnelian Room, 555 California Street; 415–433–7500) and pause at the California Street plaza. Locals nicknamed the lump of black marble in the courtyard "the banker's heart." Clad in dark-red carnelian marble, 724 feet high, at midday the building evokes the rugged Sierra Nevada. At dusk the setting sun burns in its windows like a towering inferno. Look across the street at the statues encircling 580 California Street. Poised on the rim of a glass mansard roof, twelve goddesses turn blank faces to the outside world. In local lore, the statues represent the mayor and the eleven supervisors who run the city. Press the high-speed elevator button for the Carnelian Room. The cocktail lounge boasts unobstructed bay views of Mount Tamalpais, the Golden Gate Bridge and points north. Grab a table in one of the notched corners and you'll feel as though you're in the cockpit of a plane. Order a martini with Skyy vodka. With cocktail in hand, survey the world from up above.

DAY ONE: EVENING

Dinner

Why would anyone want to name a restaurant after a Hitchcock film? Does dining at **Vertigo** (600 Montgomery Street at Clay and Washington; 415–433–7250; expensive) cause the sensation of whirling or falling? Perhaps being at the base of the Transamerica Pyramid with seating beneath its massive supports goes along with the name. Or perhaps the food induces dizziness or lightheadedness. Order the towering lobster salad and see what I mean. San Francisco, ever the trendsetter, will do anything to keep diners entertained.

Ask to sit overlooking the urban redwood grove. Look up through copper-mesh covered skylights for vertigo-inspiring views of the 853-foot pyramid, the city's tallest structure.

Although highly stylized, Vertigo's food brings contemporary French/New York cooking to California ingredients. The kitchen uses the freshest ingredients grown organically on small nearby farms. On the menu is grilled tuna with Sicilian caponata, polenta and roasted pepper sauce, and roast poussin. The favorite among the financial district crowd are the sweet potato fries, piled high, of course. Entrees range from $20 to $27.

If you have time before the show at Punch Line, stop at the glamorous Art Deco watering hole, **Bix** (56 Gold Street off Montgomery; 415–433–6300). You'll hear live jazz and taste one of the best martinis in town. Retrace your steps to join the comedy fans at the Punch Line. They don't have to push hard for laughs at **Punch Line** (444 Battery Street between Clay and Washington; 415–397–7573); it's as slick and urbane as any Manhattan venue. Seating is on a first-come basis, with two shows on weekends at 9:00 P.M. and 11:00 P.M. Call 510–762–BASS or Punch Line from 2:00 P.M. to 6:00 P.M. to reserve tickets. After the show, stroll the elevated walkways of the Embarcadero Center back to your hotel.

DAY TWO: MORNING

Your hotel is part of the largest shopping maze in the city. The circular brick walkway between the Park Hyatt and the Old Federal Reserve Bank marks the beginning of the **Embarcadero Center**. You'll be delighted by the 125 stores across the street. Stop by the front desk and pick up a map and shop directory of the Embarcadero Center, an 8-block area bounded by Sansome Street and Drumm, Sacramento and Clay. For general information call 415–772–0585; for the event hot line call 800–733–6318.

The Hyatt Regency's glass elevators and soaring atrium make it an attractive place for breakfast. **The Eclipse Cafe** (415–788–1234; moderate: buffet $15) serves California and continental breakfast in the hotel's seventeen-story glass-topped atrium lobby. Or you can help yourself to the California-style buffet, which offers fruit, yogurt, crepes, cereal, eggs, bacon, sausage, muffins, croissants, and pastries. Justin Herman Plaza also has several bakery cafes if you want to eat outdoors. **Boudin Sourdough Bakery & Cafe, Café Latté,** and **Java City Bakery Café** are adjacent to the outdoor patio.

Spend the next few hours exploring the shops on three levels of Embarcadero One (1EC), Two (2EC), Three (3EC), and Four (4EC). The buildings are connected by pedestrian bridges and walkways. Three levels from street (s) to lobby (l) to promenade (p) are linked by spiral walkways, stairs, and escalators. As you traverse the levels and buildings, keep an eye out for stainless steel sculpture. One looks like a whirlybird. You also come across quality apparel shops such as **Ann Taylor** (3EC/s), **Georgiou** (3EC/s), **Liz Claiborne** (4EC/s&l), and specialty gifts stores such as **The ParkStore** (1EC/s), **earthsake** (1EC/s), **Camelot Music** (2EC/s), **B. Dalton Bookseller** (1EC/l), and **Williams-Sonoma** (2EC/s). **Embarcadero Center Cinema** (1EC/p), shows intelligent, specialized independent films and boasts, "you'll probably never see two films from the same country at the same time." At street level at One Embarcadero Center is the SkyDeck ticket booth (888–737–5933; $6.00). The city's only indoor/outdoor observation deck offers spectacular views and interactive history exhibits on the 41st floor. They celebrate the full moon spring and summer with a jazz concert on Thursday evenings at no extra charge.

Lunch

Leaving the Embarcadero Center, cross the promenade level pedestrian bridge to **Park Grill** (in the Park Hyatt, third floor; 415–392–1234; moderate) that spans Battery Street. If the day is sunny, sit in the outdoor terrace or slip into an intimate booth, spaced for privacy. The Park Grill has the kind of soothing atmosphere that contrasts with the bustling Embarcadero Center. Soups are good, especially the sweet corn and Dungeness crab soup. Porcini crusted sea bass, a house specialty, is served with truffle-roasted yellow finn potatoes and sugar pea greens. Meal-size sandwiches are also served. Try the roasted prime rib on marble rye with horseradish cream and sauteed onions. Save room to savor pastry chef Robert Cheong's confectionery feats. He makes a prize-winning gingerbread mansion every Christmas. Try a pumpkin tart or chocolate cup filled with raspberry sorbet. Have coffee and dessert in the library and match wits at a game of chess (ask at reception for the chess pieces).

ITINERARY 3
Two days and one night

A Mandarin's Pleasures
Chinatown and Beyond

A teeming, colorful city within a city, Chinatown serves up a feast for the senses. Stone beasts roar silently at the Chinatown gateway at Grant Avenue and Bush Street. Pagoda-shaped roofs, painted balconies, and lampposts entwined with dragons create a festive atmosphere. When dim sum carts start rolling out of kitchen doors, that's your cue to sit down to a midday meal at one of the many Chinese restaurants. Elbow to elbow with boisterous Chinese families, you dine on a succession of unusual, succulent dishes.

Immerse yourselves in the exotic with abandon.

Practical Notes: You don't need the foresight of Confucius to choose an auspicious time to visit. Once a year, in celebration of the New Year, the lion tosses its mane and dances through the streets—usually January to mid-February. Consult Confucius's lunar calendar or call the Chinese Culture Center (415–986–1822) for the exact dates of the Chinese New Year Celebration and Parade. In September, the Viewing of the Moon Festival takes place. Friday is the best day of the week to start this itinerary. You can take advantage of the Mandarin's weekend rates and the small museums are open.

DAY ONE: MORNING

Leave bags and car at the **Mandarin Oriental Hotel** (222 Sansome Street between California and Pine; 415–885–0999 or 800–622–0404; $225–$520). Commercial Street, which is off Sansome Street, leads into Chinatown. Stop at the **Pacific Heritage Museum** (Bank of Canton Building, 608 Commercial Street; 415–399–1124; open weekdays). The old mint, which the Bank of Canton is built on top of and around, exhibits various artistic, cultural, economic, and other interchanges between those people on both sides of the Pacific Basin.

Romance at a Glance

♥ *View the Bay while soaking in a tub at the Mandarin Oriental Hotel (415–885–0999 or 800–622–0404).*

♥ *Roam the exotic alleys and side streets of Chinatown.*

♥ *Shop for Oriental treasures at Chinatown bazaars and at Gumps.*

♥ *Dine at Tommy Toy's for cuisine Chinoise (415–397–4888).*

♥ *View priceless Oriental artwork at the Asian Art Museum (415–668–7855).*

Lunch

"Tea time" in Chinatown, as in Hong Kong, begins early. Between 11:00 A.M. and 3:00 P.M. metal carts stream out of restaurant kitchens. The profusion of baskets, bowls, and plates emits a cornucopia of smells one associates with outdoor food stalls. Dim sum, which means "a little piece of the heart," is a late breakfast—it's also one meal not to miss.

Retrace your steps to Sansome Street. Follow Commercial Street one block to Battery Street then turn left. Dim sum at **Yank Sing** (427 Battery Street between Clay and Washington; 415–781–1111; moderate) is considered the best in San Francisco. Select plates from the small carts that stop at every table. The most popular dim sum are *cha sui bow* (steamed buns filled with barbecued pork), *ha gow* (delicate dumplings stuffed with shrimp), and *gee cheung fun* (steamed rice-noodle rolls). Bamboo steamer baskets likely contain wontons filled with meat or seafood.

Chinese characters for wontons mean "swallowing clouds." See if you think so, too. Don't pass up the custard tarts; they are a toothsome finish to the meal. **Golden Dragon** (816 Washington Street; 415–398–3920), **New Asia** (772 Pacific Avenue between Stockton and Grant; 415–391–6666), and **Canton Tea House** (1108 Stockton Street; 415–982–1032) also serve good dim sum.

DAY ONE: AFTERNOON

Clay Street leads up to Portsmouth Square into the heart of Chinatown. Chinese men gamble around benches in the lower park while grandmothers chat and children play in the upper park. Most of the three-story buildings in the neighborhood date from 1907. The Chinese rebuilt with lightning-like speed after the quake. The city had actually planned to relocate the community and claim this valuable real estate to expand the financial district.

Cross the pedestrian bridge to the **Chinese Culture Center** (Holiday Inn, third floor, 750 Kearny Street; 415–986–1822; closed Monday), which has exhibits on Chinese arts and culture and offers tours of Chinatown on Saturday at 2:00 P.M.

Stay in the alleys and old lanes of Chinatown. Waverly Place runs two blocks between Sacramento and Washington. Notice the brightly painted balconies and doorways in green, red, yellow, and orange. **Tien Hou Temple** (125 Waverly, fourth floor; 415–391–4841) is dedicated to Tien Hou, the Queen of Heaven and Goddess of the Seven Seas. It was erected in thanks for the safe arrival of Chinese immigrants in 1852. Ross Alley and Old Chinatown Lane are off Washington Street.

Golden Gate Fortune Cookie Factory (56 Ross Alley) has X-rated fortune cookies, but they're not very naughty. **Ching Chung Taoist Temple** (Lotus Garden, on the top floor of 532 Grant Avenue between Pine and California; 415–397–0707) is dominated by two portraits. One is the Jade Emperor, the reigning deity of Taoism. Next to him is the Emperor of the Eastern Mountain, who weighs merits and faults and assigns reward and punishment in this and future lives. Baskets of hand mirrors line a table. These are passed out at the appointed time during a Taoist ceremony, so people can look at themselves. Hundreds of joss sticks burn at personal shrines and atop gilded altars where people have placed fruit offerings. The stained-glass dome and carved furniture make this a pleasing albeit smoky sanctuary.

A bevy of Chinese ladies warmly welcomes you into the **Ten Ren Tea Shop** (949 Grant Avenue between Jackson and Washington; 415–362–0656). Taiwan-based Ten Ren is the world's largest tea company and offers an incredible selection of teas. You'll be surprised at what the Chinese palate considers a good cup of tea. Everything is sold here, from basic black or green tea to chrysanthemum, hibiscus, jasmine, oolong, strawberry-spice, chamomile, cinnamon-spiced, and assorted ginseng teas. If you're intrigued by the magic properties of the ginseng root, you have come to the number one authority. The Chinese consider ginseng a fountain of youth. Ask for a sample.

At the **Chinese Historical Society of America** (644 Broadway between Grant and Stockton; 415–391–1188; open Tuesday through Friday 10:00 A.M. to 4:00 P.M.) you can see photos and artifacts of old Chinatown and learn about Chinese gold fever in the exhibit, "Promise of Gold Mountain." Opium pipes and paraphernalia are on display. Gone are the opium dens that proliferated in the Barbary Coast days, but double-string firecrackers and the New Year's lion dance remain.

At the **Herbal Shop** (857 Washington at Spofford Alley between Grant and Stockton) you may inquire of the English-speaking herbalist about love potions. A three-tiered pagoda built in 1909 once housed Chinatown's phone operators. The **Old Chinese Telephone Exchange** (743 Washington Street near Grant Avenue) is now a branch of the Bank of Canton. Built by hand using an exotic variety of polished woods, **Buddha's Universal Church** (720 Washington Street at Kearny; 415–982–6116) is the largest Buddhist church in the United States. Call between 9:30 A.M. and 3:00 P.M. for an appointment so a guide will be there to greet you. A bodhi tree, grown from a slip of the one under which the Buddha is said to have found enlightenment more than 2,500 years ago, is in the roof garden beside the lotus pool. Notice the

beautiful mosaics of the Buddha and the bronze doors. Tours take place the second and fourth Sunday of every month.

Ancient mandarins often constructed resplendent strongholds atop cliffs. Modern-day mandarins would be at home in the aerial palace of the **Mandarin Oriental Hotel.** What a brilliant location for a hotel. The Mandarin Oriental moved into the top eleven floors of the twin-towered First Interstate Center, the city's third-tallest building. Glass skywalks connect the two hotel towers. Celebrate your arrival with a glass of champagne on the skywalk. You'll feel like you are on the wing of a plane. The hotel's guest rooms are bright, modern, and spacious with warm yellow, Asian chintz fabrics and Oriental-modern collages on the walls. Each guest is given a pair of Thai-silk slippers to take home.

You may want to linger in your room, or your tub, with a bottle of Cuvaison chardonnay or Codorniu sparkling wine. Mandarin rooms have tub-side picture windows overlooking the Transamerica Pyramid, Coit Tower, and the islands of the San Francisco bay. Every room offers aerial views. Afternoon fog moving in from the Pacific turns your room into a glorious viewing salon in which to watch the city disappear building by building into the dragon's white jaws. The night we watched the fog descend upon the Mandarin, it hit with such force the windows shook.

DAY ONE: EVENING

Dress for the high drama of **Tommy Toy's** Chinoise cuisine (655 Montgomery Street at Clay; 415–397–4888; expensive). Ask to sit on a banquette facing the room. The dining room brims with Chinese art and other trappings of affluence—among these are a museum-quality collection of rare paintings in sandalwood frames, lacquered carvings, and blue porcelains. "Forbidden stitch" embroidered silk from the Empress Dowager's boudoir was sold at auction and purchased by Tommy Toy to adorn the dining room walls. (These embroidered pieces were eventually "forbidden" or "outlawed" because their creation led to blindness among the women who did this fine embroidery work). Banquettes and chairs are covered in silk brocade, and tables are set with porcelain Chinese bridal lamps. This lavish dining room serves equally exquisite food. Dishes are Cantonese and Mandarin with French accents. Each course is served European-style and beautifully garnished. In the sampler feast, soup comes in coconut shells, while Peking lobster is arranged out of the shell. Trust your instincts when ordering. All dishes lead to adventure in the Forbidden City. Entrees range from $16 to $25; prix fixe $50.

◦◦◦◦

When you return to your hotel, if the fog is thick and lying low, the hotel elevator may zip you above the fog line. In that case, opening the door to your room is like entering the night sky.

DAY TWO: MORNING

Breakfast

Have buffet breakfast in the Mandarin lounge, helping yourselves to bagels, quiche, fresh fruit salad, and cereal.

After breakfast, take a taxi to Golden Gate Park, where the Asian Art Museum is located. In 1966 Avery Brundage donated 10,000 paintings, sculptures, ceramics, decorative objects, bronzes, jades, and textiles to create the **Asian Art Museum** (Music Concourse, near Eighth Avenue and

Ancient Love Potion

Herb shops proliferate around Washington Street and Jackson Street. Pause before an open door and inhale the smells that call to mind a primeval forest and centuries of humus. When you go inside you'll see mounds of herbs on white paper, bags of wood chips, bunches of dry grass, and shriveled roots. The herbalist may be filling a prescription, opening and closing small drawers, and tipping a scoop into tall apothecary jars. Many items in the Chinese drug store are used to make tonics to promote longevity and sexual vitality. The most effective tonic herbs are Chinese wolfberry, red Korean ginseng, and the potent horny goat weed.

Chinese Herbal Medicine records how horny goat weed was discovered. Once there was a goat herder in ancient China who noticed that sometimes his billygoats were especially sexually active. Curious, the goat herder observed their amorous behavior for a few weeks. He noticed that whenever they ate from a certain patch of weeds, it brought on this promiscuous behavior. The story was passed on, and before long Chinese herbalists discovered Epimedium sagittatum, one of the strongest herbs for male potency. A recipe for horny goat weed, "assorted hot pot," has been passed down and includes calf's liver, fish balls, soft bean curd, cabbage, spinach, spring onions, and, of course, horny goat weed.

Kennedy Drive; 415–379–8801; closed Monday and Tuesday; www.asianart.org). The world-famous collection represents all of Asia, but the first floor is devoted to China. The prize of the collection is a Buddha image from the year 338. This "pilgrimage piece" is the world's oldest known dated Buddha image and is a revered object of worship for many Buddhist visitors.

Lunch

After your museum visit, ask a taxi driver to take you to **Far East Cafe** (631 Grant Avenue; 415–982–3245), where you can eat Peking duck and sizzling rice soup in a private dining booth. If former patron Charlie Chan were able to revisit his old lunch spot, he would find nothing changed, down to the imported red lanterns. From this spot, you are perfectly situated for an afternoon of shopping.

DAY TWO: AFTERNOON

Grant Avenue is famed for its shops, markets, jewelry stores, and houseware emporiums. Browse through the four floors of the **Canton Bazaar** (616 Grant Avenue between California and Sacramento) for Asian artifacts. Check the time at **Old St. Mary's Church** (660 California Street at Grant). Since 1854 the clock dial on the church's red brick facade has admonished passersby to "Observe the Time and Fly from Evil." The church and its clock survived the 1906 fire and earthquake in order to remind us to enjoy life. Continue on Grant Avenue under the lion-guarded gateway, erected in 1970 as the entrance to the Chinese capital of the Western world. **Dragon House** (315 Grant Avenue between Bush and Sutter; 415–421–3693) has antique jade and Chinese antiques: decorative figurines, carved snuff bottles, teapots and other small wonders. The store synonymous with impeccable taste and refinement, **Gump's** (135 Post Street between Grant and Kearny; 415–982–1616) bears the name of the German immigrants who opened it in 1865. It is famous for its imported treasures, including jade, pearls and porcelain vases from Asia. If you are too loaded down with bags, take a taxi back to the Mandarin.

ITINERARY 4
Two days and one night

A MIDSUMMER NIGHT'S DREAM
TELEGRAPH HILL

*I*f ever a neighborhood was designed for love, this is it. At the base of Telegraph Hill, a village inn with cushioned bay windows borders a rolling green. On the Club Fugazi stage, Snow White searches for true love, getting bad advice from tap-dancing poodles. And to wile away an afternoon, you'll discover more leafy nooks and crannies in the Filbert Street gardens than in *A Midsummer Night's Dream.* But it doesn't have to be midsummer for you to enjoy this itinerary. Any season is a season for love at Telegraph Hill.

Practical Notes: For several good reasons, plan to stay here Friday or Saturday night. First, one of the treasures of San Francisco, the Coit Tower murals, is open for viewing only on Saturday morning. Second, you can poke around the North Beach Museum on Friday afternoon because it is open until 6:00 P.M. On Saturday, however, it is closed. Finally, on Friday and Saturday *Beach Blanket Babylon* has two shows, at 7:00 P.M. and at 10:00 P.M. Reserve tickets (415–421–4222) three to four weeks in advance. Whenever you come, wear comfortable walking shoes so you can climb the stairways and explore the neighborhood on foot. The area's appeal vanishes the moment you need a parking spot.

DAY ONE: AFTERNOON

Check into the second-floor, park-view rooms of the **Washington Square Inn** (1660 Stockton Street at Filbert; 415–981–4220 or 800–388–0220; $120–$200). Room 8 has pine forest chintz, and room 7 has rose chintz. Deep-cushioned seating curves beneath bay windows in both rooms. At 4:00 P.M. the staff lays out all the fixings for afternoon tea (cucumber sandwiches, fruit tarts, Earl Grey tea) or wine and hors d'oeuvres (pâté, crackers, cheese); these are served in the lobby, for hotel guests only.

Romance at a Glance

♥ *Spend the night in one of Washington Square Inn's most romantic rooms (415–981–4220 or 800–388–0220).*

♥ *Visit the Coit Tower murals and the Mediterranean gardens of the Filbert Street steps.*

♥ *Dine at Moose's (415–989–7800), a Cal-Ital trattoria.*

♥ *See* Beach Blanket Babylon *at Club Fugazi.*

When you leave the front door of the inn, turn left. At Moose's restaurant, stop and check out the dinner menu posted outside the door. Follow Stockton Street, crossing Columbus Avenue, to the **North Beach Museum** (1435 Stockton, on the mezzanine level of EurekaBank; 415–626–7070). As documented in the museum's turn-of-the-century photos, social activities in the old neighborhood formerly centered on the parish church of Saints Peter and Paul. When the Italian population of North Beach peaked in 1913, Italian feluccas still skimmed the bay, nuns in starched wimples taught grammar school, and boxers were cheered on at the Italian Athletic Club. Museum exhibits honor two famous native sons: Joe DiMaggio and A. P. Gianinni, who was the founder of the Bank of Italy, now called the Bank of America. In one museum photograph, Gianinni sits stiffly in his wedding picture. The bride and groom are not within an arm's length of one another.

Walk north on Columbus Avenue. This diagonal thoroughfare is sited on Mount Tamalpais, whose presence reminds residents of the proximity of wild places. Turn right at Union Street. Climb two blocks to Montgomery Street, looking to the left at Coit Tower. One of our favorite city views is at the Montgomery Street and Union Street corner. The

Transamerica Pyramid Building gives the financial district an Emerald City look, and the Oakland Bay Bridge leaps across the bay to Yerba Buena Island. Continue on Union one block to Calhoun Terrace. The middle house partially hidden behind a tree is believed to be the oldest house on Telegraph Hill. You can pick out the haphazard expansions over the decades.

Retrace your steps and turn right at Montgomery. At the end, **Julius Castle** (1541 Montgomery Street at the Greenwich Street steps; 415–362–3042) opens every evening at 5:00 P.M. Wedged high into the slope of Telegraph Hill, this turreted castle offers picture-window vistas of waterfront piers and the bay beyond. Now a great place to come for cocktails and to watch the light fade from the sky or the fog roll in, the castle was originally built as an elaborate mansion by Julius Roz in 1922. It later functioned as a speakeasy and private club before its 1980s conversion to a bar and restaurant. Retrace your steps to Union Street. Turn right, and right again at Stockton to return to the Washington Square Inn.

DAY ONE: EVENING
Dinner

Have dinner next door to the inn at **Moose's** (1652 Stockton Street at Filbert; 415–989–7800), a Cal-Ital trattoria everyone raves about. The open dining room is spacious and lively. The decor is purposely subdued; people are what you notice first. You can dine on gourmet pizza topped with rock shrimp and leeks or seasonal California fare such as Caesar salad, crispy Maine crab cakes with marinated remoulade and baby lettuces, and Hawaiian swordfish on truffled potatoes and leeks with chanterelle vinaigrette.

For a more Italian type of liveliness, try Antonio Latona's Sicilian dishes at **Caffe Sport** (574 Green Street at Stockton; 415–981–1251). Latona is the Bacchus of North Beach. He promotes garlic as an aphrodisiac. Caffe Sport is popular for mounds of garlic-laden pasta or tangy cioppino. Don't be intimidated by the brusque wait staff, who overrule your order with their "suggestions." Adding color to the scene, Sicilian folk art paintings and icons adorn the place, along with hanging hams, fishnets, dolls, mirrors, and kitschy bric-a-brac.

L'Osteria del Forno (519 Columbus Avenue between Union and Green; 415–982–1124; moderate; cash only) offers the refinements of a café in Siena and another dining option. This tiny twenty-eight-seat room has delicious wine served in water glasses; thin-crust pizzas; house-made pastas, such as ravioli filled with pumpkin, butter, and sage sauce; and roast meats, such as thinly sliced roast pork braised in milk.

∽✺∾

A few blocks away from the inn is **Beach Blanket Babylon** (Club Fugazi, 678 Green Street at Columbus; 415–421–4222). Since the club has open seating, you may want to line up half an hour before the show. Snow White has been singing and dancing on the Fugazi stage for twenty years and still hasn't found her prince. In her around-the-globe search, French poodles, a pizza joint waitress, and Rocky (Sylvester Stallone) enlighten Snow about true love in hilarious song-and-dance numbers. During the holidays, singing Christmas trees get into the act. Val Diamond belts out tunes á la Ethel Merman and wears the famous 12-foot city skyline hat in the finale. After *Beach Blanket Babylon*, stop at **Tosca Cafe** (242 Columbus Avenue between Broadway and Pacific; 415–986–9651) and order Tosca cappuccino, the house drink, at the antique brass espresso machine. The jukebox plays opera and Broadway show tunes and the deep leather booths invite lingering. A San Francisco original, the room hasn't changed since Bogey and Bacall sat in a booth during the filming of *Dark Passages*.

DAY TWO: MORNING

Breakfast

The sounds and smells of a city awakening may draw you to the window seat overlooking Washington Square Park. Focaccia is browning in the ovens of Liguria's bakery across the street from the inn. In the park, Chinese senior citizens move in slow motion, floating hands, arms, and legs through the air as their chief leads them through t'ai chi exercises. A limousine parked in front of Saints Peter and Paul Church means a wedding ceremony is taking place inside. Ask for breakfast to be delivered to your room so you can enjoy such choices as croissants, cereal, and Graffeo coffee in your private den.

After breakfast, join the scene below on the street. Turn right outside the inn, then right at Lombard Street. Enjoy the local flora—check the yards of the nearby homes for sights like lemon trees ripe with fruit. This Mediterranean-like microclimate supports citrus trees, hibiscus, and bougainvillea. At **Pioneer Park,** at the foot of the Lombard Street steps, rest on the Marconi stone bench before climbing the staircase. At the top of the staircase glance back at the bric-a-brac atop the corner house. A leprechaun is swinging from the chimney, and, fashioned from metal, Tweeddledee and Tweeddledum from *Alice in Wonderland* sit astride horses. The walkway at the top of the stairs takes you around the base of Coit Tower through a grove of Monterey cypress. Arrive at **Coit Tower** by 11:00 A.M. when a City Guides docent (415–557–4266) unlocks the door to the staircase and second-floor murals of Coit Tower. Street scenes of the intense 1930s fill the stairwell. Ascend slowly to appreciate the fashions, cars, and general vitality of the 1930s, spun out as a fascinating human drama in these murals. Afterward, take the elevator to the top of Coit Tower, where author Gail Sheehy was overheard gasping, "Oh, I was afraid it would be this beautiful." Now is a good time to hand your camera to a friendly bystander to have your picture taken.

When you exit, follow the circular viewing area to the right. Go down the **Greenwich Street steps**, a lovely brick staircase through the backyards and back alleys of Telegraph Hill. You'll come out at Montgomery Street at Julius' Castle. Turn right at Montgomery and make a sharp left to continue down the Greenwich Street steps. The narrow bridge overheard is a driveway. Many of these cottages at one time offered inexpensive housing for artists and writers.

And we shall walk
Through all our days
With love remembered and love renewed.
—ROBERT SEXTON

Lunch

When the staircase ends, continue ahead, turning right at Battery Street to the place where the sound of waterfalls and the smell of mowed grass announces **Levi Strauss Plaza.** Scout out a spot for a picnic. A short walk takes you past a stepping-stone fountain; red, white, and pink flower beds; a footbridge; and a stream. What you may notice next is the rich, smoking aroma of roasted red pepper, grilled chicken, and crusty bread from nearby **Il Fornaio** (1265 Battery Street between Greenwich and Union; 415–986–0100; inexpensive). We sat by the stream with a bounty of take-out from Il Fornaio: roast turkey panini, grilled eggplant and peppers, and a side of garden greens tossed with balsamic vinaigrette. The sun felt like a Mediterranean kiss. Not only a lovely spot to picnic, Levi Strauss Garden is a comfortable place to embrace on the grass unselfconsciously.

DAY TWO: AFTERNOON

On the return walk to Coit Tower, walk through Levi Strauss Plaza to Sansome Street. Cross Sansome Street to Filbert Street. As you begin to climb the Filbert Street staircase, notice the landslide on the left. An apartment building at the end of Alta Street crumbled because of it and had to be demolished. You'll see it again from the top. Ascend into the fairy-tale setting of the **Filbert Street steps and garden**. When the steep concrete stairway becomes a charming set of wooden steps, you are into the hushed domain of the Grace Marchant flower gardens and Lane. The clapboard cottages on Napier Lane once housed the families of Italian fishermen. Grace Marchant's garden thrives in this microclimate. When she moved to Napier Lane, Filbert Street was the neighborhood dump. Her legacy is this garden of roses, star jasmine, and bougainvillea bordering the steps. Added to her garden are whimsical touches from other Telegraph Hill residents: next to a fire hydrant, a painting of a French poodle toting a sign that reads: NO DOGS, ONLY TEACUP POODLES; and a white lattice arch, the kind you see at garden weddings, that leads to a secluded bench. Turn left at Montgomery and left again at Alta Street. A few years ago, an apartment building slid down the hill, leaving a gaping hole and a weeping owner. The new construction at the base of the hill may have disturbed the hillside.

Continue up the Filbert Street steps until you are at Coit Tower. Filbert Street continues as a street down the face of Telegraph Hill, but use the stairs in the center of the sidewalk. Walking downhill can hurt your toes.

People never leave North Beach without an armful of provisions. Turn left at Grant Avenue and buy Mrs. Rossi's tortas, sensual layers of cream cheese and mascarpone, pesto, and sun-dried tomatoes, at **Prudente & Company** (1462 Grant Avenue at Union; 415–421–0757). Then, stop at **Liguria's Bakery** (1700 Stockton Street at Filbert; 415–421–3786) across from the inn for the homemade focaccia bread you may have smelled in the morning.

FOR MORE ROMANCE

Artist and poet Robert Sexton's work is featured at **An American Romantic** (491 Greenwich Street at Grant; 415–989–1630). His lithographs, cards, and books honor the love, kindness, and compassion that sustain relationships. Both gallery and card shop, this establishment has a warm and welcoming atmosphere. As you browse the merchandise, you may find a poem that crystallizes your feelings for each other.

On Saturday morning you can walk the neighborhood with a City Guide (415–557–4266). Meet the North Beach Walking Tour guide at 10:00 A.M. on the steps in front of Saints Peter and Paul Church.

Only locals know about the views of Alcatraz, Angel Island, and Marin County from *Jack Early Park* (Grant and Pfeiffer Street between Chestnut and Francisco). The park was built in 1962 and is ideal for sharing a quiet moment. If you are still wandering the neighborhood at five-thirty you may find yourselves near **Zax** (2330 Taylor Street between Chestnut and Francisco; 415–563–6266). Well hidden and relatively unknown, this is one of the city's better California-Mediterranean restaurants. Their menu changes seasonally, but it focuses on healthy, garden-fresh ingredients. Try the goat-cheese soufflé, pan-fried sand dabs with roasted new potatoes and artichokes, or the roasted Sonoma duck breast flavored with grilled fig vinaigrette.

ITINERARY 5
Two days and one night

AN INVITATION FROM YOUR MUSE

RUSSIAN HILL

The Lark, a Bohemian literary publication edited by poet George Sterling, once printed a map showing the neighborhood of Little Bohemia on Russian Hill beyond Nob Hill, the so-called Hill of Plenty. With it, the free spirits, artists, and writers who once populated the neighborhood of Russian Hill were announcing their whereabouts to like-minded individuals. Here the Bohemians thrived. Ambrose Bierce, Mark Twain, and Joaquin Miller gathered at poet Ina Coolbrith's salon. For fifty years the hill sustained them. Coolbrith once dedicated a volume of verse called *Songs of the Golden Gate* to San Francisco.

This itinerary invites you to wander quiet tree-lined Hyde Street and venture forth along a century-old footpath frequented by San Francisco's literati, among the galleries of an illustrious art institute, and under vine-heavy arches of hidden lanes. It takes you to a promontory lined with the brown-shingled homes of Craftsman-style architect Willis Polk. You settle in for the night on the northern slope of Russian Hill, facing the beautiful bay. Foghorns drone at midnight and cable car bells ring jubilantly in the morning—one sound coaxing dreams, the other snatching them away.

Practical Notes: Many shops, cafes, and restaurants are closed on Monday in the Hyde Street and Polk Street area. Purchase an all-day Muni Passport ($6.00) for unlimited cable-car rides. During winter rains, avoid slippery staircases and muddy lanes.

DAY ONE: Afternoon

The **Suites at Fisherman's Wharf** (2655 Hyde Street at North Point; 415–771–0200 or 800–227–3608; $175–$195) has a mix of old-world and modern decor with terrazzo tile floors, pastel colors, and contemporary furnishings. More like home with a separate living room and bedroom, the Suites at Fisherman's Wharf also has an atrium courtyard and a roof garden to help you unwind.

Romance at a Glance

♥ *Cozy up at the Suites at Fisherman's Wharf (415–771–0200 or 800–227–3608).*

♥ *Ride the legendary Hyde Street cable car.*

♥ *Dine at Allegro Ristorante Italiano (415–928–4002).*

♥ *Visit the haunts of San Francisco's bohemians.*

♥ *Visit San Francisco Art Institute.*

Put on walking shoes and hop aboard the **Hyde Street cable car** at the corner. Stand on the sideboard together and watch the bay expand as the chain pulls the car to the top. A ballad appearing in the 1902 issue of *The Lark* captures the wind-in-your-hair freedom of riding with gripman George Ball. Gelett Burgess (1866–1951), lived in Russian Hill when he wrote a poem called the *Ballad of the Hyde Street Grip*. George Ball, a Scottish immigrant, worked as a cable car gripman along the line that ran past Ball's house at 2022 Hyde Street.

Jump off at Lombard Street. Fanny Osborne Stevenson, widow of Robert Louis Stevenson, lived at the northwest corner of Lombard and Hyde. Visit **George Sterling Park** (Hyde Street between Greenwich and Lombard). Along the path past the tennis courts is Sterling's memorial bench, inlaid with warm-hued tiles. San Francisco's foremost bohemian poet, George Sterling published eleven volumes of poetry between 1902 and 1926. While he lived at Greenwich and Hyde, no one did more to infect the hill with merriment and good fellowship. His legacy lives on prominently in the Bohemian Club. He and his pal Jack London were charter members. After acquiring forest property on the Russian River, the members reveled at the Grove in an outdoor theater in the redwoods during the summer. Sterling's verse drama, *Triumph of Bohemia*, a celebrated Grove play at the turn of the century, is still performed during July encampments. Formerly staged and acted by a group of men with talent and no money, the traditional revel is now performed by a group of men with money and talent for amassing wealth. These annual secret meetings draw from the top echelons of business and politics. David Rockefeller, Henry Ford, Henry Kissinger, and Richard Nixon have all been performers and often honorary members of the Bohemian Club.

All that most tourists know of Russian Hill is the world's crookedest street **Lombard Street**, descending from Hyde to Leavenworth. You make nine hairpin bends in one block—on a roadway with a 40 degree slope. Hydrangea bushes bloom in unison in front of each house.

In the inspirational Bohemian days of San Francisco, the arts abounded in myriad interpretations. You'll see that same spirit on display at the **San Francisco Art Institute** (800 Chestnut Street between Leavenworth and Jones; 415–771–7020), which has played a central role in contemporary art in the Bay Area. The Rivera Gallery, graced by a 1931 Diego Rivera mural, hosts weekly exhibitions of student work, with a wine and cheese reception every Thursday from 5:30 to 7:30 P.M. To find the **Cafe at the San Francisco Art Institute** (open Monday through Thursday until 9:00 P.M., Friday until 4:00 P.M., and Saturday until 2:00 P.M.; 415–749–4567), head for the roof. Sunny outdoor tables allow you to enjoy homemade soup, niçoise salad, and dessert while feasting on stunning views of Alcatraz, sailboats, Telegraph Hill, and Coit Tower. Drop in at the institute store for art books and supplies. Check out the calendar for SF Cinematheque at the Art Institute, where there is a weekly screening of experimental films at 7:30 P.M. as well as lectures by painters and poets.

*I'll sing such songs to you as never woman wrung in ecstasy from a
man's heart in all the years of art.*

> —GEORGE STERLING, who upon his death left a metal box of
> more than a hundred poems, "an enduring record of the
> fineness and worth of our love," to the woman who became
> the wife of his friend Upton Sinclair.

Back on Jones Street, watch for the **Macondray Lane** sign. Descend the wooden steps
into the shelter of foliage and lounging cats. This two-block footpath remains untarnished,
although the city hugs its borders. Bohemians of an earlier age frequented this lane to visit
their friends who lived in cottages along the path. Poets Ina Coolbrith and Charles and
Eleanore Ross were among those who came calling. The colorful life of the lane centered
on the old Macondray Street Theater, located in the basement of number 56. Number 17
was the home of the artist Cadenasso. Armistead Maupin's *Tales of the City* presents a
fictional account of Macondray Lane's residents in the 1970s. The fictional Mrs. Madrigal,
the portly den mother of the lane, chained herself to the steps to thwart a city demolition
crew that was under instructions to remove the wooden staircase. As you come down the
steps at Taylor Street, tread lightly on the ancient wooden boards. If the cars, noise, and
high-rise apartments cause your hearts to sink, turn around and go back up. Have a last
lingering look at the bucolic way of life the Bohemians loved and which has miraculously
survived.

Your return up the steps of Macondray Lane brings you back to Jones Street, which is by far the most dramatic approach to the **Russian Hill promontory** (Vallejo Street between Jones and Taylor). Ascend the ramp designed by Willis Polk, who spearheaded the Bay Area Arts and Crafts regional style. His three-story brown-shingled homes combined the need for simple dwellings with the beauty of classical elements. Investigate the three residential streets: Florence Street, Russian Hill Place, and Vallejo Street. This was Arden Forest to the Bohemians. Willis Polk also built four Mediterranean-style villas on Florence Street (numbers 1013, 1015, 1017, and 1019) between 1915 and 1916. He lived atop Russian Hill in the home on Florence where gallery owners Gretchen and John Berggruen now live. These redwood-shingled homes are architectural treasures. The view from the grassy promontory on Vallejo Street makes this a great spot to surprise someone with a kiss. At night the Bay Bridge beams a smile of white lights.

The Vallejo Street steps lead down to Taylor Street, where another Bohemian is honored with a park named for her. **Ina Coolbrith Park** is at Taylor and Vallejo Streets. A vital force throughout three generations of the city's literary history, Ina Donna Coolbrith (1841–1928) lived on Russian Hill and had a salon to which she welcomed guests such as Ambrose Bierce, Bret Harte, Mark Twain, Charles W. Stoddard, and Joaquin Miller. She held the post of the first poet laureate of the United States from 1915 to 1928. Her lyric poems celebrated life. Also a librarian at the Oakland Free Library (a job she took to support her sister's children), she directed Jack London's reading as a young adult.

Ina Coolbrith had honorary status in the Bohemian Club, serving as club librarian. The Vallejo Street steps lead down to Alta Vista Terrace, to a set of cottages much like the ones the Bohemians lived in atop Russian Hill.

Historian William Kostura regrets the gradual disappearance of Russian Hill's early-twentieth-century cottages. He unsuccessfully tried to save gripman George Ball's one-story shingled home at 2022 Hyde Street. The new owner plans to replace it with condominiums.

DAY ONE: EVENING

Dinner

Élan Vital Restaurant & Wine Bar (1556 Hyde Street at Pacific; 415–929–7309; moderate) opens at 5:30 P.M. This cozy, neighborhood French bistro has excellent wines by the glass and is a good stop on your way to dinner.

Italian-born Angelo Quaranta created a new page in the annals of Russian Hill when he opened **Allegro Ristorante Italiano** (1701 Jones Street at Broadway; 415–928–4002; moderate). The location is a storybook charmer: a quiet street corner across from the spectacular overlook atop Broadway. The prices are moderate for the fresh appetizers, pastas, chicken "baked under a brick," and veal scalloppine. Dungeness crab, a traditional New Year's dish in San Francisco, looked so fresh at the next table, we decided to share a platter. Entrees range from $10 to $20.

❦

We guarantee the view at the end of Broadway will make you tingle. Given extra sparkle from a light rain, the lights on the bridge shine brightly, and the city looks like an unwrapped gift.

If you like to dance to live bands, **Johnny Love's** (1500 Broadway at Polk; 415–931–6053) is the place to go after 10:00 P.M. It has cocktail tables, cozy booths and opposite the dance floor, a long U-shape bar where Johnny Meheny holds court. Dubbed Johnny Love by friends for excessive flirting, this celebrity bartender keeps the place packed, and the Caribbean All Stars perform a jazzy reggae that's great to dance to.

When you get back to the Suites, you may want to go up to the roof garden for a look at its view of San Francisco Bay. Listen to the foghorns. Sometimes it sounds like Prometheus sighing, at other times like Branford Marsalis's moody saxophone.

DAY TWO: MORNING

Brueakfast

The next morning take the cable car to **Hyde Street**, a small neighborhood that draws out the locals. Jump off the cable car at the **Black Rock Cafe** (1954 Hyde Street between Green and Union; 415–928–2633; inexpensive). Muffins, scones, biscotti are served daily from 6:00 A.M. The Black Rock epitomizes the place we always look for when we travel. Watch the modern-day Bohemians come and go. You can browse the cafe's magazine rack and linger as long as you please. For morning pastries try the sticky buns or apple rolls. The café is open Tuesday to Sunday.

Vallejo Street takes you right into the heart of the Upper Polk shopping district, which offers both unusual and elegant merchandise. **Tibet Shop** (1807 Polk Street between Washington and Jackson; 415–982–0326) sells lapis lazuli skulls and curios from Tibet, Nepal, and Bhutan. **Naomi's Antiques to Go** (1817 Polk between Washington and Jackson; 415–775–1207) has American pottery from the 1930s to 1960s. **Fioridella** (1920 Polk Street between Jackson and Pacific; 415–775–4065) is purveyor to San Francisco's small, personal boutique hotels. The employees will show you how to turn entryways into indoor gardens. Their clay-potted topiaries and other potted plants make long-lasting souvenirs. Browse the two floors of **Russian Hill Antiques** (2200 Polk Street at Vallejo; 415–441–5561), where you'll find early-twentieth-century jewelry and gift items as well as pine furniture.

Lunch

After shopping, have lunch at **Mario's Bohemian Cigar Store Cafe** (2209 Polk Street between Vallejo and Green; 415–776–8226). In a simple wood-paneled room you can order bruscetta, Caesar salad, lasagne, frittata, focaccia sandwiches, and pizza with gourmet toppings. Head up to Union Street to have ice cream at the original **Swensen's Ice Cream** (1999 Hyde Street at Union; 415–775–6818). You can watch the ice-cream maker cranking out the delicious flavors that launched a national corporation. Try the peppermint.

DAY TWO: AFTERNOON

As you head back to the Suites, be on the lookout for Russian Hill homes not destroyed in the 1906 quake and fire. The surviving structures reveal a fact most people don't realize: It was an elite group of citizens who settled on the northern slope here in the late nineteenth century. The house at **930 Chestnut** was the 1866 residence of attorney James Cary. All of its original detail is intact, from the balustraded balconies and square posts to the curvilinear brackets and Italianate corner blocks. What many consider the finest example of architectural expression ever built on Russian Hill is the A. A. Moore residence at **944 Chestnut.** Walk around the corner to Leavenworth Street to admire the slanted bay window. A stately Eastlake Stick home stands at **2500 Leavenworth.** The 1890 residence at **2434 Leavenworth** is also a charmer. Notice the craftsmanship of the entryway. Leavenworth Street and Chestnut Street achieve an urban aesthetic, with a charm that makes tourists dream of moving here.

ITINERARY 6
Two days and one night

PROWLING WITH YOUR PARAMOUR

NORTH BEACH

*I*f you missed North Beach during the 1950s, this itinerary, Beat-inspired through and through, will take you back to San Francisco's hippest scene. Originally an Italian community, North Beach became hallowed ground in the 1950s as the birthplace of the Beat Generation. The name Beat came from *Beatitude*, a bohemian publication from the 1920s. City Lights bookseller Lawrence Ferlinghetti, who published Allen Ginsberg's *Howl*, called the peripatetic Beats "carpetbaggers." The Beats traveled a triangle between North Beach, Greenwich Village, and Mexico City. Jack Kerouac's *On the Road*, written in a Russian Hill flat, stirred this generation, but someone else gave them a better name. *San Francisco Chronicle* columnist Herb Caen called those who broke ties and journeyed west "beatniks."

Many haunts of the Beat Generation—their coffeehouses, bars, clubs, bakeries, and restaurants—have changed little from the days when Ginsberg, the barefoot poet, tramped the streets. With its bohemian roots, North Beach is a place that is sympathetic to lovers. If you're in love, you'll feel right at home.

Practical Notes: If a fall visit fits your schedule, purchase tickets in advance to the **San Francisco Jazz Festival** (Four Embarcadero Center, Promenade Level; 415–398–5655), acclaimed as one of the three best jazz festivals in North America. Tickets for performances spanning three weeks in October and November are available by mid-August. Festival highlights have ranged from the Modern Jazz Quartet performing an elegant rendition of

Romance at a Glance

♥ *Sleep on poppies at Hotel Bohème (415–433–9111).*

♥ *Browse the poetry shelves at City Lights Bookstore.*

♥ *Hang out at coffeehouses, Beat bars, and jazz clubs.*

♥ *Picnic on Italian delicacies at Washington Square Park.*

♥ *Share* sacripantina *(an Italian dessert) at midnight.*

"Softly, As in a Morning Sunrise" to four of the world's leading saxophone players raising their horns in tribute to Charlie Parker. Here, too, Cecil Taylor has premiered his new compositions with an orchestra of the Bay Area's most innovative jazz musicians, and the jazz world's reigning divas, Abby Lincoln and Betty Carter, have joined each other on stage for a rare duet. Also as part of the Jazz Festival, John Santos, King of Mambo, has performed Latin jazz at Bimbo's 365 Club, an authentic 1950s night club.

Book two months or more in advance for a room at **Hotel Bohème** (444 Columbus Avenue between Vallejo and Green; 415-433–9111) for the Jazz Festival or four months ahead for rooms 204 or 205 overlooking Columbus Avenue during the Columbus Day Parade and Celebration. Over Father's Day weekend in June when the Upper Grant Avenue Street Faire is held, Upper Grant Avenue becomes a block party and high-end flea market.

DAY ONE: MORNING

Don black berets and slip through black-and-gold portières into **Hotel Bohème** (444 Columbus Avenue between Vallejo and Green; 415–433–9111; $125). A Victorian on the outside, the hotel could be a private enclave for poets and their paramours. It's the kind of place that masks time as well as identity. When you come inside from a bright sidewalk, adjust your eyes for a dark staircase. The black-and-white photos along the wall belong to the hotel's permanent exhibit, *I am a Lover,* by Jerry Stoll and Evan S. Connell Jr. Images of the people and culture of North Beach during the Beat era guide you up the flight of stairs to the reception desk.

The hotel borrows the colors of North Beach nights as well as coffee colors and jazz colors. Walls of sage green and cantaloupe cast a warm, moody glow along hallways, while guestroom doors are lavender trimmed in black. Step into your room onto a carpet of all those colors, and settle your eyes on muslin draping an ornamental iron bed with its headboard and footboard curved into moon-shaped bridges. The Italian armoire has been in use since the fifties; it was left by the Italian family who sold the hotel. Opium poppies seem appropriate for the bed pillow fabrics, and the lampshades are a collage of images of rare postage and ink stamps.

Ochre, black, gold, lavender—sounds like a place Beat poets might call home when they're in town for poetry readings. Room 204 was Allen Ginsberg's favorite room. Imagine the poet at the bistro table, leaning forward with the Bay window wide open. Ginsberg said what he liked best about North Beach were the trees and being able to walk to his friends' houses.

Within steps of the hotel's front door are several sidewalk cafes, bakeries, cabarets, coffee-houses, delis, and trattorias. Pick up a corkscrew and plastic cups at the front desk. If the weather is glorious, you'll want to be prepared to eat outdoors. Next, pick up the latest copies of *Poetry Flash*, *North Beach Now*, and *Jazz Times* from the hotel lobby, and then head over to **Caffé Trieste** (601 Vallejo Street at Grant; 415–392–6739).

Like other coffeehouse survivors of the sixties, it serves no hard liquor but offers espresso and cappuccino, wine, beer, and sundry aperitifs. Its walls are cluttered with scenes of old North Beach intermixed with glossies of opera and film stars, and snapshots of Trieste regulars as well as tourists. Little has changed here for decades. You can sit in the same seats once warmed by Jack Kerouac and Allen Ginsberg and look over the *Poetry Flash* calendar to see which local poetry readings you'd like to attend. On Saturday from 1:00 to 4:00 P.M., the owners of Caffé Trieste gather family and friends to sing Italian love songs and Puccini's operas. Take time for a slow cappuccino and savor being together.

Life was full of dancing, singing, poetry, parties, people, painting, music, sunshine, moonlight, rooftops, laughter, and love…These were times of plenty.

—Eileen Kaufman, wife of Beat poet Bob Kaufman, recalling North Beach in the fifties and early sixties.

A pilgrimage for many visitors, **City Lights Booksellers & Publishers** (261 Columbus Avenue and Jack Kerouac Alley; 415–362–8193) printed Ginsberg's *Howl*, giving the Beat generation its anthem. Owner Lawrence Ferlinghetti named his bookstore after the Charlie Chaplin movie because of the challenges facing the little man. Ferlinghetti printed the Ginsberg manifesto in Great Britain to save on costs. Federal agents confiscated the first U.S. shipment, and Ferlinghetti found himself in court on obscenity charges. Today you'll find *Howl* in the poetry room upstairs in the Beat section. Have a look at the bookstore's bulletin board. Gary Snyder is a Beat name you might see. Now living in the Sierra Nevada, he won the Pulitzer Prize in 1975 for *Turtle Island*. He rented a flat on the corner of Green and Montgomery and took up Zen Buddhism, distinguishing his poetry with visual energy. Look upstairs, too, for Ginsberg's, *Cosmopolitan Greetings, Poems 1986–1992*.

Lunch

The Beats loved books, jazz, coffee—and Molinari's. Look along Columbus Avenue for a display window of sausage rings, cheese wheels, and Amaretto cookie tins. In business since 1896, **Molinari Delicatessen** (373 Columbus Avenue at Vallejo; 415–421–2337; inexpensive) is jammed to the rafters with sacks, cans, bags, and tins of just about everything edible, drinkable, and Italian.

Take a number. You'll need fifteen minutes just to look at all the items in the deli cases. I like to watch them slap a few panini (sandwiches) together before deciding. Notice the smells. North Beach delis tantalize with the most intense aromas: Italian bread, pesto, garlic.

For a nice bottle of wine to accompany your lunch, head to **Coit Liquor** (585 Columbus Avenue at Union; 415–986–4036 or 800–255–COIT). It carries not the red jug wine that the Beats drank at poetry readings, but a distinguished collection of goods from small wineries, many of which are available nowhere else in the city. Tony pointed us to a Voignier from Rabbit Ridge, a winery in Russian River. We also bought bottles of Bannister Chardonnay and Benziger Merlot to take home. You may want to pick up a small bottle of Grand Marnier for a nightcap.

Take your picnic to Washington Square Park, which you'll find by walking toward the twin church spires. The sunniest spot to spread your feast is by the statue of Ben Franklin.

DAY ONE: AFTERNOON

After your picnic, cruise the shops on Columbus Avenue and Upper Grant Avenue. Check out the vogue designs at **MAC** (1543 Grant Avenue between Union and Filbert; 415–837–1604) and the 1950s postcards at **Quantity Postcards** (1441 Grant Avenue, between Union and Green; 415–986–8866). The postcard images are taken from ads, packaging material, and book covers. This kitsch emporium is open until 12:30 A.M. Stop at the Gathering Caffé (1326 Grant Avenue; 415–433–4247) to pick up a calendar and see who's playing there in the evening. At **Show Biz,** The Memorabilia Store (1318 Grant Avenue between Vallejo and Green; 415–989–6744), browse the complete collection of "all that jazz" figurines. Back at the Hotel Bohème in the late afternoon, the street scene may look different than it did in the morning. In the 1850s when a finger of the bay extended between Telegraph and Russian Hills, North Beach indeed was a shoreline neighborhood. The fog remembers and still inches along the same route, chilling Columbus Avenue as it proceeds.

DAY ONE: EVENING

The Hotel Bohème keeps a blackboard up to date with nightclub offerings. Check to see who's playing at the Jazz Workshop, the Gathering Caffè, and Pearl's, then start the evening at **Vesuvio's Bar** (255 Columbus Avenue; 415–362–3370), the quintessential Beat tavern whose history is documented on its walls. Herbert Gold's article on North Beach is framed on the left wall as you go in. Paul Kantner is frequently seen reading the paper in the corner alcove. Sit upstairs for a bird's eye view of the Columbus and Broadway intersection. Colorful only begins to describe what happens at twilight. When the sun goes down the neighborhood switches to a nighttime groove. As the night deepens, make the rounds of the clubs and coffeehouses with other North Beach habitués.

Where to eat before the jazz clubs open? Maybe with Gino at **The Cafferata** (700 Columbus Avenue at Filbert; 415–392–7544). Gino's ancestors have been rolling pasta dough in North Beach since 1886. They have a jump on the dinner scene by opening at 4:00 P.M. **Tommaso's** (1042 Kearny Street between Broadway and Pacific; 415–398–9696) put in the first wood-burning pizza ovens in the city. Walk downstairs to the dining room. The mix of people who eat here adds to the ambience of the place. The calzones and pizzas have perfectly crisp, thin crusts.

North Beach is where you can find jazz talent outside the Jazz Festival. When people want an intimate jazz club, they go to **Jazz at Pearl's** (256 Columbus; 415–291–8255), run by Pearl Wong and Sonny Baxton. Live jazz bands perform nightly from 9:00 P.M. You'll hear jazz legends along with local jazz bands. As North Beach gains notoriety for jazz, look for new clubs. The Norman Williams Quartet is the Friday night headliner at **The Gathering Caffè** (1326 Grant Avenue; 415–433–4247), which has shows from 9:00 to 11:30 P.M. They sometimes offer poetry with jazz accompaniment. Poet Ruth Weiss with bassist Doug O'Connor has performed here. Jazz inspired some of the Beat poets to experiment with improvised poetry in public performances, but Kenneth Patchen, the most vitriolic of the Beats,

Dancing with Jack Kerouac

I was drifting peacefully when Jack's voice alerted me, low yet steady, "God . . . I love you." My heart flipped, my nerves rippled, I was thrown into such turmoil I could manage hardly more than a whisper. "Let's dance," he said softly.

We floated in a close, timeless embrace; but when my joy was too full to keep up the solemn mood, he filled our glasses, chortling, affecting extravagant chivalrous gestures in my adoring eyes, loaded the record player with mambos, and we danced . . . and we danced . . . abandoned and individual, yet totally immersed in each other and the sensation of being one and together.

— FROM CAROLYN CASSADY'S MEMOIRS
Heart Beat: My Life with Jack and Neal

would have none of that. He recited from finished copies of his poems and provided sheet music for the jazz trio.

Enrico's (504 Broadway at Kearny; 415–982–6223) large sidewalk patio is also a popular jazz venue once owned by Enrico Banducci. The City Guide official who conducts a literary tour of North Beach remembers that after he read *On the Road*, Kerouac's novel of two young men's quest for the Holy Grail, he got in a car in Massachusetts and drove to San Francisco. Arriving with no money, he proceeded to bum drinks from Enrico's customers. One of those soft-touch customers was Richard Brautigan, author of *Trout Fishing in America* and other sixties Beat classics.

After a few jazz sets, wander over to **Specs'** (12 Saroyan Place at Columbus; 415–421–4112). Another legendary North Beach bar, it is presided over by local demagogue Richard "Spec" Simmons, a sort of beat version of David Letterman. Specs' is a great bar to share a drink with street poets who come in to hear the owner's stories. Spec likes to reminisce about the Beat days of North Beach. In the 25 years he's owned the bar, he has covered every inch of wall space with mementos from the past.

DAY ONE: ROUND ABOUT MIDNIGHT

If you are looking for the Holy Grail of desserts, head for **Firenze by Night Ristorante** (1429 Stockton Street between Columbus and Vallejo; 415–392–8585), which stays open until midnight. The locals are mad for Sergio's *zuppa inglese*, which is sponge cake, cream custard, chocolate, and rum. **Rose Pistola** (532 Columbus Avenue between Union and Green; 415–399–0499) also serves a late-night menu for night owls staying open until 1:00 A.M. on Friday and Saturday. Better yet, stop at **Stella Pastry & Café** (446 Columbus, next to the Hotel Bohème; 415–986–2914) *before 7:00 P.M.* Ask for a small *sacripantina*, an Italian dessert that is "una torta molto deliziosa." Thin layers of sponge cake are spread with zabaione cream made from egg yolks and sweet butter, to which the baker adds rum, marsala, and sherry wines. The Italian clerk translated *sacripantina* as an outburst of joy, equivalent to the Beat expression "cool." Ask the front desk clerk at the hotel to store the pink box in the hotel refrigerator until you return at midnight. You could do the same thing at **Victoria Pastry Company** (1362 Stockton Street at Vallejo; 415–781–2015) if you'd rather have Gateau St. Honore (choose the 6-inch), but go *before 6:00 P.M.* Whatever you choose, pick up your midnight dessert at the front desk upon your return and have it at your bay window bistro table with liqueur glasses of Grand Marnier. Then lean back on the bedspread covered in opium-poppy fabric.

DAY TWO: LATE MORNING

Greet the morning (or afternoon, if you sleep in) at **Mario's Bohemian Cigar Store** (566 Columbus Avenue at Union; 415–362–0536; inexpensive). Once a stogy shop, it is now a nonsmoking café. The lattés come with a 3-inch layer of foam, guaranteeing a white mustache just asking to be kissed away. Mario's Italian pastries come from North Beach bakeries. The biscottis he makes himself.

DAY TWO: AFTERNOON

Italians have scattered over the Bay Area, but they still return to North Beach to shop for high-quality food items. You may want to take your cue from them and stock up on provisions before leaving home. The neighborhood butcher shop since 1910, **Prudente & Company** (1462 Grant Avenue at Union; 415–421–0757) has aged pancetta and mascarpone tortas you may want to wrap up and take home with you. Then stop at **Caffé Roma** (526 Columbus Avenue at Green mail order; 415–296–ROMA) to look over their coffee bean menu. Some coffee has a smoky taste; others remind me of rich, dark chocolate. The Etruscan blend is for a light coffee drinker. Handed down in the family for three generations, the recipe produces a cup of coffee rich and unique in flavor, with a smooth, delicate finish of hazelnuts. We usually take home a pound of their special blend. Instead, you might decide to cut loose and buy a pound of Sicilian Gold, which the menu says is "wild and extremely potent." Must be the brew that generated late-night huddles at coffeehouses and ponderous Beat poetry.

FOR MORE ROMANCE

Try the new clubs opening up on Broadway. North Beach's **The Black Cat** (501 Broadway at Kearny; 415–981–2233) is decorated in low, round, leather booths, windows built for people-watching, and sensual incandescent tones. San Francisco's rich jazz heritage resonates at the Blue Bar jazz lounge downstairs. The original Black Cat was a gathering place for the black-turtle-necked Beat Generation hipsters who came to hear John Coltrane and other jazz greats.

ITINERARY 7
Two days and one night

WHEN PASSION WON'T REST

UNION SQUARE

ttending a blockbuster musical, dancing at the Starlight Room, gallery hopping, discovering hip haute couture, soaking toe to toe in a two-person whirlpool tub—this itinerary has all this and much more, if you have the energy. The three-block radius around Union Square is the city's most hyperactive district, extending to San Francisco Shopping Centre, and Crocker Galleria at Post and Montgomery. Now more than ever, this area offers the most complete shopping facilities in northern California. If you can't find it in Union Square, it may not exist.

If you are as tantalized by each other as you are by good merchandise, you'll want a hotel that matches your interests. A shopping spree that extended across continents preceded the debut of the Hotel Monaco. Open the door of this hotel to an atlas of decorative details. One detail may spark a vision of a Marrakech summer palace, another a townhouse off the cornice of Nice, another a Barcelona apartment, or perhaps a British outpost in Malaysia. The hotel lobby unifies the theme in a mural: Phineas Fogg's hot-air balloon in *Around the World in Eighty Days*. In designing the hotel, Cheryl Rowley realized her dream of "A long ocean journey in which a great ship travels the world collecting exotic, precious treasures and antiquities and returns to the port of San Francisco."

Practical Notes: Before embarking for Union Square, purchase theater tickets. Best of Broadway musicals play at the **Curran, The Golden Gate,** and the **Orpheum.** The American Conservatory Theater (ACT) stages drama and a wonderful production of *A Christmas Carol* in December. **STBS,** or San Francisco Ticket Box Office Service, is open Tuesday to Saturday (Union Square between Post and Geary; 415–433–STBS) and offers half-price tickets (plus a service charge) on the day of the performance to selected cultural events. STBS also serves as a BASS (Bay Area Seating Service) outlet. The **ACT Box Office** (405 Geary Street and Mason; 415–749–2228) sells tickets to dramas by such famous playwrights as William Shakespeare and Edward Albee. **City Box Office** (153 Kearny between Post and Sutter; 415–392–4400) is another ticketing agency.

Romance at a Glance

♥ *Luxuriate in world-class style at Hotel Monaco (415–292–0100 or 800–214–4220).*

♥ *Have pre-dinner cocktails at the Redwood Room (415–775–4700) and French cuisine at La Scene (415–292–6430).*

♥ *Attend a Best of Broadway musical.*

♥ *Buy an Armani suit or an affordable bauble at Union Square.*

DAY ONE: MORNING

The St. Francis Hotel on one side, luxury stores on two sides, Macy's on another: No wonder Union Square is the best place in town to spend money. Read the store names on shopping bags flashing by: Neiman Marcus, Saks Fifth Avenue, Nordstrom's. In one block you spot Bally of Switzerland, Gucci, Chanel, and Tiffany. Investigate the streets radiating from the square, and you find Mark Cross, Louis Vuitton, Giorgio Armani. These stores contain goods you never knew you wanted: a Hérmes saddle (1 Union Square at Stockton; 415–391–7200), Teuscher chocolates (255 Grant Avenue near Sutter; 415–398–2700), a Keith Haring T-shirt (Martin Lawrence Gallery, 465 Powell Street at Sutter; 415–956–0345).

Whether a browser or buyer, you'll appreciate the hip fantasy atmosphere of the stores around the square. An opulent multimillion-dollar redesign of a former bank built in 1911 gave **Emporio Armani Boutique and Cafe** (1 Grant Avenue between Market and O'Farrell; 415–677–9400) the look the company wanted. Racks of beautiful clothes replace tellers' cages. Ask for a table on the sidewalk and order a cappuccino. Shopping for evening clothes? Emporio Armani sells pewter satin jackets, matching pants, and satin heels. You can try on the rayon and wool crepe Issey Miyake tuxedos at **Wilkes Bashford** (Sutter Street between Stockton and Grant; 415–986–4380). This store transcends the mold by seducing you with witty, surreal surroundings. Lovely music and a glass of wine also make you linger. The designer clothes from this store show up on San Francisco's glitterati. They are beautiful and expensive, with timeless appeal. Survivor of fire and quakes, boom and bust, **Shreve & Co.** (200 Post Street at Grant; 415–421–2600) is the city's oldest retailer, selling jewelry in the six figures and handsome trinkets for under a hundred. Gems and jewelry add a little sparkle to one's attire . . . something locals have found essential since 1862. This elegant store with green marble columns takes you back to the era of extravagant living and grand style.

Since starting out this morning, the focus has been on small stores. Now switch to the grand palaces of shopping. **San Francisco Shopping Centre** (865 Market Street at Fifth; 415–495–5656) has nine floors of fashion, food, and gifts. Stores are easy to survey from spiral escalators that lead skyward toward a retractable eye-shaped dome. **Nordstrom** (415–243–8500) commands the five upper levels. The circular floors can make you dizzy.

Voted the best department store in annual readership polls, **Macy's** (entrances on Geary Street, Stockton, and O'Farrell; 415–397–3333) dominates the square, now expanded into the adjacent I. Magnin & Co. store and across Stockton Street. Rounding out the morning at prestigious retailers like Neiman Marcus and Saks Fifth Avenue, you can shop until someone cries, "Enough!" or, "Lunch."

Lunch

Take the Neiman Marcus escalator to the **Rotunda** (150 Stockton Street at Geary; 415–362–4777; moderate); by this time, you may be glad to be far from shopping bags and bustling streets. Lunch is served from 11:00 A.M. to 5:00 P.M. on the circular balcony. You sit beneath the leaded glass dome saved from the original 1896 City of Paris store. Ensconced in a cushioned booth, gaze up at the dome's seafaring scene and down at the stylishly tiered shopping floors or across Union Square. As befitting a high-class cafe, the menu offers scallop piccata, roast rack of lamb, and lobster club sandwiches. The popovers, served warm with fruit butter, are delicious. Shop in Neiman Marcus Epicure for foie gras, salmon fume, caviar, and assorted pâtés to nibble on in your hotel room.

Union Square is a crossroads of the world, but not only for its merchandise. Jamaican steel drummers perform in front of Neiman Marcus. A French guitarist sings love songs by Maiden Lane gate, and Peruvian pipe players fill the square with Andean music.

DAY ONE: AFTERNOON

Check into the **Hotel Monaco** (501 Geary Street at Taylor; 415–292–0100 or 800–214–4220; $160–$355), the *au courant* place to stay. Built in 1910 at the height of the American Beaux Arts movement, the original hotel was an all-American beauty called the Bedford. Neglected to the point of being run down, the hotel's interior has been completely remodeled. Lovely architectural flourishes of the earlier period remain in the marble grand staircase, the bronze filigree, and the two-story French inglenook fireplace. Sitting at the fireside with a glass of wine puts you in the frame of mind of Bogart and Bacall.

The hotel takes you to faraway places on the strength of its colors alone. Against a background of Chinese red, persimmon, and burnished turquoise are lustrous pieces of furniture in mahogany and satinwood. You step up to an enlarged replica of a 1920s steamer trunk to register. My husband asked, "What deck are we on?" We headed for our sixth-floor suite, guided by navigational instruments converted into light fixtures. The focal point of each

Alma Spreckels was the model for the statue representing Victory atop the monument in the center of Union Square commemorating Admiral George Dewey's victory over the Spanish at Manila Bay in 1898. The clothing she wears in the statue was considered very racy for a woman of her day—gauzy muslin revealed every curve.

guest room is the bed; ours was crowned by a half canopy rolled and held in place with grosgrain ribbons. The 68-inch convex mirror will make you feel like you're looking at yourself through a fish-eye lens. Bring your bathing suits—the Roman spa downstairs from the lobby has a steam room, sauna, and whirlpool spa.

DAY ONE: EVENING

Did you find wonderful clothes on your shopping spree? Put them on and sashay forth arm in arm and dressed to the nines. For tête-à-tête cocktails, consider the **Redwood Room** (Clift Hotel, 495 Geary Street; 415–775–4700), a great place for a pre-dinner drink. The room has carved redwood panels cut from a single tree downed in a storm. It also has a 7-foot print of Gustav Klimt's *The Kiss*. Light fixtures date from 1933, when the room was opened after Prohibition. A grand piano was recently added.

Many restaurants know how to get patrons to the theater on time and how to lure them back after the final curtain. The handiest restaurant in the theater district is just a few steps from the Curran Theatre . . . and the Geary Theater. **La Scene** (at the Warwick Regis Hotel, 490 Geary at Taylor; 415–292–6430; moderate) serves a three-course prix-fixe theater dinner for $23. Sketches of familiar stage stars decorate the bar and dining room. Ask for the table by the front window. At La Scene you may start with mixed greens with classic Dijon vinaigrette and go on to grilled chicken stuffed with aromatic vegetables and mozzarella with herb polenta.

The restaurant will allow you to postpone the final course until after the performance, thus ensuring that the evening ends on a sweet note. The lemon creme brulée shouldn't be rushed. **Brasserie Savoy** (at the Savoy Hotel, 580 Geary Street at Jones; 415–441–2700; moderate) is a traditional French brasserie; three-course theater dinner is priced at $26.

Maybe you have tickets for *Mary Stuart* at the Geary, *Phantom of the Opera* at the Curran, or *Showboat* at the Golden Gate or *Miss Saigon* at the Orpheum. The **Best of Broadway** (415–551–2000) series brings popular musical revivals and touring Broadway companies to San Francisco. The productions can be worth the hefty price of admission. Check the Pink Section of the Sunday *San Francisco Chronicle* for theater reviews. **Curran Theatre** (445 Geary Street between Taylor and Mason) is a 1,678–seat theater. Don't buy tickets in the rear balconies; they have awful acoustics. First opened in 1922, the 2,400-seat **Golden Gate Theatre** (25 Taylor Street between Market and Golden Gate) has been restored to its original opulence. Buy tickets in the mezzanine, which has better sight lines than the orchestra. **Orpheum Theatre** (1192 Market Street at Hyde) also holds Broadway musicals.

The **American Conservatory Theater** (ACT) performs at the **Geary Theater** (415 Geary Street at Mason; 415–749–2228). Check listings for other major theaters. **Alcazar Theater** (650 Geary Street at Jones; 415–441–6655), built in 1917, offers dramas, comedies, and revues in an Arabian-style Islamic temple. Imagine a Syrian facade with filigreed arches and balconies topped by a coffee ice-cream scoop of a dome. The **Stage Door Theatre** (420 Mason Street; 415–392–0569) and **Theatre on the Square** (450 Post Street; 415–433–9500) often have stellar productions.

After your evening at the theater, the night is still young. The dance band at the **Starlight Room** atop the Sir Francis Drake Hotel (450 Powell Street, 21st Floor; 415–392–7755) fills the dance floor until midnight.

As you swirl in each other's arms, city lights sparkle outside the windows. Is there a set of twin stars with your names on them? Try the chocolate martini and you'll see stars.

A Night on the Town

San Francisco bon vivant Harry Denton envisioned the Starlight Room as an elegant night spot, peopled with well-dressed city dwellers and out-of-towners looking for a great martini, a view, and a place to dance the night away to the sounds of big bands.

DAY TWO: MORNING

Breakfast

The morning my husband and I came down to the hotel's Grand Cafe for coffee, we found two cups of steaming cappuccino on the table in front of a man and woman cast in bronze, bent so their laps form seats. Are these chairs taken? Or perhaps the cappuccino is meant for the sculptures and the maitre d' is playing a joke on us. Well, this is the Grand Cafe, the former Beaux-Art ballroom of this 1928 hotel, decorated with storybook art, so don't take things too seriously. Discover more Guibara sculptures. A bear stands on a playmate's shoulders in front of the window. By the entrance, three creatures that are half human/half rabbit rock like a cradle with their hands clasped. The effect is completely enchanting, and it may kindle a desire to shop for art. Before you set out, however, fortify yourselves by lingering a while over a breakfast of crepes, omelettes, or waffles.

Since you shopped yesterday for luxuries and fancy clothing, today visit the galleries around Sutter Street and Grant Avenue. Though the works on display are for sale, you may enjoy your visits to the galleries as you would a museum. Typical hours are Tuesday to Saturday, 10:00 A.M. to 6:00 P.M. At the Sutter Street and Grant Avenue intersection, you have a number of galleries to visit. In one building, located at 250 Sutter Street between Grant and Kearny, you'll find **871 Fine Arts and Bookstore** (415–543–5155) and, on the third floor, the **Braunstein/Quay Gallery** (415–392–5532). These galleries show contemporary sculpture and paintings by

California artists. At the **Meyerovich Gallery** (251 Post Avenue between Stockton & Grant; 415–421–7171) are artists whose names we've all heard: Pablo Picasso, Henri Matisse, Marc Chagall, David Hockney, Andy Warhol. Browse on two floors plus a mezzanine.

Representing the most celebrated names in contemporary art is **228 Grant Avenue** (between Post and Sutter; 415–781–4629) where the prominent **John Berggruen Gallery** is also located. If you like Russian realism, stop at **Nevskar Gallery** (353 Geary Street between Powell and Stockton; 415–392–4932). Notice the brick archway of **Folk Art International** (140 Maiden Lane; 415–392–9999). Designed as a jewelry store by Frank Lloyd Wright in 1948, the owners were furious that he omitted display windows. The spiral ramp inside was one of the prototypes for the architect's Guggenheim Museum in New York City.

Lunch

The traditional meeting place in San Francisco is the large, ornate 1856 Magneta clock in the lobby of the Westin Saint Francis Hotel. "Meet me under the clock" is sufficient instruction to set up a rendezvous. Kick off your shoes at the **Compass Rose** (Westin Saint Francis Hotel on Powell at Geary; 415–774–0167; expensive). Sink into a damask settee and listen to a cello and piano duet in this baronial hall of mahogany, ivory-inlaid panels, fluted Greek columns, and scalloped drapes. You can order lunch or midafternoon tea, enjoying one of the prime spots to watch the pedestrian parade outside the window. For more romance try **Farallon** (450 Post Street between Powell and Mason; 415–956–6969; expensive). You're part of the drama as you join the well-dressed theater-going crowd under the giant shell-like awning. You pass the Jelly Bar with pink jellyfish light fixtures, to the pool room with a sea urchin chandelier and ceiling studded with 1920s-era mosaics. Let the Veuve Cliquot flow. It's a wonderful background for the seafood symphony coming from the kitchen: fresh Dungeness crab with truffled potatoes smoked-fish plate, mackerel tartare, roasted turbot, grilled squab. Appetizers range from $7.00 to $17.00; entrees from $19.00 to $25.00. May wonders (and passion) never cease, even after you check out of the Hotel Monaco.

ITINERARY 8
One day

FEELIN' FRISKY

JACKSON SQUARE

*T*races of the Barbary Coast and the bad, bawdy days of the gold rush await your discovery in and around the Jackson Square Historic District. This amazing collection of buildings, most dating back to the 1850s, withstood the 1906 earthquake and fire. By surviving, the music halls, saloons, and gambling houses catapult the lore and legends of the gold rush into the present.

Newcomers have kept the area vital and attractive. Antiques dealers, architects, and lawyers have moved in. Wonderful restaurants and cafes keep all these folks and their clients satisfied. Globe, a four-star restaurant across from Walton Park, is the historic district's favorite gathering spot. Lovers frequent the hillock surrounded by poplars; they gravitate here as if to an energy spot.

Wherever you go in Jackson Square, the spirit of the Barbary Coast will haunt you with earthy, mischievous excitement.

Practical Notes: This itinerary does not include lodging. It's a one-day itinerary for people who live here, who are staying with friends or relatives, or who are attending a convention. Visitors can add this one-day itinerary onto other itineraries if time permits an extra day in San Francisco. Antiques dealers are open weekdays from 9:30 A.M. to 5:30 P.M. and on Saturday from noon to 5:00 P.M. Pick up a brochure with a map on the back at any antiques shop. The Wells Fargo Museum is open weekdays until 5:00 P.M.

MORNING

Romance at a Glance

♥ *Trace the colorful history of the gold rush at Wells Fargo Museum.*

♥ *Tour a 1907 Barbary Coast saloon, now an acclaimed microbrewery.*

♥ *Relive the baudy 1850s roaming the Jackson Square Historic District.*

♥ *Have drinks at Bix, a former assay office (415–433–6300).*

♥ *Dine and revel at the unconventional Cypress Club (415–296–8555).*

The **Wells Fargo History Museum** (420 Montgomery Street near California; 415–396–2619; closed weekends) traces the founding of Wells Fargo from the gold rush era to the early 1900s. The rooms contain an intriguing assortment of photographs, gold nuggets, miners' equipment, guns, and a motorized Concord stagecoach that gives passengers a bouncy ride. A few blocks away, office high-rises suddenly give way to sun-splashed brick facades as Montgomery Street passes into the Jackson Square Historic District. The Transamerica Building, on the pie-shaped corner of Columbus, Washington, and Montgomery, is one of the city's nineteenth-century "flatiron" structures. Built to conform to lots created by the city's many diagonal intersections, this former bank is an elegant wedge of white masonry, fluted columns, and a black-and-gold circular stairway.

Before the bank stood here, the corner of Montgomery and Clay was called "Murderer's Corner." The city had built a footbridge here in 1848 as a shortcut to the docks. The name of this crossroad reflected the lawlessness that reigned at the height of the gold rush. A pueblo of 300 citizens could do without jails, courts, or sanitation services. But by 1850, gold fever brought 200,000 people from Australia, Chile, Mexico, Spain, the eastern United States, France, Italy, Germany, China, Ireland, and England. This multiethnic, multilingual onslaught turned the sleepy outpost into a noisy, bustling shantytown. A sea of white tents flapped in the breeze across hillsides, while hundreds of empty ships bobbed in the bay. It was said you could walk 4 miles in the bay, crossing from deck to deck on wooden planks.

Local officials, recovering from the onslaught of 200,000 people with 'gold' fever, got busy. Ships were dismantled. Masts became warehouse beams, sails served as tent canvas, and a ship's hull became the first jail. Because people clamored for flat land, the city also used ships as landfill. Yerba Buena Cove was replaced by the warehouses and supply stores that witnessed the rise of the Barbary Coast. This waterfront area of San Francisco, once named after the Mediterranean coastal area of the Barbary states, lived up to its reputation. In the years after the 1849 gold rush, these quiet tree-lined streets were notorious for their gambling dens, saloons, brothels, and disreputable boardinghouses.

All the 1850s buildings on Montgomery Street withstood five fires that ravaged the city between 1848 and 1853. The oldest survivor, **720–722 Montgomery Street** (at Washington), originally the Changeman's Building, was erected in 1849. Freemasons held their first meeting in California here in 1849. Irish dancer Lotta Crabtree entertained miners here when it was a theater. This three-story brick building once housed the law offices of Melvin Belli, who restored it in 1959. It is currently vacant, awaiting structural repairs to damage that was incurred during the 1989 earthquake.

A complete block of buildings on **Jackson Street** from Montgomery to Battery emerged unscathed from various disasters since the gold rush. Notice the recessed windows, a fire precaution. Shutters emerge from enclosures to completely cover the tall windows. The building at the corner of Hotaling and Jackson, dating in part from 1859, was Hotaling's whiskey warehouse, prominent in local lore.

Next to Hotaling's is a medical building, identified by the medical emblem of a staff entwined by a serpent, below the roof. A cigar factory once thrived across the street, and at Number 415–31 Domingo Ghirardelli set up his first chocolate works in 1851. Ghirardelli made a fortune selling chocolate to miners. Number 470, built in 1852, once housed the consulates of Spain, then Chile, and later France. number 472, constructed in 1850, still has ship masts supporting its interior columns. To withstand earthquakes, these brick buildings have been reinforced with steel over the years. Below the roof line you can see a large nut where a steel bar goes through the building. **Balance Street** is not named for a scale to weigh gold but for the ship, the *Balance*, used as landfill, that lies below ground. **Gold Street** is a remnant of the gold rush heyday. The Barbary Coast Assay Office, now Bix's, was at 56 Gold Street. Osgood Place, a tree-lined alleyway between Broadway and Pacific, is a historic landmark. The first block to be labeled the Barbary Coast, it was once a rakish scene with dance halls and taverns bearing names like Boar's Head, Fierce Grizzly, and Goat & Compass.

Lunch

After you've explored the streets, you may be drawn to the wonderful smells emanating from **MacArthur Park** (607 Front Street at Jackson; 415–398–5700). Barbecued meats (especially baby back ribs), great onion strings and skinny fries, Cobb salads, grilled fish and generous, juicy burgers are the Park's claim to culinary fame. MacArthur Park has been a fixture in the lively and historic Jackson Square area of the city since 1972, offering young downtown professionals an upscale after-work watering hole and good American regional cooking. Ensconced in a former warehouse, the dining room has an airy, patio-like feel, with brick walls, a profusion of potted plants and trees, and greenhouse windows overlooking the wooded square. Desserts are huge, diet-busting versions of American classics such as fruit pies, fudge-brownie sundaes, and butterscotch banana cream tartlets.

If you are lunching weekdays you have another option: **Globe** (290 Pacific Avenue between Front and Battery; 415–391–4132). The specialties at this industrial-spare restaurant with snazzy blue-and-chartreuse upholstery and large wall art are wood-fired rotisserie meat, house-made pasta, and grilled fish. This take on American/California cuisine uses seasonal ingredients largely supplied by local farmers.

You can also buy food to go from **Bon Appetite** (145 Jackson Street; 415–982–3112) and enjoy the sunshine at **Sam Walton Park.** Enter the park through the old brick arch (which was once installed at Colombo Market) near the corner of Front Street and Pacific. The centerpiece of the park is a fountain of bronze stalagmites called the *Fountain of the Four Seasons.* The rise and fall of water measures the hour. You may want to choose as your resting spot the grassy knoll encircled by poplars.

AFTERNOON

The current residents of the Barbary Coast have turned it into the center of San Francisco's thriving arts and antiques trade. Twenty-three of the finest antiques shops on the West Coast sell silver, tapestries, carpets, porcelain, and ceramics. **Jackson Square Art and Antique Dealers Association** (414 Jackson Street between Montgomery and Sansome; 415–296–8150) has produced a map and directory. When you are passing along Pacific stop at the Hippodrome, an old concert hall, at 560 Pacific. A pair of celebrated bas-reliefs of nymphs and satyrs by sculptor Arthur Putnam used to be installed at the Hippodrome. Three shops worth browsing are **Thomas Brothers Maps** (550 Jackson at Columbus; 415–981–7520), **William Stout Architectural Books** (804 Montgomery Street at Jackson; 415–391–6757), and **Arch** (407 Jackson Street near Montgomery; 415–433–2724).

San Francisco's first brew pub, **S. F. Brewing Company** (155 Columbus Avenue at Pacific; 415–434–3344), produces its own beer and names them according to Barbary Coast legends and lore. In the barroom, the famous belt-driven paddle fans of the old Albatross Saloon whirl overhead. Ask brewmaster Allen Paul for a tour. He starts with malted barley and whole-leaf hops in the style of European beers. The brewing operation in the basement is surprisingly large—bigger than the combined upstairs rooms. It extends under the street—a tip-off that you are standing in a very old space, once used, contends the brewmaster, as an opium den.

Back upstairs, take a seat in the room adjoining the bar for a ringside view of the street. Order "The Taster," which allows you to share four sample brews, one of which arrives with a lemon wedge on the rim. A huge copper tank fills the front window, the handiwork of San Francisco's last coppersmith. In front of the tank you'll spot a trapdoor cut into the floor. At one time, patrons were "slipped a Mickey" and taken out through this trapdoor and dumped into an awaiting wagon. They awoke the next morning aboard a ship, "Shanghaied to China," as the expression goes. To replace the seamen who fled to the gold fields, captains paid a bounty to bartenders to crew their ships for them by this method. It didn't stop there. One merchant was notorious for shanghaiing his competitors in this fashion.

As we sip an Emperor Norton lager, Allen Paul points to the flatiron building across the alley. "Ladies of easy virtue," as a Frenchman put it, once posed in the turret windows.

Stop at **Specs' Museum Cafe** (12 Saroyan Place off Columbus near Pacific; 415–421–4112; open at 4:30 P.M.) for late-afternoon refreshment. The display cases contain relics of global wanderings from New Guinea to the Congo, donated by seamen and

> *The ceiling, rich in fresco and gilt, was supported by glass pillars, pendant from which were great chandeliers. Entering at night from the unlighted dismal street into an immense room lighted with dazzling brilliance and the mingled sound of musical instruments, the clink of coin and glasses, and the hum of human voices, was like passing from the dark depths to celestial brightness.*
>
> —Historian Hubert Howe Bancroft's description
> of a Barbary Coast gaming house

adventurers who frequented Specs. Read publisher and historian Hubert Howe Bancroft's description of a gambling house of the 1850s.

Next head up **Commercial Street,** which was once an inlet of Yerba Buena Cove. In 1846 Americans from the sloop of war the *Portsmouth* came this way to raise the Stars and Stripes in the plaza atop the cove. You'll find very little evidence of the sleepy Mexican pueblo that was once here in the 1840s as you walk around **Portsmouth Square.** Look for the tablet commemorating the square's historic flag-raising. The first schoolhouse sat on one side. Instead of the Holiday Inn, imagine the Jenny Lind Theater, where Lotta Crabtree sang and showed her famous legs. Lotta accumulated $40 million in her lifetime. She started her fortune by high-stepping the Irish jig in miners' camps. The miners applauded and threw gold nuggets. The bronze ship in the square commemorates the author of *Treasure Island,* Robert Louis Stevenson. The city born from instant wealth drew writers like Mark Twain and Stevenson, who both observed the habits of the newly rich. Gambling was one of them.

EVENING

If you wish to dine as the newly rich, dress in your finest clothes and show up at **Bix** (56 Gold Street between Sansome and Montgomery; 415–433–6300) in the former assay office. The place evokes the clandestine pleasures of bygone eras. Art Deco lamps with beaded shades cast a golden halo of light across each table. Gold shows up in the staircase railing and in the hefty columns. On the wall upstairs hangs a large oil painting by Mark Stock, *The Butler's in Love—Absinthe*. As far as cocktails go, Bix serves one of the best martinis in town, shaken tableside and poured from a vintage silver shaker.

Dinner

After cocktails at Bix, walk over to the Cypress Club for dinner and dancing. The **Cypress Club** (500 Jackson between Columbus and Montgomery; 415–296–8555; expensive) has a spectacular interior combining set elements from *Star Trek* and a 1940s Hollywood nightclub scene. Playful elegance marks the menu as well. Entrees, ranging from $25 to $32, include salmon, roasted lobster, lamb, Sonoma squab, and Cervena venison chop. The Cypress Club is also a jazz venue where top-name jazz bands such as the Brian Melvin Trio play until 11:00 P.M. on Thursday and Friday and until midnight Saturday.

SOMETHING TO SING ABOUT

CITYFRONT DISTRICT

While most of the visitor traffic flows north to Fisherman's Wharf, this itinerary has you heading south along the bay-hugging Embarcadero to witness the birth of a new district. Banners snap in the breezes, palm trees stand regal along the center median, where the sparkling new E-line streetcar runs and pleasure craft berth at South Beach Marina. Just beyond the harbor, the San Francisco Giants will play the opening game April 2000 at their new ballpark (China Basin channel, King, Second, and Third Streets). The other end of the waterfront is also giving city officials something to crow about. People are coming from all over the city to shop for organic produce at the Saturday morning farmers' market. In every season visitors flock to Justin Herman Plaza for special events. The focal point for your special weekend is the penthouse suite overlooking the Bay Bridge and Treasure Island. You'll have a half-canopy bed draped in tapestry and a telescope you can use to watch the sailors and deck hands on the yachts crossing the bay. Take time for a kiss in front of the floor-to-ceiling windows, where only seagulls will see you.

Practical Notes: Every two years the plaza and waterfront is transformed into an outdoor ballroom for a gala charity event. You may want to time your visit to attend this special event, staged on the waterfront in May. Purchase tickets to the Black & White Ball a month in advance (415–864–6000) and pack your finest formal evening wear. Even if you can't be here for the ball, this itinerary is great at any time of year. Request one of the large, lush banquettes when reserving at Shanghai 1930 (415–896–5600).

DAY ONE: MORNING

Arrive early to visit **Embarcadero Center** (at the foot of Market Street between Clay and Sacramento). This complex of four high-rise office buildings spans eight city blocks and houses three levels of shops and restaurants as well as a movie theater, comedy club, and two hotels. The landscaped terraces and pedestrian bridges are fun to explore. If you get lost, look for the Ferry Building clock tower. Descend the spiral staircase to Justin Herman Plaza and have a seat at one of the tables on the concrete deck.

Romance at a Glance

♥ *View the waterfront from your penthouse room at Harbor Court Hotel (415–882–1300 or 800–346–0555)*

♥ *Shop at the Embarcadero Center.*

♥ *Walk arm-in-arm along the Cityfront promenade.*

♥ *Sail the bay at sunset.*

♥ *Dine at Shanghai 1930.*

♥ *Sample the sourdough baguettes, boursin, fresh raspberries, etc. at the Ferry Plaza Farmers' Market.*

The first feature of the plaza to catch your attention is a jumble of open granite cubes two stories high and the sound of cascading water. The Vaillancourt Fountain incorporates into its design staircases and concrete slabs that lead across the basin. Step onto the walkway and walk behind the cascading water. The unending tumult from upper-level cubes charges the air. The effect is exhilarating.

From the Justin Herman Plaza you'll also have a good view of whatever special event is taking place. In summer, there are noontime concerts; in autumn, a Bavarian-style Oktoberfest; during Fleet Week, the Blue Angels precision flight team, on New Year's Eve, a rockin', stompin' block party; in May, the Black & White Ball, when thousands of San Franciscans, dressed in tuxedos and black and white ball gowns, dance until 1:30 A.M.

Lunch

Both the façade and the lobby of the old **Rincon Annex Post Office** (Mission Street between Spear and Steuart; 415–243–0473) have been preserved, along with the California history mural created by Russian artist Anton Refregier. Look at his murals sequentially. When Refregier resumed painting the panels, having been interrupted by World War II, he was a confirmed communist. The timbre of his work becomes increasingly unsettling: riots, hard-set faces, communist banners, splashes of red. The entryway of the post office leads to the building's new addition called Rincon Center. Architects took the classic Art Deco post office built in 1939 and added a modern atrium-style shopping and eating complex, completed in 1988. Compare the intensity of Refregier's mural to the one you will see, by another artist, in the atrium. The staid, colorless frieze of modern San Francisco commissioned for the addition couldn't offer more of a contrast.

The food court, on the other hand, offers a colorful, palate-pleasing range of choices. You'll be able to select from such offerings as deli sandwiches, gourmet burgers, and ethnic cuisines like Indian, Korean, Mexican, and Chinese. On the day we visited, we made the rounds of the inexpensive take-out shops to help us decide. Then we spread our cartons and containers on a table by the atrium's 90-foot rain column as an indoor picnic.

DAY ONE: AFTERNOON

Check into a bay-view penthouse suite atop the **Harbor Court Hotel** (165 Steuart Street; 415–882–1300 or 800–346–0555; $195–$315). At the time Bill Kimpton bought the YMCA residence, intending to remodel it into a boutique hotel, a bi-level elevated expressway swung by the guestrooms. Now the diesel buses and East Bay commuters whizzing by the hotel's guestroom windows are gone. By demolishing the soot-encrusted freeway damaged in the 1989 earthquake, city planners gave the hotel and the waterfront a new lease on life.

Leave the hotel in windbreakers and athletic shoes to enjoy the renaissance of the waterfront, now touted as the Cityfront district. Head for the south corner of the Ferry

Building and face the financial district. After the tombstone slabs of the Embarcadero Center went up, lovers of the city pleaded with architects to give the skyline more interesting shapes. From this vantage point you see the result: a geometric cacophony that is anything but grim. There are sawtooth edges, glass silos, and mansard roofs.

From the Ferry Building south to the base of the Oakland Bay Bridge runs the **Waterfront Promenade**: ideal to jog along, to fish from, or to admire the view. Follow the promenade as it hugs the bay and notice the elegant brick and terra-cotta facade of the other side of the Harbor Court Hotel. When it was a YMCA residence, it was *the* place to stay in the city. Notice the contrasting Art Deco features of the adjacent office building. The ocean-liner curve of the upper stories is not a tribute to 1930s architecture but a concession to the curved roadway of the elevated Embarcadero Freeway. It would have clipped a huge chunk off a square building.

The Promenade is also a great place to relish the monumental anchor piers, towers, trusses, and cables of the Oakland Bay Bridge. This engineering marvel rises up with nothing in the foreground to clutter your vision. As you stroll, stop at the flagpoles and let your eyes roam over the span. During the catastrophic rush-hour quake of 1989, a motorist on the bridge saw a temblor strum those suspension cables like harp strings.

Along the Promenade are plaques and pylons recalling historical events and people of the area. Pause to read the one in front of the fireboat station: It may awaken your appreciation for these heroic vessels. The gate to the fireboat station yard may be open. If the marine engineer is working on the fireboat, he may invite you on board for a tour. Not too long ago the city considered scrapping their one fireboat to cut costs. These boats rust easily if neglected for too long, so maintenance is a costly necessity. When broken gas mains from the last earthquake set the Marina District ablaze, water mains were severed as well. Luckily, this old fireboat had been spared the scrapyard. Pumping bay water through mile-long hoses, it saved the Marina District. After the earthquake, the city bought another fireboat, just in case.

Activity on the bay never ceases: sculling boats, sea kayaks, freighters, tugs, Coast Guard power boats. Look at the names and home ports on the sterns of cargo ships—*Kokusai Maru, Jeppson*

Maersk—as they all head for Oakland, where twelve-story cranes lift the containers onto docks.

You'll be joining the parade of boats shortly if you continue to South Beach Marina, across from a new housing complex. *Sea Change* (foot of King Street), a seventy-foot-tall bright red sculpture welded in steel, marks the entrance to South Beach Yacht Harbor and the southern end of the Embarcadero. It has a kinetic piece that moves with the wind. The ship to the right has appeared in *Mutiny on the Bounty*, *Hawaii*, and *Stowaway* and is only open for private events. Walk around the yacht harbor. You can rent a 30-foot sailboat with a captain on board for $364. Or you can hop aboard the brigantine *Rendezvous* with other passengers for a sunset sail. **Spinnaker Sailing/Rendezvous Charters** (Pier 40, South Beach Harbor at Townsend; 415–543–7333) has cruises timed to catch the sunset and the moonrise. Built in 1932 and restored, the *Rendezvous* has seen sunsets in the South Pacific. Help yourselves to picnic-style hors d'oeuvres and wine early on. The skipper has to stow food and beverages before approaching Alcatraz.

DAY ONE: EVENING

Dinner

Return to your room and dress for glamorous dining at **Shanghai 1930** (133 Steuart Street between Mission and Howard; 415–896–5600; expensive) on the busy Steuart Street corridor.

The restaurant recalls a maritime link between San Francisco and this port city at the mouth of the Yangtze River where France, Great Britain, and the United States all held large concessions until 1949. Until then, splendid dining was a nightly occurrence. Delve into exotic Shanghainese cuisine such as five-spice rack of lamb, tofu crab roe, drunken squab in Shaoxing wine, and cod pillows with tree ears. For dessert try the coconut custard or pear in cassis. The sky blue back bar is a dreamy setting for nightly live jazz.

⌇⌇⌇

Back out in the fresh air, continue past the Ferry Building to **Pier 7** (foot of Broadway Street), with Victorian gas lamps to light the way. You are about as far as you can go into the bay without getting wet. The light-festooned bridge casts diamonds on the water. If Pier 7 had been here when Tony Bennett composed his tribute to San Francisco, he may have added it to the lyrics. It's a sight that tugs on the heartstrings.

On returning to your hotel, you'll notice a charged liveliness along Steuart Street. The denizens of **Harry Denton's** (at the Harbor Court Hotel) spill out into the street. Go up to your room and dress for the party. The atmosphere at Harry's is fin-de-siecle posh with Jaguar red walls, a mahogany bar, and a well-dressed crowd. Harry Denton, San Francisco's Duke of Earl, hires top bands: jazz, blues and swing, and Motown. The dance floor is tiny, so close dancing is the only kind you can do.

DAY TWO: MORNING

Breakfast

Begin Saturday morning at the **Ferry Plaza Farmers' Market** at the foot of Market Street. In front of the old-world arcaded clock tower building (modeled after the Cathedral of Seville's Giralda Tower), farmers set up by 9:00 A.M. The market showcases what few areas in the world can match: an extraordinary agricultural bounty. In great cities such as Florence, Paris, Barcelona, Istanbul, Mexico City, Vancouver, Seattle, Tokyo, and Hong Kong, the life of the city has for centuries focused on large, central markets. It took a cadre of restaurants chefs in this century to

Bed of Mizuna

You may recognize many popular menu items among the stalls at the Ferry Plaza Farmers' Market. Our favorite was "Bed of Mizuna." Wasn't that from Arabian Nights' Entertainments? *Or was it Gloria's menu again from the Big Four Restaurant? Sounds so much better than what it is: a mound of dandelion-type salad greens.*

give San Francisco this lively center. They recruited local farmers to produce a variety of superlative vegetables, cheese, bread, and poultry and sell it here in the city each Saturday.

Pick up scones or gingerbread at Healdsburg Bakery and cafe lattés from the coffee vendor. After that, nibble your way from stall to stall. Smells from the produce stalls are intoxicating. Sweet corn, heritage tomatoes, basil, Acme sourdough baguettes. At one stall, red peppers are slowly charred in a hand-cranked roaster. Whatever stall you stop at longer than fifteen seconds, you'll be feeding each other goat cheese, raspberries, pear-shaped cherry tomatoes, persimmon-colored tomatoes, orange-flavored almonds, and much more. Be sure to buy some of the wonderful olive oil grown, pressed, and bottled by Nick Sciabica & Sons. Celebrity chefs drop by at 10:00 A.M. You may spot Alice Waters signing copies of her book. She appeared on stage under the canopy, extolling the virtues of organic produce and sharing recipes.

Hoffman Game Birds sells pheasant and chukar, but their quail is the current favorite on restaurant menus. Gloria at the Big Four Restaurant atop Nob Hill brushes half a quail with rum and molasses and then grills it. I ordered it one evening as an appetizer—the tiniest fowl ever to appear on a plate.

On mornings other than Saturday market day, hop the E-Line and head down to South Beach for breakfast. **Town's End Restaurant and Bakery** (2 Townsend Street at Brannan;

415–512–0749; inexpensive) offers the best breakfast in the city. They are known for their muffins, bread, and good American fare. After nibbling on these goodies, you might want a bit of exercise. Guests of the Harbor Court Hotel can use the city's finest health club, the **YMCA,** free of charge. If you like to work out together, this club (next to the hotel) has unbeatable bay views, a lap pool, and sauna and steam rooms. Check out of the hotel, but leave your luggage at the front desk and return to the YMCA on the waterfront.

DAY TWO: AFTERNOON

Lunch

For an al fresco lunch, **Palomino** (345 Spear Street at Folsom; 415–512–7400; moderate) serves crisp pizzas, swordfish, and fresh pasta on a patio warmed by heat lamps. After lunch, your next destination is parked at a pier down the way.

Walk down to Pier 32 and board the Liberty ship, SS *Jeremieh O'Brien* (at the foot of Brannan Street; 415–441–3101). America's last unaltered Liberty ship, one of the great fleet of supply ships that operated in World War II, remains in operating condition. If you visit on "steaming weekend" (usually the third weekend of the month), the engineer cranks up the ship's triple expansion steam engine. Scenes for the film *Titanic* were filmed in the engine room. Visit the ship's store, where you can look at pictures of the busy shipyards and the female riveters on the assembly lines. The *Jeremieh O'Brien* cruises the bay the third weekend in May to give everyone the thrill of sailing on a vintage World War II vessel.

FOR MORE ROMANCE

Have an extra day to spend with only each other? You can tie this itinerary into the Sausalito waterfront getaway. Hop the Sausalito ferry and turn to Waterfront Itinerary 11. The Inn Above Tide serves binoculars with breakfast.

ITINERARY 10
Two days and one night

CHOCOLATE, CHAMPAGNE, CIOPPINO

NORTHERN WATERFRONT

*S*ometimes all I remember is the food: the chocolate, the champagne, the sourdough with cioppino. When special occasions move into the realm of memory, they take on an added luster. The same is true of special places. The city waterfront will merge with whatever images you have of port cities and their wharfside bustle. Although the docks are quiet, sea gulls and ships still own the waterfront. A poem once described these ubiquitous seabirds as the reincarnated souls of mariners.

Walk the waterfront with a poet's wondrous imagination and you may catch a sea chantey on the breeze, perhaps the deep baritone of seamen hoisting a sail in unison. Along the Embarcadero, as the waterfront road is now called, you can stop and read a few short lines of poetry on the plaques embedded in the sidewalk. Along with the poems, the plaques regale an era of the city's past when possessing one of the world's largest natural harbors meant the world docked at your doorstep.

Practical Notes: Along with all the benefits of being close to the waterfront, this itinerary features the best bargain in the city—a penthouse (complete with bay views from a stuffed and fluffed brass bed) for $125 a night. Its claw-foot bathtub, Victorian stained glass, and dark wood wainscoting retain the 1906 ambience of a waterfront lodging house. Reserve the penthouse well in advance by calling the San Remo Hotel (415–776–8688 or 800–352–7366; other rooms with a shared bath range from $60 to $75). Hornblower Dining Yachts (415–788–8866; moderate) combines a three-hour cruise, a four-course dinner, and a three-piece band. Ask for a window seat in the dining salon. Booking Hornblower's celebration package guarantees a window seat. Ask for the second-floor salon if you want to whirl around the dance floor between courses. The wind outside the Golden Gate cuts through evening clothes. While walking the decks, bring something warm to keep from shivering.

DAY ONE: AFTERNOON

Arrive early and take yourself to the waterfront, starting where it all began, at the **Ferry Building** at the foot of Market Street. Much like the Statue of Liberty in New York and Big Ben in London, the Ferry Building has served the city as a symbol and landmark. From 1898 until the bridges spanned the bay, a million people passed through its arcades each week. The Embarcadero curves north past the odd-numbered pier sheds—warehouses that once were filled with goods from Indonesia, China, and Thailand. Pier 35 is the cruise ship terminal. Summertime cruises through the Northwest Passage to Alaska are usually booked to capacity. Although the ships that dock along the waterfront nowadays carry people rather than cargo, an abundance of exotic goods, which used to fill the hulls of ships, now overflow the shelves and cavernous space of **Cost Plus Imports** (2552 Taylor Street between Bay and North Point; 415–928–6200). This import store is an ideal terminus for an afternoon walk.

Romance at a Glance

♥ *Sleep in a brass bed at the* San Remo Hotel penthouse.

♥ *Take a dinner dance cruise on the bay aboard the* California Hornblower.

♥ *Stroll along the beach at Aquatic Park.*

♥ *Lunch at the birthplace of cioppino, on the pier.*

♥ *Shop Ghirardelli Square.*

Check into the penthouse of the **San Remo Hotel** (2237 Mason Street at Chestnut; 415–776–8688 or 800–352–7366; $60–$70) as much for its view and privacy as well as its unique ambience as a vestige of the old waterfront. Working men, Alaskan fishermen, artists, and writers all have lodged here. The current owners have spiffed up the brass fixtures, redwood wainscoting, stained-glass skylights, and tile floors and refinished the antique furniture for your comfort and pleasure. So kick off your shoes and dash for that brass bed.

DAY ONE: EVENING

As twilight approaches, it's time to cross the tracks. Before boarding the *California Hornblower* at 7:00 P.M., walk along Bay Street to the Embarcadero and turn right. Near Battery Street, cross the Muni streetcar tracks to **Pier 23 Cafe** (The Embarcadero at Battery; 415–362–5125). Flicka McGurrin's funky hangout has been around so long, it may have inspired the 1963 hit by Jimmy Gilmer and the Fireballs: *"There's a crazy little shack beyond the track. And everybody calls it the sugar shack."* Sit on the patio with a cocktail and enjoy live jazz, world beat, Motown, Latin-salsa, and reggae from 5:00 P.M. on Tuesday, Wednesday, Thursday, and Saturday, and from 10:00 P.M. on Friday.

Dinner

After drinks at Pier 23, retrace your steps to Pier 33 and **Hornblower Dining Yachts** (the Embarcadero at Sansome Street) to board the 183-foot *California Hornblower*. (Boarding begins at 7:00 P.M.; departure is at 7:30 P.M.) This newly built replica of an opulent turn-of-the-century steamer is the perfect vehicle on which to enjoy the city's ever-changing skyline. Tables are handsomely set with fine china, crystal, and silver. The dinner dance cruise is like being on a cruise ship, without the dip and roll of the open sea. On our cruise, my husband popped the champagne and filled our glasses. Foam tumbled over the rims and we toasted each other as the ship slipped out of the pier. Bon voyage.

Each course of our dinner emerged from the galley at thirty-minute intervals. I predict you, too, will start on the salad just as the skipper steers slowly past the waterfront. The city skyline dazzles at night. The name Ghirardelli in marquee lights illuminates Aquatic Park. A long municipal pier curves into the bay like a question mark. You'll visit these places tomorrow on foot. North of the Golden Gate Bridge, the Marin Headlands loom dark and distant. Then, suddenly, the scenery closes in. Residences in Sausalito sit precariously over the edge of hillsides, allowing the ship to pass close by. I looked up during dessert and saw a man watching television in his condo on the Sausalito waterfront. After dessert near Sausalito, take a turn on the deck, for at this point Richardson's Bay is out of the wind and often balmy in warm weather. Stop by the wheelhouse and watch the skipper guide the *California Hornblower* through Raccoon Straits.

Choose an isolated stretch of the deck to pause at the railing. If it's a perfect night for stargazing, the heavens will shine for the two of you. In Raccoon Straits, out of the reach of city lights, stars beam more brightly.

The excitement among passengers heightened ours. The band played well enough to make us linger on the dance floor. The bandleader may ask you for "your song," or you can write down your request and slip it to the bandleader to make it a surprise for your companion.

Be at the prow of the ship for the long, slow return to the pier at about 10:00 P.M. These moments may be the ones you treasure the most. It looks like someone blew fairy dust over the waterfront from the way the lampposts and office lights sparkle. Your penthouse is a short stroll from the pier.

DAY TWO: MORNING

Breakfast

When you awaken in the morning, prepare for a day of shopping, beachcombing, and other waterfront delights. Stroll leisurely or briskly to Fisherman's Wharf, where the smell of

crab pots fills the morning air. Have breakfast at the **Eagle Cafe** (Pier 39, second floor; 415–433–3689; inexpensive), a wharfside eatery rescued from demolition and lifted by crane to Pier 39's second level. San Remo lodgers from days of yore also ate here; if only the rafters could speak. The cafe has outlived the demolished Embarcadero Expressway, whose construction forced the Eagle's relocation. The quintessential "salty dog" hangout, the Eagle is still today the haunt of stevedores, longshoremen, and waterfront lovers.

☙☙☙

Skip the rest of Pier 39 and the cheap souvenir shops of Fisherman's Wharf, and save your shopping money for **Ghirardelli Square** (900 North Point Street; 415–775–5500). Walk north on Jefferson Street 3 blocks. A splendid location for eighty shops and restaurants, the fine old brick buildings of the square reopened in 1962 as the city's first theme shopping center. The **Ghirardelli Chocolate Factory** (Clock Tower Building; Beach Street and Larkin; 415–771–4903) has occupied the same site since 1895. Italian-born Domingo Ghirardelli arrived in San Francisco during the peak of the gold rush and opened his confectionery. Ghirardelli mint chocolate . . . now *that* will get you through a hard day of panning for gold. They still sell the creamy, rich chocolate miners packed up to the gold fields, as well as ice cream sundaes with all the trimmings and toppings. View the chocolate factory works, then stroll through Ghirardelli Square. A sign-posted walking tour starts at Fountain Plaza, where a mermaid family cavorts with sea creatures in Ruth Asawa's beloved fountain.

A reminder of San Francisco's seafaring past, **Hyde Street Pier** (Hyde Street at Jefferson; 415–556–3002; open daily) has six historic ships moored to its docks. Board the *Balclutha,* a full-rigger that rounded Cape Horn seventeen times. The *Eureka,* a ferryboat, has a vintage car exhibit, and *C.A. Thayer,* a lumber schooner, holds sea chantey songfests the first Saturday of every month from 8:00 P.M. to midnight. The **National Maritime Museum** (Beach Street at the foot of Polk; 415–556–3002; open daily) has scale models and shipping relics on the first floor alongside carved and painted figureheads.

Kick off your shoes in the sand of **Aquatic Park,** the city's first municipal beach. Don't wade by the rocky end unless you want to slice a toe on "souvenirs." When the tide is out, you can see the rubble that was dumped along the seawall ninety years ago. Apparently, cartloads of rubble from the 1906 earthquake and fire ended up at Aquatic Park. Later on, this natural cove was the site of several water-oriented spectacles. Harry Houdini once released himself from chains and escaped from a trunk tossed into Aquatic Park. His head broke the water's surface in fifty-seven seconds. Today the most activity takes place out on the municipal pier. Walk out and mingle with the Asian families reeling in lines or pulling up crab baskets; it may give you an appetite for seafood.

Lunch

Have lunch at **Alioto's** (8 Fisherman's Wharf; 415–673–0183; moderate) in the terraced upstairs dining room overlooking the fishing basin, once the heart of a huge commercial fishing fleet. Today we are here to visit the birthplace of cioppino, a fish stew that reminded Rose "Nonna" Alioto of her Sicilian homeland. Joe and Nunzio have put Nonna Rose's recipes back on the menu after discovering that people like regional Italian cooking. The Sicilian food served here is hearty and spicy and features ingredients such as lemon, raisins, pine nuts, figs, and lentils, and, since Sicily is an island, seafood is plentiful—swordfish, prawns, red mullet, baby scallops.

Try Sicilian salmon or the aforementioned cioppino. Balking at the bib the waiter offers? My advice is, enjoy the tomato broth, don't wear it. Entrees range from $9.00 to $32.00 (which is for the abalone).

If you want something sweet on the walk back to the San Remo, stop at **Ben and Jerry's** on the waterfront. Enjoy a cup of "Heavenly Hash" and linger at your penthouse view before checking out. Take home memories of "the times down at that crazy little sugar shack."

ITINERARY 11
One day and one night

MOONLIGHT SONATA

SAUSALITO WATERFRONT

*R*oom 314. Now that was a night to remember. Of the hundreds of hotels within a 10-mile radius of San Francisco Bay, we happened to be in the only hotel *on* San Francisco Bay. The moment we crossed the lobby threshold, we left dry land. It was hard to believe until Verena, the general manager, pointed out the 100-year-old seawall in the courtyard. We timed our visit to the full moon. Wine glasses in hand, we sat before a floor-to-ceiling window in our hotel room. Richardson Bay, as still as the hour before dawn, took upon its surface a swiftly growing arc of white moonlight.

Practical Notes: Arriving by boat makes you feel much farther from the city than 5 miles. Ferry across the bay to Sausalito from either the Ferry Building or Fisherman's Wharf. The **Golden Gate Ferry** departs nine times a day from the terminal behind the Ferry Building (at the foot of Market Street; 415–923–2000). The Blue & Gold Ferry shuttles visitors from Fisherman's Wharf (Pier 41; 415–773–1188) to Sausalito from 11:00 A.M. on weekdays and from 10:40 A.M. on weekends and holidays. Time your stay at the Inn Above Tide for a special event. If you can't make it in December for the Lighted Yacht Parade or in April for the Opening Day on the Bay, at least plan ahead for a full moon. Keep in mind this itinerary is geared toward water buffs.

DAY ONE: AFTERNOON

Disembarking from a ferry and checking immediately into a hotel is something I haven't done since a trip to Greece. Driving over the Golden Gate Bridge can't compare with the exhilarating thirty-minute ferry ride from the city proper to Sausalito. As you smartly descend the gangway at Gabrielson Park, know that you've chosen the most magical way to enter Sausalito. This is how affluent turn-of-the-century San Franciscans retreated from the city. Victorian cottages still grace the Sausalito hillside, some dating from 1890. **The Inn Above Tide** (30 El Portal; 415–332–9535 or 800–893–8433; $195–$445), built over the water on the shore of Sausalito, is next to the ferry landing in the center of the village. This three-story inn is redefining the meaning of "panoramic view."

The thirty rooms and suites all face the bay. Most of the rooms have gas jet fireplaces and private decks over the water. Reserve a corner suite to have a view of the bay on two sides. The room rate includes continental breakfast and a wine-and-cheese reception in the evening. Noted hotel interior designer Nan Rosenblatt's decor blends with the watery vista at high noon, at twilight, and in the misty morning. Whisper-soft blues, sea greens, and shell whites spread across walls, bedspreads, lounge chairs, ottomans, and drapes that barely interrupt the view.

After checking in, walk north along the waterfront park to the marina, a massive concentration of yachts. The beauty and expense of the boats reveal the passion of Sausalito sailors for their sport. Anchored at the end of a pier, you'll see a stark,

Romance at a Glance

♥ *Take a ferry to the Inn Above Tide (415–332–9535, or 800–893–8433), where your fireplaced room provides a panoramic water view.*

♥ *Visit Schoonmaker Point Marina, a haven for water buffs.*

♥ *Watch the moon rise while dining on Mediterranean-inspired cuisine at Mikayla (415–331–5888).*

♥ *Sail a catamaran under the Golden Gate Bridge.*

♥ *Stroll along the seawall in the moonlight.*

white miniature of the Taj Mahal. It's a houseboat that's also rented for parties and weddings. Wander back to the inn to enjoy wine and cheese in your room.

Binoculars are provided in each room, as is evening wine with grapes, cheese, baguettes, and crudités. Because The Inn Above Tide is on the water, your room is a ringside seat for colorful water-oriented events. You'll see an endless cavalcade of pleasure craft: yachts, catamarans, tall-mast schooners, along with swift wooden sculls and kayaks. Snack on hors d'oeuvres in your room, and watch the moon rise over the East Bay Ridge. It seems the moon above the open bay casts a path of diamonds leading directly to Room 314. Book a window table at the Mikayla restaurant for after the moonrise.

DAY ONE: EVENING

Dinner

Walk to the **Casa Madrona Hotel and Restaurant** and take the elevator up to **Mikayla Restaurant** (801 Bridgeway; 415–331–5888; moderate) which has gorgeous views from the glassed-in porch. As stunning as the moonlight is, you'll stop in mid-sentence when the food arrives. Chef David Buttons romances the Mediterranean theme with rack of lamb with eggplant couscous torte, pan-roasted rock cod with saffron risotto, and striped bass inside a crust of potatoes. Entrees range from $11 to $19.

⸎

The rise of a full moon brings romance to the old seawall. Stroll the parapet as far as you can go, out toward the Chart House Restaurant. At this distance, night encases San Francisco in luminous crystal. An infinity of lights shines forth. Along the seawall couples are seated among the rocks, sharing, perhaps, a bottle of Pinot Noir along with this marvelous night.

Water laps at the sides of Benny Bufano's bronze sea lion. Scullers row noiselessly home.

DAY TWO: MORNING

Breakfast

Scullers may be the first sight you see the next morning, rowing single file in front of the window. Sea kayakers are usually out, too, paddling figure eights close to the shore. Seagulls fuss and squawk above the ferry while visitors disembark. After juice and coffee in front of the window, ask at the front desk for a Sausalito map. En route to Schoonmaker Point, stop at **Caffé Trieste** (1000 Bridgeway; 415–332–7770), a branch of the famous North Beach coffeehouse. Sit outside if the sun has appeared. Afterward continue walking on Bridgeway Boulevard for about ten minutes. You can also hop aboard a bus that frequently makes its way along Bridgeway, but the driver requires exact fare. If you want a more substantial breakfast, stop at **Fred's Coffee Shop** (1917 Bridgeway Boulevard at Spring; 415–332–4575). This casual coffeehouse about a half mile from the touristy section of Bridgeway is a locals' spot serving home-style breakfasts since 1966. Fred's French toast is addictive, as is the steak and eggs with golden hash browns. Swedish pancakes, omelets, and scrambled whipped eggs are also on the menu. Don't worry about the calories: You'll burn it off paddling on Richardson's Bay. Cross the street to the **Bay Model Visitors Center** (2100 Bridgeway Boulevard at Marinship Way, Gate 6 Road; 415–332–3871), a working model of San Francisco Bay and Delta simulating the bay's tides and currents.

❧

Go down the hill at Liberty Ship Way and walk toward the water. Sausalito supports a thriving artists' community. At the **Schoonmaker Building** (10 Liberty Ship Way; 415–331–6466) check the "We're in" board for artists accepting visitors that day. Artists were drawn to the beautiful natural setting with its fog and light as well as to the promise of affordable art studios. They set up shop in these industrial buildings vacated after World War II when the shipyard was closed. You may see handmade paper jewelry, Chinese brush painting, watercolors, and nature photography.

All types of sport centers moved into the remaining buildings. A paradise for water buffs, **Schoonmaker Point Marina** keeps you wet and wild with kayak rentals, water-bike rentals, as well as sailboat and powerboat charters. **Captain Case's Powerboat & Waterbike Rentals** (85 Liberty Ship Way, off Marinship Way and Bridgeway; 415–331–0444) rents powerboats, unsinkable Boston Whalers that go from 25 to 40 miles per hour. You can also scoot around the bay on a high-tech waterbike that you pedal yourself. At Schoonmaker Beach you can rent sea kayaks and take classes with **Sea Trek** (415–332–4465 or 415–488–1000). Turn right at the palm tree. You'll catch the Sea Trek staff at the beach all day seven days a week during the busy season from May to October. They offer the best option for exploring the Sausalito coastline on your own, paddling into the community of floating homes (locals don't like to call them houseboats). Those who live freely out in the water are called "anchor-outs": floating junkyards to city officials who have tried for years to oust them.

If you're wondering "what next," from the beach you'll see the most adventurous way to spend the rest of the morning. *Apparition*, a catamaran, and skipper Stan (**Sausalito Waterfront Tours;** 415–331–8730) are the perfect combination for a spectacular sail through Richardson Bay, under the Golden Gate Bridge, past the San Francisco waterfront, and between Angel Island and Tiburon. The ride is smooth and stable, and Sausalito Waterfront Tours offers complimentary pickup and return within Sausalito. The back of the hulls have steps that you can sit on. Being so near the wake may give you some playful ideas. Take off your shoes and drag your feet in the water. The skipper will let you steer under the Golden Gate Bridge and help with the sails. On the way in, you'll spot your hotel room and the restaurant where you plan to have lunch.

Rowing in Eden—
Ah, the Sea!
Might I but moor—Tonight—
In Thee!

—Emily Dickinson, from *Wild Nights*

DAY TWO: AFTERNOON

Lunch

Back on land, return to the village via the **Sausalito Shuttle** at Easterby Street and get off at **The Spinnaker** (100 Spinnaker Drive; 415–332–1500; moderate). Lunch is served over the bay from 11:00 A.M. to 3:00 P.M. Halibut California comes with mango salsa, but a hearty sandwich may be more what you're looking for. Try the smoked Black Forest ham on sourdough baguette. Entrees range from $7.00 to $15.00.

Walk back to the hotel along the bayfront **Gabrielson Park.** The residents may strike you as dog lovers, since their pets can quench their thirst at an ornate doggy fountain. Sally Stanford, a legendary madam in the 1920s and 1930s who ran her operation from a mansion in San Francisco, bequeathed money to the town to erect the fountain. She ran the former Valhalla Restaurant, which is now the Chart House you saw last night, at the end of Bridgeway. A much-beloved citizen, Sally later became mayor of Sausalito; she died in 1982.

Leave your bags at the Inn and browse in the galleries, boutiques, and handicraft shops in the village. Outside the door of the inn is **Sausalito Designs** (22 El Portal; 415–331–0588), where you can pick up nautical gear. Windbreakers, jackets, and sweaters come in all weights to cover all types of weather conditions on the bay. Anyone with the sea in his or her blood will want to stop at **Armchair Sailor Bookstore** (42 Caledonia Street between Johnson and Pine; 415–332–7505). Ship models mounted on the walls range from $175 up to $900 for the half-hull model hand carved in teak. Look over the collection of new and used nautical books, international charts, cruising guides, and navigation instruments. Continue on Bridgeway and before returning to your hotel take a short detour to explore the shops on Princess Street. Princess leads to the back streets, which are lined with lovely homes.

For More Romance

Rather than take the 5:20 P.M. ferry back to San Francisco, stay an extra night at The Above Tide Inn. If you want one more intimate experience of the bay, go out tonight with **Sea Trek** (415–332–4465) for a moonlight adventure. They lead a group of sea kayakers to Margaritaville (a restaurant in Sausalito) for a lively dinner and then back into the bay again. When the full moon shines on the bay, you glide through a gem-strewn landscape. Enchantment rules the night.

Consider this twist on a typical sunset sail: a 1790s trading vessel from teak trim to mahogany paneling brings alive the days of Spanish explorers and pirates. **The Hawaiian Chieftain** (Marina Plaza Harbor, 2310 Marinship Way off Bridgeway; 415–331–3214) is run by a six-person crew dressed in old-time British naval uniforms, who control the ship's ten sails. Even Disneyland can't compete. Brunch, sunset, and educational cruises leave Sausalito from April through October, although the Friday sunset sail is the best for couples.

THEME
ITINERARIES

ITINERARY 12
Two days and one night

PUTTIN' ON THE RITZ

PARIS OF THE WEST

"What does Paris have that we don't have?" asked boastful San Franciscans in the 1890s. We have the Ritz, we have *les maisons des couturiers* of Paris. We have haute cuisine. To which the French minister of culture replied, "Ah, the touching arrogance of cities born only yesterday." A hundred years later, San Franciscans are still crowing. "We have those Martian green kiosks and automatic toilets, only ours are three feet higher than the ones in Paris."

San Francisco, since its abrupt inception, has benefited from the largesse of people who made their fortunes here. To early resident Alma Spreckels (wife of the heir of the huge fortune of sugar king Claus Spreckels) and others, French culture could be purchased, packaged, and imported. One of Spreckels's friends introduced her to the sculptor Auguste Rodin, suggesting that she buy his sculptures for her "little museum in San Francisco." Alma's (and her husband, Adolph's) museum stands on a majestic bluff in Lincoln Park, a replica of the Legion of Honor in Paris. One of the first casts of "The Thinker" stands in the courtyard. This itinerary, while paying a compliment to the city many regard as the standard-bearer of culture, shows you a city that still wears the accolade Paris of the West so well.

Practical Notes: The Ritz-Carlton retains its glow from one season to the next. Ask for an inside room overlooking the garden courtyard. You'll enjoy the fresh air in the morning fog or the clear skies of twilight. Jazz brunch in the courtyard is held from May to October.

Romance at a Glance

♥ *Delight the bon vivant in you at the posh Ritz-Carlton (415–296–7465 or 800–241–3333).*

♥ *Shop and browse les maisons des couturiers.*

♥ *Dine on haute cuisine at Fleur de Lys (415–673–7779).*

♥ *Ride in a town car to San Francisco's most breathtaking viewpoints.*

♥ *View French masters at the Palace of the Legion of Honor.*

DAY ONE: LATE MORNING

Breeze across the threshold of **The Ritz-Carlton** (600 Stockton at California Street; 415–296–7465 or 800–241–3333; $295–$675) and you are a guest in a *petit palais* off the Champs Elysée. Call this place home for a few days, and you'll be addressing each other as "Daahling." So posh are the surroundings, so monumental the floral displays, so lilting is the harp music in the drawing room, that it's enough to make you swoon onto a settee as soon as you arrive.

"To the manor born," I was not, nor probably were you, but this blend of gentility takes no time at all getting used to. The harpist, china, silver tea service, portrait paintings would be so out of place in a typical home (the 10-foot paintings, if hung from my ceilings, would crash against the floor), yet are so essential to a born-again bon vivant. Museum-quality art is not the only reason we love staying here. One Ritz-Carlton executive sums it up, "At the Ritz you can have whatever . . . whenever . . . wherever." Whichever occasion you are coming here to celebrate, take full advantage of its pleasures.

DAY ONE: AFTERNOON

Lunch

Walk down Stockton Street, turning left at Bush. Pause a moment in front of Notre Dame des Victoires, the church of the French community once centered here. The French church was rebuilt after the 1906 earthquake, but the original residents scattered. **Cafe de la Presse** (352 Grant Avenue at Bush; 415–398–2680) is at the next corner. They should hang a sign: FRENCH SPOKEN HERE. In fact, you'll probably hear every major European language among the patrons on a summer afternoon. You can leaf through French editions of *Vogue*, *Elle*, or choose from an extensive collection of foreign newspapers.

One of the pleasures of a sunny Parisian afternoon is dining at an outdoor cafe, wallowing in the chicness of it all. When the sun shines, Francophiles flock to **Plouf** (40 Belden Place between Bush and Pine, Kearny and Montgomery; 415–986–6491). Look for Plouf among a sea of umbrellas, tables, and chairs in this quaint downtown alley. Simply while away the hours with a glass of Pinot Blanc or Meursault and a bowl of mussels while dreaming of the Left Bank.

After a leisurely repast, you are in the center of French and European haute couture. Follow Grant Avenue to Post Street to **Cartier** (231 Post Street at Grant; 415–397–3180) for a look in the new designs in watches, leather goods, jewels, silver, and crystal. On Claude Lane you'll find adjacent him-and-her stores that include the hip Paris design firms as well as French accessories: **MAC** (Modern Appealing Clothing) is for men; it's at 5 Claude Lane between Bush and Sutter near Kearny (415–837–0615). **Diane Slavin** at 3 Claude Lane is for women (415–677–9939).

Cafe Claude (7 Claude Lane; 415–392–3515) is next door if you feel like a quick espresso. Wind your way back to Grant Avenue. French-made items for the home are available in a few of the shops here. France's premier silversmith, **Christofle** (140 Grant Avenue; 415–399–1931) has great martini glasses. Fabric and furniture from Provence are at the **Pierre Deux** showroom (134 Maiden between Stockton and Grant; 415–296–9940).

Save the rest of the afternoon for some European-style pampering. Where Maiden Lane intersects Kearny Street is the most sybaritic salon this side of the Western Hemisphere. With a look reminiscent of Paris in the late thirties (Art Deco designs right down to the metal buttons on the tufted sofas), **77 Maiden Lane Salon** (77 Maiden Lane, second floor; 415–391–7777) pays equal attention to both genders. While he is having the "Tune Up for Men," she could be getting the "Belle of the Ball." Both last four hours. The menu of services includes French seaweed facials, French manicures, massages, and aromatherapy body wraps; the charge for these services ranges from $35 to $200. Era is a stylist who has trained in France if you need a trim.

DAY ONE: EVENING

With renewed vitality and *esprit*, have dinner at Hubert Keller's **Fleur de Lys** (777 Sutter Street at Jones; 415–673–7779). Walk halfway up California Street and turn left onto Joice Street. It comes down a staircase, a garden-like oasis to end at Pine. Turn right at Pine, then left at Powell. If the cable car is coming down the hill, hop on. Get off after two blocks, at Sutter Street and turn right. Window-shop the galleries of Sutter Street en route to dinner. **Pasquale Iannetti** (522 Sutter Street between Powell and Mason; 415–433–2771) often displays Rembrandt, Toulouse-Lautrec, Miró, Renoir, Matisse, and Chagall in the window.

Dinner

Fleur de Lys's four-star dinners, served under a canopy of cascading old-world fabric, represent the pinnacle of San Francisco's haute cuisine. Chef-owner Hubert Keller, an Alsatian born into a family of pastrymakers, has gone as far as the White House to cook. Cooking with the panache of a renegade, he eschews butter and cream in favor of vegetable reductions. His Vegetable Feast or Tasting Menu hits all sensual triggers simultaneously. You'll dine on a symphony of flavors such as chilled asparagus soup with a timbale of Imperial caviar, crab meat and avocado; Maine lobster tail and salsify *en tartelette* with a pinot noir sauce; or boneless quail stuffed with ris de veau, morels, and spinach with a spicy nutmeg sauce. Entrees range from $30 to $35. Dining here will only amplify your *joie de vivre*.

❧⁓❧⁓❧

If you make arrangements earlier in the day (or before your weekend begins), you can be picked up by a limousine at the restaurant door after dinner. Call **Bauer's Limousine Tours**

(415–522–1212 or 800–546–6688) and ask for the Romantic Evening tour. You'll ride out to Inspiration Point, across the bridge to Marin Headlands, and along the Embarcadero. After returning to the Ritz-Carlton, link arms and stroll in the rose garden. You'll likely have this glorious spot all to yourselves.

DAY TWO: MORNING

Brunch

Have brunch outdoors in the Ritz-Carlton's courtyard **Terrace Restaurant,** possible from May to October. Listen to a jazz quartet while dining on oysters and caviar-topped cornmeal pancakes and sipping champagne from Épernay. The dessert table always has a centerpiece of spun sugar. Once it was a woodland scene with a family of swans floating on a lake.

⌘⌘⌘

Spend the rest of the morning at the **California Palace of the Legion of Honor** (Lincoln Park, Thirty-fourth Avenue at Clement; 415–863–3330; closed Mondays). Tell the taxi driver to take the scenic route to Lincoln Park through the Presidio and Baker Beach. Atop a bluff commanding sweeping views of Marin Headlands, the bay, and the ocean is a fine arts museum perfect for Francophiles. Modeled after the Palais de la Légion d'Honneur in Paris, the museum has European and ancient art with an emphasis on the French Masters of the

A woman is closest to being naked when she is well dressed.

—Coco Chanel

eighteenth and nineteenth centuries: de la Tour, Boucher, Fragonard, Watteau, Manet, Monet, Renoir, Cézanne, and Degas. French decorative arts are presented in three period rooms. You'll come upon the Rodin sculpture collection bathed in natural light in one of the skylit galleries. Head toward the museum's inner recesses to admire the fifteenth-century tapestries of Flanders.

DAY TWO: AFTERNOON

End the day at Union Square. Shops are open from noon until 5:00 P.M. on Sunday. The silk scarves and ties at **Hérmes** (212 Stockton at Maiden Lane; 415–391–7200) have been haute couture for a hundred years. Food, insects, Germany: If it's on the planet, it's been on a Hérmes tie or scarf. A full collection of clothing, accessories, perfume, cosmetics, fine watches, and jewelry are under one roof at **Chanel Boutiques** (155 Maiden Lane between Stockton and Grant; 415–981–1550). Elegant women's wear from the internationally renowned Parisian maison de couturier **Celine** (155 Post Street at Kearny; 415–397–1140) can be either purchased or coveted. Celine polo shirts for men are the height of international fashion.

The biggest "French" news locally is the ninety very French automatic toilet and advertising kiosks installed all over the city. A half dozen alone surround the intersection of Market and Montgomery. In spite of their practical nature, they add to the aura of our Paris of the West.

At the end of the afternoon, don't rush home. Knowing how reluctant you are to leave the Ritz, I suggest you linger awhile. Order a Kir Royal in the lobby lounge and toast a culture dedicated to *Romantisme:* "Vive la France!"

ITINERARY 13
One day

A BAY IN THE LIFE

ON SAN FRANCISCO BAY

*F*rom vantage points around this hilly peninsula, San Francisco Bay shimmers in grand prominence. As spectacular as the city is, sooner or later you'll be tempted to leave its shores. You don't have to be an Aquarius to have an affinity for water nor be a sea nymph to respond to fresh ocean air and a mile-long flotilla of afternoon fog heading inland. This itinerary, a tour of Angel Island in a sea kayak, satisfies that urge. When the day is over, the bay will be more than a lovely backdrop. Together in double kayaks, you'll synchronize your paddles, getting a good workout amid the natural elements with which the Bay Area is so well endowed.

Practical Notes: Sea Trek (415–488–1000; $110) provides all-day guided trips with lunch on Saturday, Sunday, or holidays from May to October. A few days ahead, make reservations. They set you up not only with stable, fiberglass kayaks but waterproof jackets, life preservers, and drybags for stowing cameras and a change of shoes and shirt. You pull out (kayakese for "return to land") for lunch on the beach and to tour various historic sites. Blue & Gold Ferries to Angel Island are scheduled May to October (415–773–1188 or 415–705–5555).

DAY ONE: MORNING

Head for Fisherman's Wharf and Pier 41 at the foot of Jefferson to the **Blue & Gold Ferry Terminal.** Board the Angel Island ferry and turn your back to the wake, where sun glints off steel and polished granite. Within minutes the green arms of Ayala Cove engulf you.

Centuries have barely blemished the forested slopes, open meadows, and tranquil coves of **Angel Island,** a California State Park and Wildlife Preserve. After leaving the ferry, head toward the sea kayaks lined up on the beach of **Ayala Cove.** Paddling instruction and safety orientation begins at 9:30 A.M. A quick cup of coffee and a muffin at the Cove Cafe may be a good idea before joining the other kayakers. Don yellow slickers and strap on spray skirts. (Your companion may look like Big Bird in a tutu, but don't let on that you think so.) The lightweight paddles have an easy grip. In unison, weave figure eights through the air, turning smoothly on the dip. Once tucked into the kayak and shoved off the beach, the guide shows the rear paddler how to operate the rudder with the foot pedals.

In the eighteenth century a party of Miwok Indians paddled tule canoes into Ayala Cove to barter with the Spaniards. Sailors aboard the *San Carlos* ridiculed the Indians, for the canoes looked half-sunk and the Indians appeared partially submerged in water. The *San Carlos* was the first European vessel, under Miguel Ayala's command, to enter the bay and name the islands.

Leaving the still waters of Ayala Cove, point your kayak tips east, putting Raccoon Straits on your left. Here, the water of the Pacific Ocean flows through the Golden Gate, churns through Raccoon Straits, and continues to San Pablo Bay, finally reaching the Sacramento Delta. Richmond Bridge spans the bay on your left and connects Marin County to east bay towns along the opposite shore.

All else remains unpredictable. Each shift in direction alters the impact of the wind and the tide and changes your vistas. As powerful as the tides are, you'll be glad to have a guide along. On approaching our first turn, the wind whipped us toward the rocks. Within seconds the guide had attached a tow rope to our kayak and paddled us away from harm. The danger passed before we had time to panic.

Lunch

Can you believe lunch on a deserted beach? Within sight of the city? No road or trail connects this beach to the perimeter road of Angel Island. The Sea Trek guides provide a picnic table and all the fixings for lunch: Our recent trip offered a feast of ham and turkey sandwiches, pasta salad, and chocolate chip cookies.

⤜◈⤛

After lunch, our hosts shooed us away from the clean-up chores, pointing out a path leading up to Blunt Point lighthouse. Like us, you'll have time to explore. In a small cove down the beach, harbor seals tilt their heads shyly.

DAY ONE: AFTERNOON

After an hour, you push off again with the island on your left. The next stop is the Immigration Station, where you can tour the barracks and read translations of poetry scratched onto the walls by detainees. As you follow the curve of the island to the left, notice a 5-foot brass bell in a grassy area. It once rang from the end of a long pier, now gone, signaling the arrival of the primarily Chinese immigrants, who were considered a threat to the nation's economy. Steer toward the sandy beach and glide to a smooth landing. Dale Ching, who gives tours up the hill at the men's barracks at the **Immigration Station,** first saw the bell when he stepped ashore in 1924, an eight-year-old craning his neck for a glimpse of his father. All immigrants were detained here and interrogated by officials who weeded out the spurious "paper sons" and "paper daughters" possessing tampered documents. Unlike Ellis Island, this port of entry had all the trappings of a prison: guard towers, nightly lock-downs, and rations so meager they provoked a food riot.

Read the translations of the detainees' poems on the barracks' walls. The entire compound was slated for demolition until these poems, because of peeling paint, came to light. Experts trace the origin of Chinese-American literature back to this wall.

Leaving the Immigration Station, a short 30-minute paddle brings you back to Ayala Cove. If you want to cap your adventure with some fun, try surfing the wake of the motor boats. Paddle hard and fast, in unison, to ride the wake like Tsunami rangers. Approaching the corner of the island, you are soon back in the maelstrom of Raccoon Straits. No doubt you'll have to fight the wind on the way back, but in a moment it's all over. In Ayala Cove you glide to the shore effortlessly.

DAY ONE: EVENING

Dinner

You can catch the 4:20 P.M. ferry to Tiburon, a budding St. Tropez, disembarking at Main Street. Have dinner on the upper deck of **Tutto Mare** (9 Main Street; 415–435–4747; moderate), where the waiters sport ponytails and rock-star sunglasses. You would think you were in a fashionable Mediterranean port if the skyline wasn't sparkling silver in the sun. Seagulls wheel S-curves outside the railing, yacht sails press into the wind, riggings clang against the masts in the marina. Tutto Mare's food is a good match for its location. Try the crisp, salty shrimp with a glass of Orvietto or the Dungeness crab cooked to order. Grilled halibut and spinach ravioli filled with crab and shrimp are both excellent, as are the sea bass and seafood pasta. Entrees range from $10 to $19.

❧❧❧

After dinner, explore the Main Street shopping district. Tiburon, which means "shark" in Spanish, was first a railroad town and then a summer resort. Along Ark Row you can shop in a

Paddling together in a tandem kayak, the tides and the seabirds, added to the hypnotic dip of the paddle, shrink the world outside your aquatic realm. It's just you and your love, locked in rhythm.

restored "ark," what Victorians called a houseboat 100 years ago. **Windsor Vineyards** (72 Main Street; 415–435–3113) is a wine-tasting room and gift shop. This award-winning Sonoma County vineyard has thirty wines open for tasting. They print personalized messages in the middle of the label as a free service. Several people have used this method to propose marriage. You have three lines and forty-five characters—plenty of room for a short poem or declaration of undying love. **For Paws** (90 Main Street; 415–435–9522) stocks everything imaginable with a canine or feline theme.

When you cross over to Beach Road at the next intersection, you leave Tiburon and enter the tiny hilltop haven of Belvedere. The town was laid out at the turn of the century. Fewer than a hundred homes, some barged over from San Francisco cluster around a hillock that faces Belvedere Cove on the east and Richardson Bay on the west.

Within five minutes, you'll spy a staircase on the right. Climb up under a canopy of foliage and enjoy the backyard gardens and New England–style homes. Belvedere homes are linked by a series of staircases and lanes. These pedestrian lanes make it easier for residents to run to the ferry in the morning. You'll have no such worry. The 8:20 P.M. ferry back to the city allows plenty of time for a leisurely return to the Main Street docks.

ITINERARY 14
Two days and one night

ROMANCE IN THE AIR

AN AERIAL FANTASY

*S*an Francisco is serious about putting you on cloud nine. The question is: How high will you go? . . . 1500 feet aboard a vintage DC-3 or 781 feet via a trail to Angel Island's summit? To the top of the skyrooms, like the Fairmont's Crown Room, the Top of the Mark, and the Bank of America's Carnelian Room, all of which have vied for the highest-in-the-city trophy? Since you'll be visiting them all, judge for yourself. You'll see the views from their windows in sunlight, twilight, or moonlight. The play of clouds, light, and fog is always mesmerizing. Sometimes the fog cascades like a waterfall over Twin Peaks; other times it rips through the Golden Gate like water freed from a dam. The lofty skyrooms, observation decks, and airplane windows may make you feel like singing Jimi Hendrix's line, "Excuse me while I kiss the sky," from his song "Purple Haze."

San Franciscans slowly developed a passion for heights. The summits of San Francisco, forty-two hills of 200 feet or more, were not always sought-after addresses. Living here meant schlepping uphill the daily provisions. Cable cars gave the hills their cachet. From that time on, to reside on a hill instantly established one's social status. Here's an itinerary that gets you off the ground and puts you on track, as Tony Bennett sang, "halfway to the stars."

Practical Notes: Book a DC-3 sky tour at least two weeks in advance with **Otis Spunkmeyer Air** (800–938–1900, $120 per person). Ask the booking agent for information on airport shuttles to Oakland Airport North Field (Kaiser Air Jet Center, 8433 Earhart Road), from which point you'll fly. Flights are canceled in heavy fog and added in gorgeous weather.

The DC-3 flies four tours per week during the winter and ten during the summer. Sky tours are usually booked Saturday and Sunday. Ask about the moonlight-and-roses flight and check availability of the pilot observer seat.

Two other ways to satisfy your aerial fantasies: **San Francisco Helicopter Tours** (800–400–2404) take off from San Francisco International Airport and include shuttle service from the city in the price of the tour. **San Francisco Seaplane Tours** (415–332–4843; $89) leave conveniently from Pier 39. You'll get a hybrid of aviation and seafaring fun on board a wood-paneled seaplane originally built for use in the Canadian bush. All rides include bridge views, bay islands, Mount Tamalpais, the Marin coastline, and the San Francisco skyline.

DAY ONE: AFTERNOON

Let your lover know that the sky's the limit by beginning your weekend aboard a champagne flight on a historic DC-3. Music from the 1940s fills the cabin and flight attendants wear perky red-and-white uniforms of that decade. You'll probably be touring the sky in Otis Spunkmeyer owners Ken and Linda Rawling's DC-3 C-41, the first military Gooney Bird outfitted with an executive interior. It once served as the personal transport

---

Romance at a Glance

♥ *Stay in the Fairmont Hotel's twenty-two-story tower (415–772–5000 or 800–344–3550).*

♥ *Fly 1,500 feet over the city in a vintage DC-3 (Otis Spunkmeyer Air; 800–938–1900).*

♥ *Dine on the 52nd floor of the Carnelian Room, in a private room if you like (415–433–7500).*

♥ *Dance at the Starlight Room atop the Sir Francis Drake Hotel.*

♥ *View San Francisco Bay from the crest of Mount Livermore on Angel Island.*

of General Hap Arnold and was the oldest piece of war equipment in the historic June 6, 1994, fly-over of the Normandy beaches during D-day celebrations.

Check into the twenty-two-story tower at the Fairmont Hotel (950 Mason Street at California; 415–772–5000 or 800–344–3550; $295–$625). "Bonanza Jim" Fair bought the property on which the Fairmont Hotel now stands to shake off his burly miner image. The most expensive view in the city, and possibly in the world, is from the "Persian Court" terrace of the Fairmont's $8,000-a-night penthouse.

DAY ONE: EVENING

Nob Hill is a romantic aerie unto itself. For an overview of the neighborhood and an afternoon cocktail, stop at the Top of the Mark at the Mark Hopkins Inter-Continental Hotel (1 Nob Hill; 415–392–3434). After drinks, catch a cable car on the corner of California Street and Mason. Hold on tight as the **California Street cable car** brakes before tipping over the edge of the hill. What better way to take the plunge than swinging together from a cable-car pole? The height of the hill catches the fresh bay breeze, adding to the heady sensation of flying downhill.

Dinner

Get off the car at Kearny Street for dinner at the **Carnelian Room** (Bank of America; 555 California Street, 52nd floor; 415–433–7500; expensive), which has the highest 360° view in the city. Ask the maitre d' to choose a north-facing table for dinner. The menu includes fresh dill-cured salmon, Sonoma rack of lamb, and fat-free passion-fruit baked Alaska. Entrees range from $12 to $23. For the utmost in romance, dine in the Tamalpais Room, a private dining room available for an extra charge. It's expensive, but the room is yours alone, and *you* summon the server only when you're inclined to do so. The height of the restaurant ensures a magnificent view. You're at eye level with Mount Tamalpais, but shouldn't you be gazing at each other?

After dinner, walk down Kearny Street to Sutter. Take a right and walk three blocks to Powell Street. The flashing lights of the **Starlight Room** atop the Sir Francis Drake Hotel (450 Powell Street, 21st floor; 415–392–7755) announces the next stop. A skyroom doubles as a ballroom where dancers step together to a big-band orchestra playing jazz, tango, and West Coast swing. You can dance under the stars at **Cityscape** in the San Francisco Hilton & Tower (333 O'Farrell Street, 46th floor; 415–771–1400). The retractable ceiling slides open in good weather. If you want quiet, intimate conversation, go to the **Club 36** at the Grand Hyatt (36th floor; 415–398–1234), where jazz pianist Larry Vuckovich performs six nights a week.

One special way to end the night is to ask the taxi driver to take you to **Twin Peaks,** the most famous vista of the forty-two hills. Dark mountains loom on every horizon—the Marin Headlands, the East Bay Ridge, the San Bruno Mountains—while a luminescent city lies at your feet. The amber lights along Market Street shine like "a path of gold," a tribute to the city's incandescent beginning.

DAY TWO: MORNING

Brunch

The next morning have buffet brunch (Sunday from 10:00 A.M. to 2:00 P.M.) in the **Crown Room** at the Fairmont Hotel (24th floor; 415–772–5131; $36 per person). The highest public observation point in the city, the Crown Room offers an endless flow of clouds and champagne. The seafood station has fresh clams, oysters, prawns, and smoked salmon. Entrees from the hot buffet range from roast sirloin of beef and veal medallions to fruit crepes and pancakes. Omelettes are assembled from the ingredients you select.

DAY TWO: AFTERNOON

In the middle of San Francisco Bay, another 360-degree view awaits you. This one is at the end of a moderately steep trail atop Angel Island. After brunch, put on hiking clothes, then

The idea for Otis Spunkmeyer Air was conceived in 1979, when Ken and Linda Rawling took a flight in a DC-3 back east. They loved it so much, they bought the plane and decided to make the experience possible for other couples.

check out of the hotel, leaving your bags with the bell captain. Next, hop the Powell-Taylor cable car to Fisherman's Wharf. Walk down Taylor Street to Jefferson Street and turn right. Plan to arrive at Pier 41 a half hour before departure. The **Blue & Gold Ferry to Angel Island** (415–773–1188) departs Saturday, Sunday, and holidays at 9:30 A.M. off-season and every two hours during the summer.

Once you've debarked at Angel Island, ask the staff person at the kiosk for directions to the island's Northridge Trail. It takes you through groves of oak, bay, and madrone along a 1.7-mile, self-guided trail to the summit of **Mount Livermore.** From the crest, 781 feet above sea level, you can see up San Pablo Bay, the Golden Gate Bridge, Mount Tamalpais, and, beyond the East Bay Ridge, the peak of Mount Diablo, the highest point in the bay area. While you are waiting for the return ferry, have lunch or a light snack at the **Angel Island Cafe** patio on the beautiful crescent-shaped Ayala Cove.

❧☙

Return to the Fairmont and retrieve your bags from the bell captain. If you live in a flat region of the States, I guarantee you'll have aerial dreams of San Francisco for quite some time.

ITINERARY 15
Two days and one night

GOLDEN MOMENTS OF THE GILDED AGE
HISTORIC MARKET STREET

*T*he Palace Hotel invites you to step back to San Francisco's Gilded Age. If the walls could speak, you'd hear ladies dining in the Garden Court and the "Bonanza Kings"—owners of Nevada's silver mines—calling for more oysters at the Pied Piper Bar. You'd hear it whispered that Lillie Coit Hitchock staged a boxing match in her suite.

Reserve a Palace suite for a night, and home becomes a set of rooms favored by the silver barons. The magnificent bank of windows scores a bull's-eye on the central hub of San Francisco. Three rival newspaper offices located on each corner kept this intersection buzzing with word of scandals, bankruptcies, murders, and disasters. Where Geary, Kearny, and Market Streets converge, look for Lotta's Fountain. An event that lived long in the memories of San Franciscans took place there on a crisp December night.

Practical Notes: If you go for the full effect and reserve a Palace suite, specify Room 738, 638, 538, or 438. Ask for room 438 if you like the idea of trotting just down the hall to the sauna, Jacuzzi, and pool. Keep in mind that guests in standard rooms enjoy these amenities as well. Reserve a Tuesday or Wednesday tour at the **Historic Levi Strauss Factory** (415–565–9159).

DAY ONE: MORNING

On the morning of the day you plan to check in, park your car with the valet of the **Palace Hotel** (2 New Montgomery Street; 415–392–8600 or 800–325–3535; $225–$625).

Beyond the lobby is the Garden Court. This glass-domed Victorian atrium gives you the feeling of standing indoors in full sunshine. A **City Guide** sweeps through the Palace Hotel every Tuesday, Wednesday, and Saturday at 10:30 A.M. and Thursday at 2:00 P.M. Join the Palace Hotel tour in the lobby for the 45-minute tour of the ballrooms and Garden Court. Toward the end of the tour, you'll walk down the hotel corridor toward the Market Street entrance, stopping at the Pied Piper Bar to see the children of Hamlin happily following the piper in a luminous original Maxfield Parrish mural. In the dining room of the Pied Piper are paintings of Emperor Norton, a much-loved San Francisco vagabond, and Lotta Crabtree, the toast of vaudeville dance halls for whom the fountain at the intersection outside the hotel is named.

Leave the hotel through the Market Street entrance. At one end of Market Street is the **Ferry Building,** the tallest structure in the city when it was built in 1894. Before the city's bridges to Oakland and Marin were constructed, one million ferry passengers passed through the Ferry Building every week. At the other end of Market Street is Twin Peaks, two pointed hills that suggested another name to Spanish explorers: the breasts of the Indian Girl. Walk right toward the Ferry Building. Heraldic lanterns flank the **PG&E** (Pacific Gas & Electric) doors. This fireproof, steel-frame building with metal windows and cream-colored terra-cotta exterior is representative of the post-1906 quake-and-fire building boom, when the entire length of Market Street was in ruins. It took 15,000 cartloads just to clear the rubble of the original Palace built by Billy Ralston in 1875, touted in its day as the world's largest and most luxurious hotel. The **Matson Building,** once headquarters of the Matson shipping line, bears the symbols of the merchant marines and has a cupola on the roof.

At the corner of Market and First, the first street of the old shoreline, wait for the streetcar F-Line. Use a **Muni Passport** ($6.00), available from your hotel concierge, so you don't have to fumble for dollars and transfers. Part of a $50 million project, the F-Line runs vintage streetcars from the 1930s up and down Market Street. On special occasions they roll out the "big green boat," a convertible streetcar from Blackpool, England. Each streetcar in the fleet wears the colors of the flag of the city that they came from. Los Angeles, St. Louis, Boston, and Philadelphia are among the cities whose trolleys you may board.

Take the trolley to Valencia Street and head for the **Historic Levi Factory** (250 Valencia Street at Clinton Place; 415–565–9153) a few blocks down Valencia Street. Ninety-minute tours are held Tuesday and Wednesday at 9:00 A.M., 11:00 A.M., and 1:30 P.M. The museum and tour of the factory floor are a rare glimpse into the historic beginnings of the world's largest apparel company.

Like many prosperous nineteenth century merchants, Levi (born "Loeb") Strauss made his fortune supplying miners. Strauss began making button-fly "waist overalls," as jeans were called, from indigo cotton twill imported from Nîmes, France. "Serge de Nîmes" or denim waist overalls appeared in the Levi Strauss catalog as lot number 501. This factory turns out 1,500 pairs of 501 Levis a day. For a quick lesson in the evolution of attitudes regarding Levi's 501 jeans, check out the ads in the factory museum from 1853 to the present. In a 1980s ad, Brooke Shields purrs, "Nothing comes between me and my Levi's."

DAY ONE: AFTERNOON

Lunch

Return to Market Street and cross over to **Zuni Cafe** (1658 Market Street between Franklin and Gough; 415–552–2522). What started in the early 1980s as a tiny cafe has evolved into one of California's most distinguished restaurants. Chef Judy Rodgers presides over the kitchen, which produces great Italian and southern French menus and a superb menu of fresh seafood. Sit by the window to take in the street scene. Zuni Cafe is in the heart of a small enclave of antiques shops and curio shops. Directly across Market Street is the Brady Street collection of tiny shops, one with imported ribbons, another for flowers and plants. Wander back to Market and catch the F-line trolley to Dolores Street. Walk to **Mission Dolores** on the corner of Dolores and Sixteenth Streets (415–621–8203). The basilica is on the corner, and the mission is next to it. Nearly 500 years ago, Spain conquered Mexico and sent Catholic missionaries into Alta California to establish settlements. Take a self-guided tour of this structure, the oldest building in San Francisco. The mission, which still offers services, contrasts with the adjacent 1910 rococo basilica. The former is very simple; the latter elaborate, like the churches of Mexico and Spain. Indian laborers set 4-foot-thick adobe walls and lashed roof timbers with leather. The bell at the apex still rings, and the Doric columns haven't collapsed despite three major earthquakes. Inside, the walls and ceiling have been repainted with designs taken from traditional Indian basketry.

Also tour the mission's cemetery, which contains graves of the early pioneers and merchants and their families. The grandest monument marks the remains of a man hanged for murder. True, James P. Casey had been a fireman, but having become a politician and publisher, he shot and killed a rival. You'll also find the graves of two lovers, Charles and Arabella Cora.

The pair was married (see "Love's Last Request," page 119), right there on the spot, and though Arabella tried to save her lover's life by pleading with the vigilantes, in the end Charley swung from a warehouse's third-story gallows for killing William Richardson. The lovers are buried together. All around them, the cemetery gardens bloom with native wildflowers.

Love's Last Request

In 1856 members of the audience twittered when gambler Charles Cora escorted Arabella, a brothel beauty, to the theater. William Richardson protested by promptly leaving the theater with his wife and friends. Cora and Richardson exchanged gunfire a week later, leaving Richardson dead. The vigilantes who apprehended Cora asked him for his last request prior to a public hanging. He said, "I want to marry Belle."

From Mission Dolores, turn left at Sixteenth Street, then right at Church Street where the upper Market shopping district begins. **Just Desserts** (248 Church Street between Market and Fifteenth Street; 415–626–5774) is a local bakery cafe with a vine-covered patio in the back. Once refreshed, visit the shops that line both sides of Market Street. Local designers and artists have free rein here.

Walk to Market Street's center meridian and take an F-Line trolley back to the Palace, getting off at New Montgomery Street. Now you can check into a Palace Suite overlooking Market Street. Fourteen-foot ceilings and five windows nearly as high puts a sizable chunk of the cityscape on view. At night, the bowed corner window reflects the room's furnishings. You have to push hard on the black button inside the tub to get the Jacuzzi jets rolling. Yes, you can both slide into the tub with some creative positioning, or you can slip down the hall to the hotel's Health Club Jacuzzi.

DAY ONE: EVENING

Dinner

After a long soak and perhaps a leisurely rubdown, dress for dinner and head for **Boulevard** (One Mission Street at Steuart; 415–543–6084) in the historic Audiffredd building,

A Magnificent Marriage

Boulevard chef Nancy Oakes, who cooks by intuition, is the crowned queen of potatoes. Her signature dish everyone clamors for is potato Napoleon. She married the Sausage King, Bruce Aidell. They come together in a dish: rabbit stuffed with chicken/turkey sausage and potatoes.

south of the Ferry Building. Originally designed by and named for the French architect Hyppolite d'Audiffred in 1889, the exterior and interior blend. In an age when restaurants have become the place to go for evening entertainment, designer Pat Kuleto bids you welcome to Belle Époque Paris. The restaurant's mascot, an iridescent peacock, lies in mosaics at your feet. Flower-shaped wall lamps of amber glass cast a sultry glow. A vaulted ceiling of red brick is the handiwork of old-world artisans. Add to this cushioned banquettes in bay windows. Tables 5 and 6 place you a little way out of the bustle and allow you to sit side by side. Dining at Boulevard will convince you that San Francisco is the reigning culinary capital of the West.

At Boulevard, the conversation, food, wine, and celebrity patrons create an electric atmosphere.

⌘

Return to the Palace Hotel, and stop at the Pied Piper bar before going upstairs.

DAY TWO: MORNING

The next morning swim in the pool under a skylit atrium. The sauna leaves a fresh, clean feeling. I love the smell of the untreated wood covering the sauna's ceiling, walls, floor, and benches. Ask room service to deliver your breakfast to a poolside table. Wrap up in your terry-cloth robes and sit down to fresh orange juice and French roast coffee with brioche, scrambled eggs, and sausage, or perhaps waffles topped with fresh berries and yogurt.

From your hotel suite window look for a **rooftop garden** across Market Street (Post and Montgomery), maintained for the enjoyment of all courtesy of Wells Fargo Bank—with a little arm-twisting from the city. Creating a public space was a condition of the bank's building permit for the adjacent tower. Enter the bank on Post and Montgomery, taking a look at the soaring 50-foot-high coffered ceiling. Take the elevator to the garden and enjoy the view on all sides. Next, walk up Post Street to the **Crocker Galleria** on Post between Montgomery and Kearny (415–393–1505). Three levels of shops offer a mix of European and American fashions. The boutiques high on our list are Nicole Miller, Gianni Versace, and Polo/Ralph Lauren.

When you return to Post Street, turn left at Kearny and cross Market Street. The entrance of the Monadnock building (685 Market Street between New Montgomery and Third) has a barrel-arch ceiling with a Greco-Roman balcony scene. Among the famous San Franciscans in Roman attire is an opera singer with raven black hair. She sang at Lotta's Fountain, at the corner of Kearny and Market, on a clear December night. Because so many people were turned away from her sold-out performances, Luisa Tettrazini decided to sing in the street, defying the orders of her promoters. Twenty thousand listeners gathered as silvery notes filled the air—music to make the angels sigh. If ever the gates of heaven opened, witnesses said, surely they did that night.

The diva had worked up an appetite, *bien sûr*. A saloonkeeper on Market Street offered to make a light supper for her. All he had on hand were noodles and turkey. The dish has come down from that night as Turkey Tettrazini. Beyond the gallery to the left is a small courtyard and sculpture garden. At Christmastime or anytime you can slip in here to escape the crowds of shoppers. After a quiet interlude here, return to the Palace Hotel to check out.

Lunch

Before rushing headlong back into the present, have lunch in the hotel's **Garden Court.** Depending on the hour, the Garden Court serves breakfast, lunch, afternoon tea, or Sunday brunch. Every seating area is handsomely furnished. Potted palms, crystal chandeliers, and gold leaf throughout the room keep the spirit of the Gilded Age alive. The great dome, glistening from the removal and cleaning of its 17,000 panes of glass, makes this room the city's most splendid indoor setting.

ITINERARY 16
One day and one night

S.F. AVANT-GARDE

SOUTH OF MARKET

*W*hen I edited a city guide ten years ago, South of Market wasn't on the map. Why would I now send couples to a former "blighted area" for a romantic getaway? Love Among the Dung? On opening night of the Yerba Buena Gardens and Art Center, my husband and I lay on the grass and watched floodlights christen the buildings and the sky above an urban rebirth.

South of Market now not only has its own map but also it boasts a tourist attraction that topped all others in attendance this summer: SFMOMA. Scan the skyline for a building that looks like the acronym MOMA and you've found the San Francisco Museum of Modern Art.

Do you fancy yourselves a thrill-seeking couple, drawn to the fresh, the new, the unexpected? South of Market, with its "fringe" fashion designers and experimental art, bistros and night clubs, will satisfy your curiosity about the underground scene.

Practical Notes: Although SOMA (South of Market) extends south of Market Street to King Street and from the Embarcadero to Twelfth Street, light industry still characterizes the area. Luckily, SOMA's offbeat galleries, designer lofts, and bistros cluster around Yerba Buena Gardens, Multimedia Gulch (the center of digerati trendiness), South Park, and the nightclub district. Stick to these areas. And don't wear anything boring; that way, you'll be assured of

Romance at a Glance

♥ *Stay at the Armani-inspired Hotel Milano (415–543–8555 or 800–398–7555).*

♥ *Be inspired at the San Francisco Museum of Modern Art.*

♥ *Learn the meaning of irresistible at your luncheon venue, Bizou (415–543–2222).*

♥ *Be where it's happening on the nightclub circuit.*

assured of fitting in. Call these hotline numbers or visit these web sites for calendars of events. Yerba Buena Center for the Arts (415–978–2787; www.YerbaBuenaArts.org) is an exciting venue for evening entertainment and only 1 block from your hotel. SFMOMA (415–357–4000) lists current exhibits and lectures. Check the *San Francisco Bay Guardian's* daily calender at http://www.sfbg.com. Metreon Sony Entertainment Center (Fourth and Mission) is new to the SOMA scene. Check out the Microsoft SF store and exhibits.

DAY ONE: AFTERNOON

Check into the **Hotel Milano** (55 Fifth Street between Mission and Market; 415–543–8555 or 800–398–7555; $109–$189). The neon-colored mobile and collage obelisk in the lobby and the modern Italian guest room decor (copied from Giorgio Armani's Milan apartment) set the tone for a foray into avant-garde South of Market. Ask the concierge for the Center for the Arts (at Yerba Buena Gardens) calendar listings for the galleries and theater.

Walk down Mission toward the **Center for the Arts Gallery and Theater** (701 Mission at Third; 415–978–2787), venues for multicultural and/or nontraditional artists. In the lobby, buy tickets to the gallery and theater if you wish. A recent headliner, the Paul Taylor Dance Company performs modern dance that "mystifies, shocks, and diverts." So do the exhibits at the Center for the Arts. In one gallery we looked up at a cello strapped to the ceiling face down. From it a string ran 16 feet to the floor onto a cast-iron bathtub. As a sign instructed, I ran my palm lightly along the string. On the third try, it made a sound like wind passing through a harp.

Yerba Buena Gardens and Esplanade outside the gallery playfully challenges your senses as well. A walk-through granite fountain has gray streaks that turn metallic in the afternoon sun. Hop from stone to stone behind the fountain, stopping to read the glass plaques on the wall memorializing Martin Luther King Jr.'s "I have a dream" speech. Let animal tracks cast in the walkway lead you to a butterfly garden. When you spot a green glass structure jutting like a ship's hull, look inside. The moss-covered ledges will make you think of a giant petri dish. One end protrudes into the convention space beneath the garden. Yes, you've been walking over the Moscone Convention Center's Exhibition Hall. A layer of Styrofoam between the roof of the hall and the garden helps reduce the weight. On the upper terrace, look through the glass pyramids onto the heads of conventioneers. Does the briefcase-toting *Shaking Man* erected at the entrance to the upper terrace convey the motion you see below? Quite so, if a mega-convention is in town.

Cross Third Street and go into the lobby of **SFMOMA,** acronym for the San Francisco Museum of Modern Art (151 Third Street between Mission and Howard; 415–357–4000; closed Monday). Designed so people are on exhibit, the museum boasts a staircase from which you can survey the entry hall. Judge for yourself if architect Mario Botta succeeded. In the galleries, the artwork takes center stage. Paul Klee's landscape paintings are dense Cubist abstractions while Willem de Kooning has created some of the most fluid, sensual, and celebratory works in the twentieth century. How about a celebratory kiss under the circular skylight on the 5th floor catwalk before departing?

On the way back to the Hotel Milano, stop at the **San Francisco Marriott's View Lounge** (55 Fourth Street, 39th floor; 415–896–1600) to get a perspective on the entire SOMA District where your wanderings will lead tonight and tomorrow.

DAY ONE: EVENING

Back at your hotel, slip into swimsuits and terry robes and take the elevator to the health club. The whirlpool's soothing jets will make you forget you've been on your feet all day.

Dinner

When you're refreshed, dress for dinner and nightclub hopping. A recent addition to SOMA is an ultra-hip row of bistros, dishing up the city's most inventive cuisine at moderate prices. The Basque owners of **Fringale** (570 Fourth Street between Bryant and Brannan; 415–543–0573) call their food "Gallic exotic" and named their restaurant *fringale*: French for "I'm starving." Close seating makes it easy to spy on what others are eating. Let yourselves by tempted by the goat cheese galette, foie gras, and sauteed prawns in Pastis; and for your entrees fricassee of lamb sweetbreads, chicken with caramelized parsnips, or duck leg confit. Entrees range from $12 to $19.

Across the alley from Fringale is a contemporary American bistro, **Cyrus on Fourth** (564 Fourth between Brannan and Bryant; 415–227–4700). Très stylish with rosewood bar, marble-topped tables, open kitchen and wood-burning oven, this is the newest bistro on the block.

⊷◌◗∾

Feel like dancing? Every musical venue outside the mainstream seems to be located in the nightclub district near Eleventh Street and Folsom. Check the *San Francisco Chronicle's* Sunday Datebook for nightlife listings, then take a cab to the intersection of Eleventh and Folsom and begin a nightclub crawl at Boz Scaggs's premiere music club, **Slim's** (333 Eleventh Street near Folsom; 415–522–0333 advance tickets at http://ticketweb.com). Slim's books nationally famous acts. You could spend the night, let's say, with Mermen or the Nick Lowe Trio. End up at **Eleven** (374 Eleventh Street at Harrison; 415–431–3337) for improv jazz, or **Paradise Lounge** (1501 Folsom Street at Eleventh; 415–861–6906) to take in the counterculture scene on a large dance floor. **El Bobo** (1539 Folsom Street, between Eleventh and Twelfth; 415–255–8552) rocks every night with jazz, blues, and alternative bands.

1. *Le Baiser (The Kiss) is Auguste Rodin's bronze sculpture of a couple embracing. The man rests his hand lightly on her thigh while she reaches up and clasps the back of his neck, pulling his lips to hers.*

2. *In* The Joy of Living *Matisse has sketched a buoyant celebration of life.*

3. *The Petunia is erotica in a natural state. Georgia O'Keeffe's painting invites intimacy with the purple blossom.*

4. *Anything by Mark Rothko. His monumental canvases are rhapsodic color abstractions, with softly blurred rectangles of luminous, eye-filling hues.*

5. *Photographs of Georgia O'Keeffe done in 1922 by her long-time lover Alfred Stieglitz.*

DAY TWO: MORNING

Breakfast

Next day, retrace your steps to Yerba Buena Gardens to have breakfast on the upper terrace at **Pasqua** (730 Howard Street; 415–541–9962). What better way to welcome the day than to rest your eyes on a garden! Plan the day over smoothies, cafe latté, muffins, and scones. Then take a taxi (from in front of Moscone Center) to the exhibition space at **California College of Arts & Crafts** (CCAC, 450 Erwin, off Seventh, entrance at Eighth; 415–703–9500). Along with student and faculty exhibits you'll see the Capp Street Project's avant-garde, often monumental installations in this former Greyhound garage.

What's next on the menu for the day? Third Street takes you through the heart of SOMA's **Discount Shopping District** (between Bryant, Brannan, and Townsend). I like to stop at **Tower Outlet** (660 Third Street near Townsend; 415–957–9660).

Lunch

Bizou (598 Fourth Street at Brannan; 415–543–2222; moderate), our favorite South of Market bistro, is on the next block. Loretta Keller's food registers an 8.6 on our moaning scale. Start with her signature appetizer: flatbread. No, really—it's wonderful. She sprinkles it with carmelized onions. Entrees range from $9.00 to $14.00. Try the baked halibut with cranberries and fava beans, or the wild king salmon with sweet corn. Bizou means "kiss" in French, and the restaurant is so named for the effect eating here has on you. No matter how hard you resist, let your server talk you into ordering the Vacherin. While this bittersweet chocolate and coffee confection is passing by, conversation stops. The staff anticipate a flurry of orders for "whatever *that* was."

—∞—

Finish the afternoon investigating the shops around **South Park** (between Third and Second, Bryant and Brannan), a quiet, tree-lined oval. Stop at **ISDA & Co. Outlet** (29 South Park; 415–512–1610) for savings on French-inspired knitwear. **Jeremy's** (2 South Park at Second; 415–882–4929) sells vintage wear for men and women. Take a cab back to your hotel or to the **Thirsty Bear Brewing Company** (661 Howard Street, between Second and Third; 415–974–0905) which has a two-story state-of-the-art microbrewery on view behind glass. Seven microbrews and a seasonal ale are on tap every day. Though the Spanish tapas garner much praise, this pub prides itself on its brews. On tap may be Anchor Steam by the city's Anchor Brewing Company; which also brews Liberty Ale; Old Foghorn Ale, a barleywine-style ale; and Anchor Porter, an old-fashioned dark brew with a smoky, toasty aroma and rich flavor. You'll find British-style ales, Guinness-style stout, porter, and bitters. And since this is California, fruit-flavored beers are making a splash with Marin Brewing Company producing some of the best. Blueberry Flavored Ale and Raspberry Trail Flavored Ale both have appealing aromas and a subtle hint of fruit.

NEIGHBORHOODS

ITINERARY 17
Two days and two nights

FOR MUSIC LOVERS AND TIME TRAVELERS
HAYES VALLEY

*T*his itinerary is an invitation to unfetter your romantic soul in Hayes Valley, San Francisco's glorious performing arts district. Its exuberant mix of restaurants, shops, galleries, and cafes entertains by day and by night the curtain rises in one of the world's greatest opera houses. Not since the early nineteenth century has Hayes Valley enjoyed such popularity. Back in the 1850s it offered first-time homeowners country air and quiet streets. An event in 1989 helped the area regain its charm. Because of earthquake damage, an elevated freeway that cut through the area was demolished. Once again the sky over Hayes Valley spans clean and uncluttered.

Maybe you and your love are looking for a fresh start like others who are among the new faces on Hayes Street. Two Texans opened Momi Tobys Revolution Cafe, named for one owner's 92-year-old great grandmother who ran away from home to cook for Pancho Villa. Down the street from the cafe, Richard Hilkert holds court in his front parlor like a bookseller of yore, befriending everyone who comes in. Like Richard, wine bar owners Deborah Chalsty and Pamela Busch are passionate about their inventory. They taste 3,000 wines a year in compiling a menu for Hayes and Vine Wine Bar. They'll invite you to sip a glass of cabernet while reclining on their crinkled velvet banquette. Then follow the crowd to Davies Symphony Hall to spend the evening with a musical time traveler, which Michael Tilson Thomas once said his initials stand for. Get ready to toast a weekend of music, love, and new beginnings. Here, in a two–night itinerary, is Hayes Valley.

Practical Notes: Purchase opera (415–864–3330), symphony (415–864–6000), and ballet

Romance at a Glance

♥ *Sleep on a featherbed at the Inn at the Opera (415–863–8400 or 800–325–2708) and in French Empire–style splendor at the Archbishop's Mansion (415–563–7872 or 800–543–5820).*

♥ *Shop up-and-coming Hayes Street.*

♥ *See an opera or a ballet or the San Francisco Symphony—or all three.*

♥ *Dine in old-world Style at Vivande Ristorante (415–673–9245).*

tickets (415–865–2000 or 415–861–5600) months in advance so as not to be disappointed. Tickets go on sale August 21 for the opera, August 28 for the symphony, and October 28 for the ballet. The subscription season runs September to December for the opera, September to May for the symphony, and December to May for the ballet. The ebullient *Nutcracker Suite* ballet is a December favorite. Performances are generally not scheduled in August or on Monday and Tuesday. Reserve a mezzanine table at Jardinière (415–861–5555) to enjoy a relaxing three-course dinner before attending the ballet, opera, or symphony. Hayes Valley extends from the Performing Arts Center at Franklin Street to the Alamo Square Historic District of turn-of-the-century homes.

Patronize the arts for one day and book a room at the **Inn at the Opera** (333 Fulton Street; 415–863–8400 or 800–325–2708; $165–$280) across from the opera house. The next day surround yourself in Victorian-era opulence at the **Archbishop's Mansion** (1000 Fulton Street; 415–563–7872 or 800–543–5820; $149–$419) on Alamo Square. Whichever end you wake up in, the rich variety of Hayes Valley lies before you.

DAY ONE: MORNING

Arrive early to have a full day. Once a month on a Wednesday morning from October to March, the San Francisco Symphony invites the public to an open rehearsal (for tickets, call

415–864–6000). Michael Tilson Thomas fans can see the maestro at work. Throughout the year, on Monday (and Wednesday and Sunday on request) tours of **Davies Symphony Hall** depart the Grove Street entrance from 10:00 A.M. to 2:00 P.M. on the hour and half hour. Call 415–552–8338 for tour information.

Along Hayes Street and its tributaries, you'll mark a spirited élan among shops, restaurants, galleries, and cafes. The Franklin Street end of Hayes Street caters to patrons of civilized pleasures. **Nuts About You** (325 Hayes Street; 415–864–6887) has a cache of handcrafted anniversary and birthday cards, fruit-infusion tea from Switzerland, and great sweets to place on pillows. Chocolate-covered blueberries, strawberries, and cherries are displayed in tall glass jars—ask for a sack of each. Open the Dutch door to **Richard Hilkert**'s booklined parlor (333 Hayes Street; 415–863–3339). Richard, a bespectacled, bow-tied bookseller, greets you from behind a stack of books. He sells hardcover books on interior design, art, cooking, and anything his educated clientele ask for. Cross the street to a trio of galleries: **S.F. Women Artists Gallery** (370 Hayes; 415–552–7392), **Art Options** (372 Hayes Street; 415–252–8334), and **de Vera Glass Gallery** (386 Hayes Street; 415–861–6480).

The **S.F. Performing Arts Library & Museum** (399 Grove Street at Gough; 415–255–4800) is open Tuesday through Friday from 10:00 A.M. to 5:00 P.M. and Saturday from noon to 4:00 P.M. It has a small gallery and reference library to satisfy every conceivable interest concerning the opera and symphony. The staff asks you to make an appointment to use the library. **Vorpal Gallery** (393 Grove Street; 415–397–9200) next door exhibits Escher, Allen, and a host of modern California artists. The next stop is **Star Classics** (425 Hayes Street at Gough; 415–552–1110) to add some musical masterpieces to your CD collection. The store stocks Broadway, jazz, opera, and classical. Not only can you browse among 50,000 hard-to-find CDs, you can hear local artists perform. Chamber music or a piano concert is performed every Friday at noon and every Sunday at 2:00 P.M. in the store's recital hall.

Lunch

Lunch choices vary with the day. Monday through Friday head for **Hayes Street Grill** (320 Hayes Street at Franklin; 415–863–5545; moderate). Ask for a window seat. The crab cakes, Alaskan halibut, and grilled fish are popular among locals as well as visiting opera and symphony stars, many of the latter of which appear in the restaurant's photo gallery. Because I have a penchant for alley restaurants, I lunch at **Vicolo's** (201 Ivy Street between Gough and Franklin; 415–863–2382; inexpensive) whenever I am in Hayes Valley. Vicolo's cornmeal crust pizza is made for adult tastes; it's topped with gourmet ingredients such as grilled vegetables, sausage, and wild mushrooms. Healthy salads are lightly tossed with balsamic vinegar and herbs. But on Saturday or Sunday, to imbibe the neighborhood spirit, clink beer glasses at **Suppenküche** (601 Hayes Street at Laguna; 415–252–9289; moderate). The German brunch includes sausage, cold cuts, and German ravioli with scrambled eggs. Just the right repast to put you in the mood for *Die Walküre*.

DAY ONE: AFTERNOON

On your return walk to the Inn, two stores showcase the inventiveness of Hayes Street designers. **Darbury Stenderu** (541 Hayes Street between Laguna and Octavia; 415–861–3020) is a Seattle designer who has spurred the revival of hand-dyed silk velvet. The dressing room is draped with remnants of Darbury's best brocade, a cocoon of silk velvet. The body-skimming dresses equal the quality of garments found in museum collections from the 1910s and 1920s. Slip one over your head and you'll feel like waltzing. **Bella Donna** (539 Hayes Street; 415–861–7182) carries bridal gowns and dresses in the winsome shades of magnolia summers. Why not buy something shimmery to wear to the opera? Return to the inn, where your bags should be waiting for you in your room.

The White Lady

The upstairs boutique at Bella Donna on Hayes Street features a wardrobe of white inspired by a century of fashion from the turn of the century, the 1920s, the 1930s, and modern times. I wish I could be married again just to wear a dress from the Camille DePedrini collection.

DAY ONE: EVENING

Dinner

The warm weathered brick outside **Jardinière** (300 Grove Street at Franklin; 415–861–5555; expensive) is the backdrop inside for decor that signals a classy celebration. Backlit champagne buckets are built into a ribbon-like railing. The dome over the bar is fitted with fiber-optic lights as tiny as champagne bubbles. The celebratory tone of champagne carries over to by-the-glass menu, where you can choose from Billecart-Salmon Brut Rosé or California sparkling wines such as Iron Horse Brut or Gloria Ferrer Brut. Chef Traci Des Jardins, who was "born into a family that took pride in eating well," changes the menu daily. Starters usually include lobster-leek-chanterelle strudel, and entrees range from pan-roasted squab with baby turnips and tatsoi to lamb loin with squash blossoms, cranberry beans, and tomato confit. An inventive cheese course offers flavors as peppy as a Mardi Gras band, as smooth as a jazz trio. Aged Gruyére, farmhouse cheddar, alpine chevre, and fifty others are kept on the first floor in a temperature-controlled "cave." For dessert try the bittersweet Scharffen Berger chocolate torte or brown butter walnut cake with creme fraiche and caramel ice cream. Dessert wines are increasingly popular, and you may want to try the Bonny Doon Vin de Glacière Muscat. I admit if I wasn't theater bound I'd put myself in the chef's hands and order the $65 five-course tasting menu.

Do opera singers pledging oaths of undying love make you sigh? *Madame Butterfly, Ruslan and Lyudmila,* and *Rusalka,* the Dvořák opera inspired by Hans Christian Andersen's *The Little Mermaid,* are scrumptious productions, the most lavish in the city. Cross Franklin Street and go through the park. **War Memorial Opera House** (Van Ness and McAllister) is on the left, a mere three-minute walk from the Inn.

The symphony here is vigorously alive, which is why San Francisco attracted as prodigious a talent as Michael Tilson Thomas, called the "greatest American conductor since Leonard Bernstein." Under his direction, the symphony presents *Harmonielehre* by Adams, *The Martyrdom of Saint Sebastian* by Debussy, and a concert version of the 1944 musical comedy *On the Town* as a tribute to Bernstein. The San Francisco Symphony performs at **Davies Symphony Hall** (Grove Street between Van Ness and Franklin), a five-minute stroll from the inn.

The San Francisco Ballet season begins with a holiday favorite, the *Nutcracker Suite*, at the **War Memorial Opera House** and continues in repertory February until June.

DAY TWO: MORNING

Breakfast

The sound of young artists at work may awaken you in the morning. One side of the inn shares an alley with the Ballet Association. Dancers jetée past rehearsal room windows, but their activities won't prompt you to leap out of bed. Featherbeds at this inn exert a gravitational force to keep one prone. Besides, rising late is part of the genteel pace of life. Downstairs at the **Act IV** breakfast table, fresh daisies, yellow roses, and button chrysanthemums are as perky as the baroque music piped into the room. Halfway through brioche and coffee, you may catch yourselves humming to Berlioz's *Scheherazade*.

∽∾∾

Check out of the inn and drive five blocks on Fulton to the **Archbishop's Mansion** (1000 Fulton Street at Steiner; 415–563–7872 or 800–543–5820; $149–$419). Crystal chandeliers hang from coffered ceilings, and an oval leaded-glass dome glitters above a three-story oak staircase. This French Empire—style manor is in the heart of the city's finest collection of nineteenth-century homes. Leave your bags if your room isn't ready. Stroll around the hillside park, stopping at the crest to view the most photographed sight in San Francisco after the Golden Gate Bridge. The Painted Ladies of San Francisco are not women of Alamo Square but six matching Victorian town houses that outdo the city skyline.

Begin at Pierce and Hayes to explore the Alamo Square neighborhood. Follow Hayes to Steiner. The Queen Anne mansion at 1057 Steiner Street, the **Chateau Tivoli** B&B, halts everyone in their tracks. Imagine Moroccan red and Wedgwood blue with light-catching gold leaf. The details are extravagant: patterned slate roof, witch's cap turrets, rounded bay windows. Painted resplendent so that no detail escapes the eye, the house is a grammar of Victorian architecture. Visitors are welcome to view the first floor rooms. The visual feast continues through the entrance and grand staircase, front parlors, and dining room. Best of all, Bradbury & Bradbury wallpaper ornaments walls and ceilings. According to the Victorian credo, no surface is left undecorated. Retrace your steps back to Grove Street, and turn left. Then take a right at Laguna to return to the Hayes Street commercial district.

Lunch

I suggest lunch at a 1900s bakery whose interior has survived intact only because it was closed up for forty-five years. It was unboarded in 1982 and brought back to life by appreciative owners. Soup, salads, pasta, and daily specials cross the bakery counter at **Momi Tobys Revolution Cafe** (528 Laguna Street between Hayes and Fell; 415–626–1508; inexpensive). This could have been a Berlin cafe, but you won't spy an anarchist among the mostly local crowd. Want to tango? is the question painted on the pavement outside the cafe door. Follow the footsteps on the sidewalk for an impromptu dance on the sidewalk.

In old Kiev, a beautiful princess and a handsome knight fall madly in love, but a sorcerer has evil on his mind and the young couple is plunged into a fantastic world of wicked fairies, sleeping spells, magic swords, giants, dwarfs, and enchanted rings."

—synopsis of *Ruslan and Lyudmila* from the program
at the War Memorial Opera House

DAY TWO: AFTERNOON

Stop at **Victorian Interiors** (575 Hayes Street at Laguna; 415–431–7191) to visit a veritable shrine to Victoriana. Silk-screened wallpapers, moldings, lace panels, cornices, plaster crowns, and much more are for sale here. The shop is filled to the rafters with designs and details for restoring Victorian homes.

By late afternoon, as you wander down Hayes Street, you'll be close to our favorite wine bar. **Hayes and Vine Wine Bar** (377 Hayes Street between Franklin and Gough; 415–626–5301) is not an intersection but a mecca for wine lovers. Order the white wine flight or the red wine flight—selecting from the eighteen-page wine list can be a bit overwhelming. The "flight" is presented as four glasses of wines in the order determined by the connoisseur owners. Caviar is reasonably priced. This is a good place to linger as the day winds down.

Before returning to the Archbishop's Mansion, stop at **EC Studio** (347 Hayes Street at Gough; 415–621–1015). Owner Hal Brandes designs journals, sketch books, photo albums, and writing folios in embossed papers, fabrics, and rich leather. If a soak in your hotel room's claw-foot tub is part of the plan tonight, **Worldware**'s (336 Hayes Street; 415–487–9030) aromatherapy bar leads you through a sampling of earthly delights. Patchouli, musk, or lavender added to your bath water will banish any lingering concerns.

DAY TWO: Evening

Do you remember the impressionist paintings of absinthe drinkers, slumped in lifeless stupors? **Absinthe** (398 Hayes Street at Gough; 415–551–1590; moderate) the restaurant, as opposed to absinthe the beverage, bustles with energy. The liveliest bar and most sensuous dining room in Hayes Valley, Absinthe is where San Franisco cafe society gathers at the turn of the millennium. Follow the host into a red room of burgundy walls and banquettes and a long red mural of cafe-goers. Among them sits a pitchfork-toting elf, green like the dangerously potent absinthe. Risking health and sanity, artists and poets sought the green liqueur for the hallucinations it induced. Absinthe, they said, lay bare the soul. What are we doing at the dawn of the third millennium to pull us deeper into our experience of life? Feasting, of course, with our lovers.

From the kitchen issues a melange of tastes. The well-dressed crowd is cracking Dungeness crab, slurping Tomales Bay oysters, calling for another bottle of wine while servers scurry past armed with plates of rack of lamb and enormous bowls of pasta (you can catch the smell of olives, capers, red pepper, anchovies, and tomo tuna as they whiz by). Pissaladière, south-of-France pizza, arrives heaped with carmelized onions on a thin crust with slivers of olives and anchovies. It tastes smoky and sweet. French fries spike from a silver tumbler. Glasses of white Bordeaux set off the fresh shellfish elevated on a stand. Around your feast, candlelight spins a cocoon. Save room for the tempter appearing on the Absinthe dessert menu: it's the color of creme brulee. Entrees range from $10 to $17.

Zen and the Art of Rejuvenation

Japantown

$\mathcal{O}$n their densely populated island, the Japanese devote a portion of their scarce acreage to cherry blossom orchards. The height of the flowers' showy glory is so brief, and even a strong breeze can strip a tree in seconds. Still, the Japanese nurture their beloved trees. These people have a thousand ways of that making us wonder. They have a formal school of aesthetics devoted to flower arranging. They find great beauty in rocks, which are chosen according to what they mimic—a dragon or volcano—and are carefully arranged in gardens. They sleep on the floor. They soak in hot water until they reach a state that translated means "an octopus out of water."

You can do all of the above in Japantown.

At San Francisco's Miyako Hotel, you can gain a sense of Japanese ways. While you lie on a futon, you can admire a rock-and-bamboo garden. Jasmine, burning in a stone lantern, lightly scents the air. An alcove contains flowers in a raku vase and a scroll of a mountain stream rendered in black ink. A haiku written on hotel stationery leans against the phone:

> *Getting up again*
> *To look at cherry blossoms*
> *In the moonlight.*

Romance at a Glance

♥ *Stay in a futon room or sauna suite at the Miyako Hotel (415–922–3200 or 800–533–4567).*

♥ *Have a shiatsu massage at a Japanese bathhouse.*

♥ *Participate in a Japanese tea ceremony.*

♥ *Dine on Japanese tapas at YoYo Bistro (415–922–3200).*

♥ *Shop for kimonos, rice-paper stationery, Japanese country furniture, and "fortune cats."*

Practical Notes: Make massage appointments with a Japanese practitioner at Kabuki Hot Spring (415–922–6002). The styles of shiatsu used at Kabuki Hot Spring (Amma, classical, and Zen) provide you with a thorough, comfortable, full-body massage, leaving you both relaxed and revitalized. Or you can book in-room massages at the Miyako Hotel ($35/half hour, $70/hour) with a Japanese practitioner who has been with the hotel for thirty years. You may also make appointments at **Mount Fuji Shiatsu** (1723 Buchanan Mall; 415–346–4484; $39/hour) for authentic Japanese massage. For an in-depth look at Japanese culture in San Francisco, join the **Japan Center tours** Saturday at 2:00 P.M. at the Peace Pagoda (off Buchanan between Post and Sutter; 415–557–4266).

Schedule a tea ceremony with Mrs. Sakino (415–751–9676) after your bath and massage.

When you make your reservation at the Miyako Hotel, have the clerk go through the room options with you. Better yet, check the pictures of guest rooms at the hotel's Web site: www.miyakosf.com. If you've never slept on the floor, this is the place to try it. Futon rooms have a Western-style tub; you can still enjoy the Japanese bathing ritual at Kabuki. Be sure to ask for a garden-facing room—they're the quietest.

DAY ONE: AFTERNOON

Check into the **Miyako Hotel** (1625 Post Street at Laguna; 415–922–3200 or call Radisson reservations at 800–533–4567; $209–$300). Ask for a room in the five-story Garden Wing, the west rooms of which overlook the hotel's greatest asset: a Zen garden outside the lobby.

Stepping-stones floating in a sea of gravel lead to a koi pond. In these monotone surroundings, the goldfish startle the eye. Bodies of orange or pink opal flash by with fins that look like silk scarves caught in the wind. A blue tile-roof supports a torii-type gate flanked by dwarf conifers, or *bonsai*. Color is conspicuously absent.

> *The sharp points,*
> *A soft pine needle bed*
> *And the smell of it.*

Like the above lines from the hotel's stationery, Miyako Hotel reminds one of a polished haiku that subtly awakens the senses. In a futon suite, the act of opening the door begins an adventure. Shoji (rice paper) panel doors glide open to another room. Heavy tatami mats cover the floor. Kimono silk is tucked over a down comforter and a cotton-padded queen-size futon. Typical clothing is not suited to rooms where chairs have no legs and bedrooms no bed. As soon as you can, change into the hotel's cotton robes (*yukatas*) designed for lounging, and you complete a cultural submersion that is supremely relaxing.

You could ask for the sauna suite and idle away an afternoon with a Japanese ritual. Fill the deep soaking tub with hot water. Empty into the water a packet of jasmine bath salts provided by the hotel. The bathing ritual begins with a scrubdown while sitting on a stool, then rinsing with a hand-held shower. Stretch out in your private redwood sauna for ten minutes. Rinse again in the shower area, and slip into the hot tub. When you have finished soaking, be sure to go to the shower area again for a final scrub with a washcloth and soap. Rest. If this is your first introduction to the Japanese bath, rest and cool off every ten to fifteen minutes because the heat tends to increase your heart rate. Once you get used to the heat, you will require less resting time between the sauna and hot tub.

Walk to the Geary Street entrance of **Kabuki Hot Spring** (1750 Geary Boulevard; 415–922–6000). Thousands of San Franciscans have become aficionados of Japanese bathing and shiatsu massage by coming here. Shiatsu is the age-old Japanese art of using finger-pressure massage on acupressure points identified 5,000 years ago by the Chinese. Japanese shiatsu removes obstacles so energy flows unimpeded throughout the body. Shiatsu massages are given privately every day of the week or communally depending on the day of the week. On Monday, Tuesday, Thursday, and Saturday men have use of the bathing facility; on Wednesday, Friday, and Sunday women have use of it. The public area includes hot and cold tubs, a spacious sauna, a steam room, showers, and a Japanese-style washing area. The private rooms include a deep soaking tub, a steam cabinet, and a twenty-five-minute (allow one hour) or fifty-five-minute massage (allow one and a half hours). No oil is used, and you wear underwear. *Arigato* is a word you'll hear often. It means "thank you."

After a bath and massage, you've achieved the perfect state to appreciate the sanctuary of Mrs. Sakino's teahouse (1759 Sutter Street between Laguna and Buchanan, third floor; 415–751–9676 or 415–921–1782). For thirty years she has been performing the centuries-old **Japanese tea ceremony** with skill and grace. As you are being served, know that every movement is significant and has been precisely prescribed. A sixteenth-century Zen priest, Sen no Rikyu, perfected the tea ceremony so that people would observe the beauty of nature, simplicity, and spiritual tranquility. The small teahouse, as well as the larger one, was constructed in Kyoto, then dismantled, and later reassembled in this setting. It rests upon river stones taken from Kyoto. Only natural materials are used, and these are often unfinished or asymmetrical, in keeping with the teachings of Sen no Rikyu.

Walk back to the hotel through the **Buchanan Street Mall.** This cobbled lane resembles a countryside village. **Soko Hardware Company** (1698 Post Street at Buchanan; 415–931–5510) is Japantown's prime importer of all Japanese goods, from rice paper shades to sandalwood, patchouli, and jasmine joss sticks. Cast-iron teapots for single servings of leaf tea, such as Republic of Tea, are a good value.

DAY ONE: EVENING

Dinner

Begin the evening on the mezzanine level of **YoYo Bistro** (Miyako Hotel; 415–922–7788; moderate) overlooking the Zen garden. *YoYo* means "a wide expanse of ocean." Lemon Drop cocktails, made with Absolut citron, come in a martini glass. The tsumami menu offers twenty small dishes from a rotating selection of about sixty and is available from 11:30 A.M. to 11:00 P.M. *Tsumami* is "a little snack you eat while drinking." If you order four small tasting dishes, they arrive stacked in a tower. Can't imagine yourself eating "spicy glassy noodles" without injuring yourself? The chef is having fun, and your taste buds won't mind. I picked oysters and a delicate ginger-pickled salmon with wasabi créme fraîche and gingered shellfish salad on cabbage. My companion was more daring. He ventured into the East-West theme, ordering the rich duck confit on black lentil galette and braised fennel with star anise and olives.

Go downstairs to the dining room for the full Franco-Japanese menu. The decor is part Zen, part Provence: slate floors, warm umber and deep blue walls, glass angelfish in the windows, patterned shoji screens, and Japanese lanterns and sconces in sweeping curves. As the sky darkens, streetlights shine through the stars and leaves on the rice-paper screens.

Our server, wearing loose-fitting black pajamas, suggested a few befuddling but sensually rewarding dishes—tamarind-caramelized pork tenderloin with rice noodles and green-tea rice with barbecued eel and condiments. My favorite dish was wide rice noodles with gingered tomato confit, chilies, and strips of basil. Entrees range from $12 to $25.

⌘

The current nightclub that has a good karaoke crowd, **Shinjuku** (Japan Center, 1581 Webster Street between Post and Geary; 415–922–2379), is a cozy Japantown karaoke bar. Just punch in the song you want to sing and the bartender passes the microphone. If you're familiar with karoake, you know that a video monitor provides you with the words of the song you pick, but you can also sing whatever you know by heart.

On the way back to the Miyako, stop at **Benihana of Tokyo** (415–563–4844) in the Kintetsu Mall. The cocktail lounge could serve as a museum, for it displays handsome panels and antiques. An open-sided porch surrounded by a koi pond is a great place to sip sake in thimble-size glasses. The bear with the large round tummy is a lucky panda. You can rub his tummy and make a wish—unless you have everything you wished for already.

DAY TWO: MORNING

Brunch

An interesting stop for weekend brunch is **Now & Zen Bistro and Bakery** (1826 Buchanan Street between Bush and Sutter; 415–922–9696). They serve organic coffee, French toast, benevolent Caesar salad, and tofu veggie medley. It's a welcome contrast to last night's exotic foray.

⌀⌀⌀

Wander in the neighborhood alert for unusual sights and sounds. The city added the area west of Van Ness Avenue, naming it the Western Addition. Japanese immigrants built homes and shops on and around Geary Street. **The Japanese Cultural and Community Center** (1840 Sutter Street between Webster and Buchanan; 415–567–5505) holds classes on karaoke singing, ballroom dancing, ikebana flower arranging, and sushi making. In the gym you may catch the Saturday morning class of Japanese-style fencing with bamboo swords called *kendo*. You're likely to hear judo, karate, and aikido being practiced in church basements. Church bazaars and fairs, held in the spring and fall, are wonderful opportunities to mix with locals. Neighborhood activity is frenetic in April when preparations for the Cherry Blossom Festival are underway.

We saw a wedding party on the church steps of the **Konko Church** (1909 Bush Street; 415–931–0453). The Japanese have their weddings in the Konko church and their funerals in the Buddhist church. Konko is the older of the two religions and teaches that a bountiful universe under the benevolent eye of the Principal Parent is available for all to enjoy. A minister sits patiently all day to the right of the altar waiting for people to come in. His job is to offer comfort and guidance, a practice called toritsugi meditation. He also holds monthly appreciation services for the "Blessings of Life."

Next turn your attention to **Japan Center.** Occupying three blocks, Japantown's shopping, dining, and entertainment hub extends from the Miyako Hotel at Laguna to the AMC Kabuki Theatres at Fillmore. Cross Post Street at the Peace Plaza, opposite the Buchanan Street Mall. The focal point of the plaza is the five-tiered **Peace Pagoda,** inspired by the miniature, round pagodas dedicated to eternal peace more than 1,200 years ago in Japan's ancient capital of Nara. The five roofs decrease in diameter as they increase in height. Atop the highest roof is the *durin*, a nine-ringed spire symbolizing the highest virtue. The durin is topped by the *hoshu*, an ornamental golden ball with a flaming head. The Peace Plaza is an outdoor performance area, thronged with people during the Cherry Blossom Festival (on the last two weekends in April) and the Nihonmachi Street Fair (on the first weekend in August).

Take a moment to orient yourselves. On the left is **Tasamak Plaza** and the fifteen-story Miyako Hotel; on the right is the **Kintetsu Mall** and the **Webster Street Bridge** to the **Kinokuniya Building** and the AMC Kabuki 8 Theatres. More than thirty shops sell items such as antique kimonos, pearl necklaces, rice paper stationery, bonsai trees, tea utensils, shoji lamp shades, and dojo drums. You'll also find a branch of Japan's largest bookstore chain in the Kinokuniya Building.

Off the Peace Plaza on the left is the back door to **Genji** (Tasamak Plaza; 415–931–1616). The owner collects furniture of a style still in use in the Japanese countryside. Several pieces, including a staircase dresser, are carved from the honey-colored hinoki wood of the Japanese cypress. The dresser is as high as a typical room, 7½ feet, and fitted with cabinets and drawers in the hollows of steps. Try on happi coats and kimonos, another specialty of the store. Unlike the

Japanese, who wouldn't wear a stranger's clothing, we appreciate vintage garments. The owner imports the pick of the bunch, including exquisitely made kimonos and men's happi coats.

Lunch

As you enter the Kintetsu Mall, straight ahead is a cluster of restaurants. No single type of Japanese food claims more enthusiasts than sushi, a culinary marriage of raw fish and sticky rice. **Isobune Sushi** (415–563–1030) has seating around a racetrack. In this case the thoroughbreds are slow-moving sushi boats. Parading by are dishes of barbecue mackerel, California rolls, octopus, salmon roe, sea urchin, yellowtail, and red snapper, all in bite-size portions. Stir into the soy sauce a dab of green horseradish. This makes a great dip for yellowtail sushi. Use the pickled ginger (*gari*) to refresh your palate. In the middle of the oval, sushi chefs sharpen knives, snap rice cooker covers, and flip bamboo mats. Order sake and peruse the boats.

Sushi Bar Japanese

♥ Welcome: *Irashaimase*

♥ Good evening: *Konban wa*

♥ Bon appetit!: *Itadakimas*

♥ To your health, a toast: *Kanpai*

♥ Excuse me (waiter!): *Sumimasen*

♥ I have eaten well: *Gochiso-sama deshita*

♥ Thank you very much: *Domo arigato gozaimasu:*

Mifune (415–922–0337), a venerable noodle house, is the place to lunch on noodles. Choose thin soba (buckwheat flour) or wide udon (rice flour) in a vegetable-laden broth. Much more appetizing than the plastic version on display in the window, tamago (egg) donburi is warm and filling on a misty day.

DAY TWO: AFTERNOON

Retrace your steps to the Kintetsu Mall entrance. At the corner, across from the Murata Cafe Hana, stop at **Murata Pearl Company** (415–922–0666). Saltwater pearl necklaces, lustrous and expensive, range in price from $800 to $10,000. Seiko watches come in a variety of

styles. Kintetsu Mall shops also carry the essentials of Japanese life. At **Mikado Gift Shop** (415–922–9450), you can buy a fortune cat for only $5.00. A white cat with the palm up signifies success. If you throw coins in a fountain to no avail, try your luck with a Daruma doll, actually a monk, whose eyes are blank. You paint one eye and make a wish. If it comes true, you paint the other eye.

As soon as you see flowers, you've arrived at the **Ikenobo Ikebana Society**'s display windows (415–567–1011). Painting with flowers, an art called *ikebana*, reflects 1,400 years of Japanese traditions and philosophy. Three styles are usually displayed in the windows. *Rikka* expresses the beauty of a natural landscape. *Shoka* expresses life's perpetual change and renewal. Free Style expresses the arranger's inventiveness in using plant materials to convey a mood. Most of the effects are achieved with a few stems. I recognized my backyard weeds in one arrangement. Visitors are welcome in the showroom. Peek in the back room where Ikenobo masters may be at work. Stop at **May's Coffee Shop** (415–346–4020) in Kintetsu Mall for an afternoon snack of tai-yaki, fish-shaped griddlecakes filled with sweet bean paste and cooked to order.

Step up to the Webster Street Bridge. Stop at the **Taiko Dojo Showroom** (415–928–2456) to learn more about Taiko, the sacred art of traditional Japanese drumming originally practiced by monks. Posters in the showroom capture modern-day drummers in passionate abandon and graceful movement. Cassettes and CDs of their concerts introduce you to this exciting, athletic percussion music. **Shinge Nishiguchi** (415–346–5567) sells antiques, vintage kimonos (including a stunning wedding kimono in the window), and men's lounging robes.

The bridge deposits you on the upper floor of the Kinokuniya Building, near the door of **Kinokuniya Bookstore** (415–567–7625). If you have any interest in bonsai, rock gardens, origami, sushi-making, shiatsu, or haiku, this is the place to browse. **Izumiya** (415–441–6867) is where I was introduced to Japanese pizza one foggy night after a movie next door at the Kabuki Theatres. Called *okonoyaki*, Japanese pizza looks just like the plastic version in the window. It's a rice pancake with a nice crunch to it from bean sprouts and shrimp.

Kinokuniya Stationery & Gift Store (415–567–8901) carries handmade birthday and anniversary cards and sheets of paper for lining drawers or making origami. Downstairs, you'll want to look at the bonsai at **Katsura Garden** (415–931–6209). Passed down from generation to generation, trees that take well to the dwarfing process are juniper, elm, boxwood, maple, and pine. Return to the Miyako via Post Street so you can stop at **Maruwa Supermarket** (Post and Webster; 415–563–1901) for take-home treats. You'll find Mrs. Sakino's tea cakes, imported sake and beer, pearl rice (for sushi), and a jar of pickled ginger. You'll also be taking home memories suffused with Japanese gentleness and simplicity of living.

ITINERARY 19
Two days and one night

IT'S MAGIC
UPPER FILLMORE

A cross between the Garden District in New Orleans and Montmartre in Paris, Upper Fillmore's pleasures are truly cosmopolitan. Two stunning hilltop parks command its borders, its architecture reeks of civility, and its shopping district transcends the ordinary. Words are as ineffective as postcards in capturing it, so you have to come in person.

Every store and restaurant is cut from a different mold, as are the people who run them. Meet the eccentric who sells architectural salvage and the most riveting paintings, priced too high, he admits, for he can't bear to part with them. With the care of one handling a newborn, a Swedish shopkeeper introduces the damask duvet you admire. At one of the ladies' auxiliary shops, you may find a barely worn Halston, Chanel, or YSL. Tiptoe to the checkout counter with your treasures; someone may be spying over your shoulder.

The most original personality you'll encounter belongs to the magician owner of The Mansions Hotel—a perfect overnight for all you worldly hotel hoppers. Take the next two days at a leisurely European pace. Let curiosity and the promise of surprise lead you through this itinerary.

Practical Notes: Reserve the Josephine Suite at **The Mansions Hotel** (2220 Sacramento Street between Laguna and Buchanan; 415–929–9444 or 800–826–9398;

$189–$225) if you have a penchant for Empire furniture and want to decide for yourselves if the room is haunted, as is reputed. This room is also a good choice for tall guys; the shower is 7 feet high.

DAY ONE: LATE MORNING

Check into **The Mansions Hotel,** by all appearances a stately mansion in a staid neighborhood. When you bed down at this home of a magician, however, nothing is as it seems. Once inside this house, questions zip around your head as fast as a billiard ball. What's a macaw doing in the hallway? Are those pigs on the ceiling? Just clear your mind and go exploring. Beniamino Bufano sculptures are scattered among the grounds. His statue of St. Francis is an obelisk with a mosaic inlay. A bronze panel of the Crucifixion in the rear garden shows a transcendentally serene Christ. It can be too mesmerizing. Put your hotel adventure on hold and head down to Fillmore Street.

Romance at a Glance

♥ *Stay at the truly magical Mansions Hotel (415–929–9444 or 800–826–9398).*

♥ *Shop at the unique stores along Upper Fillmore Street.*

♥ *Attend the Haunted Mansions Magic Show.*

♥ *Stroll through an elegant Beaux Arts neighborhood.*

♥ *Enjoy a gourmet picnic at a hilltop park.*

Lunch

True to its international leanings, Fillmore Street has food from Brazil, Arabia, New Orleans, Sicily, and Mexico. A perfect repast can be enjoyed at **Vivande Porta Via** (2125 Fillmore Street between California and Sacramento; 415–346–4430). If the day is sunny and warm, take a picnic to the park. Vivande's prepares picnics to go.

The restaurant is set up like Carlo Middione's private kitchen. The atmosphere is casual, but the food is not. Layers of flavor characterize each dish, from the lemon risotto to the anchovies and olives that spice the pasta puttanesca. Internationally popular from his cookbooks and television show, Middione fills the deli case with southern Italian tortas, roasted chicken, polenta, and white bean salad.

DAY ONE: AFTERNOON

If you had wine with lunch, now is the time to clear your head. Whatever suits your fancy, you'll find it in some form or other on Fillmore Street. Be on the lookout for that perfect purchase, but browse the shops as much for the unique offerings and the chance to hobnob with the locals. Two distinct categories of merchandise predominate: home and garden accessories and European boutiques. Shop downhill on one side of Fillmore then uphill on the other; numbers decrease on the downhill and increase on the uphill.

Pick up the neighborhood paper, *The New Fillmore* at **Juicy News** (2453 Fillmore Street at Jackson; 415–441–3051), where you can also flip through copies of *Corriere Tella Sera* from Italy and *Le Monde* from France. **Cielo** (2225 Fillmore Street; 415–776–0641) carries European designers So, Paul Smith, Alberta Ferretti, and Dries Van Noten for both men and women. Rick Herbert, who owns **R.H.** (2506 Sacramento Street at Fillmore; 415–346–1460), is noted for his herb topiary trees of English myrtle and lavender. Three floors at **Fillamento** (2185 Fillmore Street between Sacramento and California; 415–931–2224) carry trendy decorative pieces and locally designed glassware. Visit the imported bath products section on the second floor.

Cosmopolitan chic reigns at a handful of women's and men's stores: **Bebe** (2133 Fillmore near Sacramento; 415–771–BEBE); **L'Uomo International** (2121 Fillmore Street; 415–776–0669); **Mio** (2035 Fillmore between California and Pine; 415–931–5620). At **Victorian Annex Thrift Shop** (2318 Fillmore Street at Clay; 415–923–3237) you may discover a bit of froufrou to wear to the magic show tonight, although **Betsey Johnson** (2031 Fillmore Street between California and Pine; 415–567–2726) may be more to your liking. **Cedonna Artful Living** (1925 Fillmore Street near Pine; 415–474–7152) and **Zinc Details** (1905 Fillmore Street at Bush; 415–776–2100) cut to the heart of accessorizing a home. Bringing luxury to the bedroom, **Duxiana** (1803 Fillmore Street at Sutter;

415–673–7134) sells top-of-the-line bed linens from Missoni, Hecking Royal Damask, and Bon Jour.

Surely the prospect of a climb up Fillmore sparks the thought of sustenance—just as you pass the windows of **Delanghe Patisserie** (1890 Fillmore Street at Bush; 415–923–0711). Cafe au lait with raspberry swirl scones or custard brioche? The windows of **Mike Furniture** (2142 Fillmore at Sacramento; 415–567–2700) give you an idea of how a well-dressed upper Fillmore residence might look. European taste predominates on every block. French and Italian lingerie and sleepwear can be purchased at **Toujours** (2484 Sacramento Street at Fillmore; 415–346–3988). You may find last season's cast-offs in secondhand stores. Try **Next-to-New Shop** (2226 Fillmore Street between Sacramento and Clay; 415–567–1628). **Zoë** (2400 Fillmore at Washington; 415–929–0441) sells designer clothing for women. The second-time-around phenomenon shows up in other permutations. Treasures may lurk in the dust at **Mureta's Antiques** (2418 Fillmore Street between Washington and Jackson; 415–922–5652) and **Repeat Performance Thrift Shop** (2436 Fillmore Street between Jackson and Washington; 415–563–3123). Jocasta Innes, the British paint magician, has single-handedly revived the decorative use of paint. You can watch people at work in the studio of **Paint Effects** (2426 Fillmore Street between Washington and Washington; 415–292–7780) learning trompe l'oeil, metallic finishes, craquelure, and gilding.

DAY ONE: Evening

Before you know it, it's time to dress for dinner. Spiritualism was a major hit around the turn of the century. Well-to-do citizens probably held seances in the very parlor where you'll attend tonight's magic show. Continue exploring the maze of rooms. Two mansions have been inconspicuously joined. When you step up into a short hallway you are crossing over to another house. Piano music leads you to the bar where an elegantly stuffed Barbra Streisand sits. After you get a glass of wine, walk around the front and rear gardens to see Bufano's bronze and marble sculptures. Then settle into the front parlor where other guests are gathering.

This room, as is the entire hotel, is an extension of its eccentric owner, Robert Pritikin. He scoured the city looking for a mansion to buy. When he found Utah Senator Charles Chambers's Queen Anne mansion, he converted the front parlor into a small venue for his nightly magic shows. A case full of historic documents, such as letters from Houdini, Lincoln, and Thomas Edison, takes up one wall. A priceless J. M. Turner oil painting, *The Ancient City*, shares wall space with marauding pigs. Claudia, the resident ghost, has a passion for pigs and kept them as pets when she lived here with her uncle. Robert Pritikin is a magician first and innkeeper second. He introduces Claudia as his invisible sprite. You'll see some wonderful sleight of hand and card tricks. His magic show features him playing Beethoven on a saw and conversing with a human head on a platter.

Dinner

One guest enthused in the comment book, "The most insane, fabulous, implausible, magnificent hotel in the world." The fabulous part applies to the dining room and food. A four-course dinner follows the magic show in a room set with a stained-glass mural titled *Garden in Heaven*. These were originally designed for a villa in Barcelona. The beef Wellington and salmon in parchment match the opulence of the setting. A four-course dinner and one-hour magic show is $57.

DAY ONE: LATE EVENING

If you'd like to stroll for awhile, walk down to Fillmore Street. Night alters its character. **Harry's Bar** (2020 Fillmore Street between California and Pine; 415–921–1000) has a live band that can be heard from the sidewalk. Tell the bartender your room may be haunted and you need a drink to put you out fast. He'll probably serve you a Cosmopolitan.

Cosmopolitan

1¼ ounces vodka
¼ ounce triple sec
1 tablespoon lime juice
dash cranberry juice

Serve in chilled martini glasses. Garnish with sugared cranberries or lime zest.

DAY TWO: MORNING

Breakfast

You slept like a baby, I bet. Rise late for croissants and cafe au lait at 11:00 A.M. Want something more substantial? A full American breakfast is the forte of **Pauli's Cafe** (2500 Washington Street at Fillmore; 415–921–5159; moderate). They are well known for their pancakes with real maple syrup and bowls of granola, fresh fruit, and yogurt.

◌◌◌

Formal staircases sweep up to **Alta Plaza Park** (bounded by Scott and Steiner, Jackson and Clay), where the whole world is on view. The high gloss of the scene atop Alta Plaza Park is reflected in the neighborhood's mix of mansions, Victorians, and row houses, each one a polished gem. Spend an afternoon appreciating the work of an elite group of San Franciscan

architects. Along the crest of Jackson Street you encounter a rich pocket of architectural styles attributed to graduates of École des Beaux Arts in Paris. At the turn of the century, this was the Western world's top architectural training ground.

The Beaux Arts vernacular is evident in the symmetry and grandeur of the facades. Look for basket-weave brickwork, Venetian loggias, Austrian pitched roofs, classical dentil moldings, arched doorways, Mission revival tile roofs, and Craftsman brown shingle. **Whittier Mansion** (2090 Jackson Street at Laguna), a sandstone residence completed in 1896, is a notch above the others. At this thirty-one-room, red sandstone dwelling, a Hong Kong businessman now lives.

Turn right at Octavia and climb the hill to **Lafayette Park,** where another hilltop view spreads before you. The **Spreckels Mansion** (2080 Washington Street at Octavia), also called "the Parthenon of the West," boasts the largest private indoor swimming pool in the United States. Alma Spreckels preferred to swim her daily laps in the nude. She also wanted her husband to enjoy his afternoon nap peacefully, so she finagled a permit from city officials to install the park below the crest of Octavia. To this day the park's location dissuades drivers from using the street. The facade of the mansion is sorrowfully crumbling. Architect George Applegarth chose to build the house with limestone, a material that weathers badly in San Francisco. Now, the house's decorative cherubs are losing their features. The white limestone edifice was a suitable reminder, though, of the "white gold" that made sugar czar Claus Spreckels a wealthy man.

⤫

In a moment, you are back at The Mansions Hotel's front door. If you have a comment, write it in the guest ledger. It may end up in a display case—especially if it tantalizes the host. That memorable trysts take place under his roof is a point of pride.

ITINERARY 20
Two days and one night

BEAUTISSIMO!

PACIFIC HEIGHTS

*T*his single-word title leapt off the guest book page, so exuberantly written it caught my eye. I felt the couple wasn't merely referring to the ambience of their lodgings. Other entries indicated the Sherman House was a popular place for wedding nights and anniversaries. To ensconce yourselves on "Millionaire Heights" in San Francisco's lushest hotel, a special occasion is nice but not necessary. What you need is an unexpected bonus, a business venture that pays off, or an anonymous benefactor (remember the 1950s television show *The Millionaire*?). Yes, to pull this off you'll need more than extra pocket change.

If it's time for a well-earned indulgence, give this gift to yourselves. Call it the ultimate date. Pull out the stops. When darkness descends, lights flicker on at the Coconut Grove, San Francisco's most elegant night club. That's where you'll be tonight. A well-cut tuxedo, a whisper of silk charmeuse, the glitter of rhinestones on an ankle strap. You're walking in now. Fame, fortune, and a heartthrob on your arm.

Practical Notes: Call **Coconut Grove Supper Club** (1415 Van Ness Avenue; 415–776–1616) and ask for the entertainment lineup. Book early at the **Sherman House** (2160 Green Street; 415–563–3600 or 800–424–5777; $310–$775). Every room has canopied feather beds, full drapes, and fireplaces; one has a terrace, another a private garden. Two have private decks. Like a designers' showcase house, every room is different. When you call the Sherman House, ask them to fax you descriptions of the French Empire, Biedermeier, and English Jacobean suites. The Paderewski Suite on the second floor, once Sherman's billiard room, would be my choice on a foggy summer night. It has a fireplace in the bathroom and a deeply cushioned window seat. The details of the room recall the reign of Henry VIII: wood-beamed ceiling, pictorials of fox hunters and Ascot races, gate-legged table, Hyde Park-style furniture. In the clear weather of late winter, spring, and fall, I would book the Sherman Suite at the top of the house, once the master bedroom. The bed is in an alcove behind 18-foot drapes. The English sitting room, with a delicate frieze painted above the molding, opens to a vast brick terrace. You might also like the gingerbread carriage house, which was completely gutted so everything is new. Movie stars like Meg Ryan prefer the carriage house for privacy.

Romance at a Glance

♥ *Sleep by a glowing fireplace in a canopied feather bed at the Sherman House (415–563–3600 or 800–424–5777).*

♥ *Shop in colorful Victorian buildings along Union Street.*

♥ *Dance at Coconut Grove Supper Club (415–776–1616).*

♥ *View patrician homes along the Broadway bluff.*

DAY ONE: LATE MORNING

Check into the Sherman House. If you chose the Sherman Suite, you are enjoying one of the world's most beloved panoramas. The drama of the bay never ceases, from morning sunlight to wisps of afternoon fog to evening moonlight. Add to this the finery of the Golden Gate Bridge and the Palace of Fine Arts, as well as tiled Mediterranean roofs, a yacht harbor, and the Sausalito hillside cloaked in vacation cottages.

Lunch

Chef Maria Helm, from the Sherman House, took over the kitchen at **PlumpJack Cafe** (3127 Fillmore Street between Filbert and Greenwich; 415–563–4755; moderate), where her popular pairing of California and Mediterranean cuisine garnered a four-star rating in the first year. Open Monday to Friday for lunch, this cafe has a blue-blood pedigree. J. Paul Getty's grandchildren own it, and they hired the same people to design the restaurant who did the Gettys' private jet. The oval shape of the gold lighting fixture reappears on the waiters' vests and the buttons of tufted banquettes. Try the mustard-seed crusted steelhead salmon, risotto, or duck confit. Entrees range from $9.00 to $13.00. If it's Saturday, **Pane e Vino** (3011 Steiner Street at Union; 415–346–2111) serves an exceptional lunch. They have superb pastas and fresh seafood.

DAY ONE: Afternoon

San Francisco's most colorful street is **Union Street.** From Steiner to Gough, its Victorian buildings have been transformed into designer boutiques, shoe emporiums, jewelry shops, art galleries, cafes, and restaurants. You'll even come across an occasional farm building, a reminder of when this area was pastoral Cow Hollow. Between Fillmore and Webster, **Three Bags Full** (2181 Union Street; 415–567–5753) has handknit sweaters, **Lorenzini** (2149 Union Street; 415–346–2561) men's clothing. Between Webster and Buchanan, **Armani Exchange** (2090 Union Street; 415–749–0891), **Kenneth Cole** (2078 Union Street; 415–346–2161), and **Bebe** (2095 Union Street; 415–563–2323) have elegant clothing and footwear.

The Victorian Court (the first residence to be converted into shops), with a century-old palm in front, has a red barn housing a gallery in back. The door to the hayloft is visible from the street. Between Buchanan and Laguna, **Peluche** (1954 Union Street; 415–441–2505) has women's clothing. Jewelry stores also line the block: **Patronik Designs** (1949 Union Street; 415–922–9716), **Puffins** (1945 Union Street; 415–931–4918), **Glamour** (1931 Union Street; 415–775–6622), and **Paris 1925** (1954 Union Street, second floor; 415–567–1925). Between

Laguna and Octavia, **Fenzi Uomo** (1801 Union Street; 415–563–9700) is also worth a stop for European men's clothing.

Allyne Park (Gough Street at Green) is a pastoral retreat, thanks to the Allyne sisters. Their home once stood inside the picket fence that surrounds this natural garden of redwood, pine, and rhododendron. Beside the park stands an architectural fad that never caught on: the **Octagon House** (2645 Gough Street at Union; 415–441–7512). The shape admits more light into the house, but you need to build on a large lot.

Before walking back to the Sherman House along Green Street, stop at the corner and look down Gough Street. In 1850 you would have been looking directly into a lagoon, which was the city's laundry basin. The name Cow Hollow, as this section of Pacific Heights was once called, conjures a bucolic scene of lowing dairy cows. The truth is, the stench of Cow Hollow, from thirty dairies, slaughterhouses, tanneries, and a soap factory caused hand wringing from the folks up on the hill. The city made a clean sweep. With the cows banished, industry banned, and the malodorous lagoon filled in, homes of the prosperous soon sprouted up.

In a city whose aristocracy were self-made people, it is possible for a Pacific Heights resident to trace his or her roots back to a squatter. That Cow Hollow squatters fared so well was a freak occurrence. Land grant papers verifying ownership disappeared en route from Mexico. If the land obtained by building a house and erecting a fence remained in the family's possession, a Pacific Heights realtor once calculated, its value since 1850 increased 75,000 times.

The first examples of the Bay area regional style can be seen in the homes at 1635 and 1639 Green Street. The Queen Anne tower home (Green Street and Octavia), painted blue and white, evokes the colors of Wedgwood china. Ernest Coxhead designed the library (1801 Green Street) in the shape of a Roman basilica. It still has the early name of the district, Golden Gate Valley. Turning into the walkway of the Sherman House, you may feel like you are visiting friends in the neighborhood. The bell captain snaps to attention. The Count and Countess of Cow Hollow have arrived.

DAY ONE: EVENING

Even couples of ordinary means have fantasies to live out and the Sherman House is your willing accomplice. The house chef prepares a five-course dinner only for hotel guests. And in these elegant surroundings a tuxedo and silk evening dress would not be out of place. Hors d'oeuvres are served in the upstairs gallery while the finches chirp in their chateau and you clink champagne flutes by the fireside. The food, superbly prepared and presented, fits the high-class drama of the setting, Mr. Sherman's dining room. Entrees range from $29 to $38; prix fixe menu $65.

After dessert, call a cab for the **Coconut Grove Supper Club** (1415 Van Ness Avenue between Pine and Bush; 415–776–1616), where Hollywood's golden era is alive and swinging. Dance under a coconut palm with green-painted metal fronds, coconut lights, and lighted trunks. On Thursday, Saturday, and Sunday, dancing continues after 11:00 P.M. when Motown, salsa, or swing takes over.

Back at the Sherman House, the hotel mascot Boots, a black cat with a white face, purrs a greeting. You can light a fire, watch the stars, listen to tinkling of the courtyard fountain. Then, climb into bed and draw the drapes.

DAY TWO: MORNING

Breakfast

Breakfast is served in the Sherman House solarium. A basket of warm muffins and scones comes with homemade raspberry jam and apricot jam spiced with cloves, cinnamon, allspice, and nutmeg. Eggs, omelets, and waffles are served with fresh fruit. After breakfast you are invited to visit the greenhouse, where the gardener grows orchids. The grounds are lovingly tended. Two dwarf citrus trees bearing bright oranges flank the carriage house. The Sherman House is painted sparkling white, the traditional color for Victorians.

❦

Victorian homes are the fanciful, joyful gifts of the late nineteenth century to our city streets. Few finer displays exist anywhere of this ebullient architecture. On this **Pacific Heights walk,** you'll encounter a hundred Victorians with gingerbread inside and out, displaying the status and success of the homeowner. So get ready to take inventory. Take Webster to Vallejo, turn left, and walk to Gough. Broadway is one block to the right. Among the profuse ornamentation, most of it ordered from millwork catalogs, are dentils, beading, finials, brackets, cornices, porticoes, pressed sunbursts, etched and stained glass, gables, French caps, mansard roofs, newel posts, balustrades, wrought-iron picket fences, lace ironwork, decorative shingles, columns, pilasters, doorway pediments, and arched spoolwork. See how much you can spot on each house.

On Sunday or Wednesday, when the house is open for tours, walk the extra three blocks to the **Haas-Lilienthal House** (2007 Franklin Street between Jackson and Washington; 415–441–3004). The romantic clutter of this magnificent Queen Anne house is always on view from the side driveway. It was built in 1886 at the height of Victorian excess, which dictated that no two stories could be alike. The sunflowers, witch's cap tower, and fishtail shingles are all finely preserved.

Follow the Broadway bluff starting at Gough and ending at Lyon. One of the city's great patrician walks lies ahead. The **Flood Mansion** (2120 Broadway at Buchanan), where lions guard the entrance, was built by silver king James C. Flood for his daughter in 1901. The exterior is not stone, but painted wood. James L. Flood, son of James C., built the white marble palace at **2222 Broadway** (between Webster and Fillmore) in 1912, commissioning the intricate grillwork of the front door. It houses an exclusive girls' school. At each street corner you have the same unobstructed views that these spectacular homes possess.

Broadway ends at the top of the **Lyon Street steps.** From here you see the tiled roofs of the Marina, the Palace of Fine Arts, the Golden Gate Bridge, and hundreds of sails billowing across the bay. You see why Jim Carrey chose the location to propose to actress Lauren Holly. The marriage may have crumbled, but the allure of the scenery lives on. This bucolic staircase, the longest in the city, follows the eastern wall of the Presidio. As you walk down, notice the contrast of wilderness on the left and gracious homes on the right. At Green Street a small oval park fronts a Classical Revival home. Turn right onto Vallejo Street to witness again the height of the Victorian craze for decoration. This street has the best examples of Queen Anne row houses and Queen Anne tower houses. Go up Pierce to see the **Casebolt Mansion** (2727 Pierce between Vallejo and Green), built in 1865. Casebolt sailed around the Horn with his wife and eleven children and set up a wagon factory in Cow Hollow. He made enough money from a cable-car grip he invented to build this Italianate home. Don't let the facade fool you. Casebolt painted it this way to deceive his eastern friends into thinking it was granite. Saint Mary Episcopal Church (2325 Union), built in 1891, brings the English countryside to Union Street. In the courtyard beyond the lych-gate is a tile fountain fed by the last free-flowing spring in the area.

Take a well-deserved rest at **Rose's Cafe** (2298 Union Street at Steiner; 415–775–2200). On a typical weekday afternoon commotion reigns at curbside tables where dogs owners feed their pets the remaining crumbs of a panini or focaccia. Inside, the Episcopal minister is bent over a bowl of Ligurian minestone soup, while neighborhood teenagers pass around a strawberry focaccia, breaking off pieces and dipping them in lattés. At the counter, sandwiches line the board: grilled steak, peppered salmon; and the house specialty, stuffed focaccia with crescenza, a creamy cow's-milk cheese. Rose's has the ambience and menus of countryside cafes in France and Italy that chef Reed Hearon frequently visits. A friend I had lost touch with met me for lunch one winter afternoon at Rose's Cafe. We laughed, looked at wedding photos, and filled the fifteen-year gap in our friendship. We shared platters of tuna, arugula salad, spring vegetables and focaccia stuffed with Italian prosciutto and cheese. How did we get along without each other?

Turn off Union at Webster. The structure at Webster and Filbert is a Vedanta monastery.

Among its features are a Moorish minaret, a replica of the Taj Mahal, a Russian onion dome, and a Norman tower. They coexist in surprising harmony. Hindu monks brought the Vedanta philosophy to the West in the 1890s. Their building reflects Vedanta's reverence for the great prophets and religious leaders whose teachings lead people, they believe, to the same eternal truths. This Vedanta Victorian produces a more immediate experience. The pleasure of setting your eyes on beauty—which abounds in Pacific Heights—is one of the joys of life.

ITINERARY 21
Two days and one night

DISCOVERY ZONE

THE MARINA

*G*ear up for zany, spontaneous fun in this itinerary. Even if you've been coming to the city for years, you'll find something here you haven't tried before. The Marina district traces its genesis to a shoreline extravaganza held more than eighty years ago. The 1915 Panama Pacific Exhibition drew eighteen million visitors to nearly a hundred pavilions radiating from its fabled Jeweled Tower. To ready itself, the city filled 600 acres of marshland with sand from the bay. Afterward it was carved into housing lots. So much of the shoreline had been dredged, the San Francisco Yacht Harbor could establish itself with little more than the addition of piers and slips. Homes went up; yachts moved in.

An afternoon stroll takes you along the old fairgrounds, around the yacht harbor, and into the neighborhood. There you step back to 1930. Art Deco architecture gives Marina streets the panache of Hollywood. Evening gets off to a spicy start with southwestern cuisine on Chestnut Street, then continues at San Francisco's Magic Theatre for innovative drama. No stage performance, though, can match the most spectacular event in the Bay Area—the migration of the gray whales. Driven nearly to extinction in the twentieth century, gray whales have now

Romance at a Glance

♥ *Stay in a carriage house apartment at the Edward II Inn (415–922–3000 or 800–473–2846).*

♥ *Attend the Saturday morning "West Coast Live" radio show (415–664–9500).*

♥ *Dine at the all-organic Greens Restaurant (415–771–6222).*

♥ *Awaken your sense of touch in the amazing Tactile Dome (415–561–0362).*

♥ *Get a rare thrill viewing the gray whale migration (Oceanic Society Expeditions; 415–474–3385 or 800–326–7491).*

regained their historic population level. Seeing them is a thrill worth sharing with someone you love.

Practical Notes: This itinerary sounds great, doesn't it? Here's the hitch: You have to look good in jogging clothes. Only kidding. Even so, Marina Green is the closest thing we have to L.A.'s Venice Beach. The drawback is that you have to reserve everything in advance. So much for spontaneity. But a half hour on the telephone will pay off. A copy of the **West Coast Live** show schedule; (Cowell Theater; Pier 2, Fort Mason Center; 415–664–9500 www.wcl.org) may include a legendary author or musician. If Isabel Allende is your hero, you can hear her read from *Aprodite, a memoire of the senses*. Blues guitarist Jon Hammond was on the show recently to celebrate his new CD.

I've known people who cry when they're turned away from **Greens Restaurant** (Fort Mason Center, Building A; 415–771–6222) for lunch. Make Saturday reservations between 12:30 and 1:00 P.M. Reserve four to six weeks ahead for the **Tactile Dome** (Exploratorium; 415–561–0362; http://www.exploratium.edu), requesting a late Saturday afternoon appointment. Get a performance schedule from **Magic Theatre** (Fort Mason Center, Building D; 415–441–3687). Book a carriage house apartment at the **Edward II Inn** (3155 Scott Street at Lombard; 415–922–3000 or 800–473–2846; $225). With all that said, the keystone of this itinerary is **Oceanic Society Expeditions** (Fort Mason Center, Building E; 415–474–3385 or 800–326–7491). Whale watching cruises depart Fort Mason from December to April; Farallon Islands cruises depart from late May to November. Call the **Golden Gate National Recreation Area** for a map that includes the Golden Gate Promenade (GGNRA; 415–556–0560; http://www.nps.gov/goga).

DAY ONE: MORNING

If you're arriving on Saturday, drop your car at the Edward II Inn and take a cab to Fort Mason. "San Francisco's Live Radio Show to the World" is broadcast from the heart of the Marina district every Saturday from 10:00 A.M. to noon. Sedge Thomson, who hosts the *West Coast Live* variety show in front of an audience, is fast becoming identified as Mr. San Francisco. The mix of entertainment and interviews is a slice of San Francisco. Guests as disparate as the Gyuto Tantric Monks, Calvin Trillin, the Kronos Quartet, and Spalding Gray have appeared. When he asks for volunteers at the beginning of the show, charge onto the stage. It may be your one opportunity for stardom.

As you exit Cowell Theater, a trio of small museums are open to visitors: African-American Historical and Cultural Society (Building C; 415–441–0640), Museo Italo-Americano (Building C; 415–673–2200), and Mexican Museum (Building D; 415–441–0445). Each of these has exhibits on the people and cultures of the ethnic group for which each is named.

Lunch

When you come back out into the wind, a bowl of delicious soup is right around the corner. At **Greens Restaurant** (Building A; moderate) it is not an ordinary bowl of soup that appears before you, but a virtual garden: broth infused with herbs, chunks of vegetables perfectly simmered, heavenly rolls from Tassajara bakery to soak up the last drop. I remember telling my dad, halfway through Sunday brunch, that this was a vegetarian restaurant. He took another bite of the breakfast sausage he had just been raving about. "Ya gotta be kiddin' me," he said. We chose Greens for the sun-splashed view of yachts, the Golden Gate Bridge, and the

A Romantic Rescue

One of the most romantic movie scenes set in San Francisco was filmed at the Fort Point seawall. In Vertigo, Jimmy Stewart rescued Kim Novak from the bay, cradling her in his arms as she regained consciousness.

sparkling bay. The truth is, the patrons of Greens are not typically vegetarians, just lovers of good food. Some may not even be health-conscious, but I feel if I ate like this every day, I'd live to be a hundred.

DAY ONE: AFTERNOON

Alas, I don't have 100 years to travel the world. Neither do you. But if you concentrate your senses, the 3 miles stretching before you will be so rich in discovery, it will seem like the whole world is yours. After lunch, go up the staircase to the great meadow, dedicated to Philip Burton, father of the Golden Gate National Recreation Area (GGNRA). The **Golden Gate Promenade** stretches open and free in contrast to the dense and attached houses of the Marina district. This walkway follows the water's edge all the way to Fort Point, the Art Deco bridge never leaving your sight. Follow the spit of land out to the entrance of the **yacht harbor.** A sandy beach makes a great spot to watch skippers hoist sail. When the tide comes in, a water organ, installed in the adjacent slope by artists, emits a low tone.

Windsurfers out in front of **Crissy Field** are also fun to watch. The experts sail as fast as 60 miles per hour. Crissy Field was a grass airstrip when the hangars were built. Biplanes carried mail and later passengers, becoming San Francisco's first airport. This area is slated for change. On your next visit the pilothouses on the hill may be converted to B&Bs and the shoreline restored to marshland. Beyond the wharf, the walkway deposits you at the sally port of Fort Point. Notice how the waters at the bay's entrance, a 1.2-mile strait, grow more turbulent.

Fort Point is the most spectacular historical site of the Presidio (a former Army base). Not a brick of the fortress has been altered, not even to accommodate the overhanging bridge. The fort was erected near the abandoned Spanish Castillo and shows very few signs of wear. Enter through the sally port onto the quadrangle sheltered by three stories of red brick and granite. Each of the arched gun casements contained a cannon capable of hurling thirty-two-pound cannonballs 2 miles into the bay. Climb the spiral staircase to the top for a view of the shining girders and the arch supporting the bridge.

Retrace your steps to Marina Boulevard. Long after the lights of the 1915 Panama Pacific Exhibition's Jeweled Tower were turned off and the fair's pavilions dismantled, the curved colonnades and classical rotunda of the Exhibition's **Palace of Fine Arts** (Lyon Street between Bay and Jefferson) continue to draw visitors.

It's Saturday, so the bridal brigade is out in force. Newlyweds line up for their turn. Satin gowns billow, a geyser spurts to life, swans sail on cue, and the photographer says "Smile." The fine arts exhibit hall now houses the **Exploratorium** (3601 Lyon Street between Bay and Marina; 415–563–7337 or 415–561–0362), where you can explore the science behind technology.

Hidden in a back corner of the Exploratorium is another very special dome—one that will make you smile like a newlywed. Behind the **Tactile Dome**'s blue curtain, you are instructed to remove earrings, watches, chains, keys, shoes. Everything can come off if you reserve the dome for yourselves—"except for undergarments," the staff member decorously informs us. She gives us the signal to enter. Crawling around in pitch blackness is one of the most sensual experiences you can imagine. Not only your hands but your entire body responds to smooth, fuzzy, rubbery, cold, and pebbly surfaces. I grope my way through the maze, then suddenly my feet find the first step of a vinyl-covered rope ladder. I pull myself into a circular room with a slide. What happens at the bottom of the slide I am forbidden to tell. Though you share your hour-and-fifteen-minute session with fourteen other crawlers, people enter at fifteen-minute intervals. It costs $180 to reserve the entire session for yourselves; otherwise it costs $12 each.

You'll love the location of your carriage house apartment owned by **Edward II Inn** (3155 Scott Street at Lombard; 415–922–3000 or 800–473–2846; $225). The motels lining Lombard Street cater to families who prefer the convenience of a motel. The carriage house apartments across the street from Edward II have four-poster beds and whirlpool tubs for two. Check into this haven for couples. If you are concerned about traffic noise, the second bedroom in the rear is quieter.

DAY ONE: EVENING

Marina district homes hide the most marvelous gardens. On an entire block, neighbors agreed to remove their fences to have an unbroken green sward behind their houses. Neighbors showed the same cohesiveness during the 1989 earthquake. Residents pulled a mile-long fireboat hose from the bay and extinguished the fires threatening to engulf the district. You won't see any earthquake scars or, unfortunately, the gardens, but you can spend a rewarding hour before dinner scouting out the architectural treasures and oddities of San Francisco's most homogeneous district. Aesthetics of the 1920s and 1930s stray as far as possible from Victorian ideals.

In the nineteenth century undecorated space signaled a lack of wealth, but in the Art Deco era, restraint conveyed good taste. Look for medallions, black vitrolux glass, molded bay windows, chevrons, and a general lack of ornament. The building at **1700 Bay** shows off Art Deco at its flamboyant stage. The lobby ceiling is painted to look like aluminum. Peer into apartment building lobbies for stenciled ceilings and glazed entryway tile in tropical colors. The intersection of Webster and Beach has two apartment buildings built in 1932 painted to highlight their Art Deco details. Ladies with cubist breasts flank the building at **3665 Scott,** corner of Beach. Think of them as the goddesses of Moderne Marina. Unique for its blue

mirrors, **165 Malloca** shows a dash of Hollywood. Look for plumed serpents on square columns, which began appearing in the Marina soon after the Mayan pyramids were discovered in Mexico.

Dinner

The Marina hasn't lost its reputation as a trendsetter. Chestnut Street is at the peak of a food craze. The pungent aroma of chili wafts from doorways. Complimenting the Art Deco storefronts are restaurant interiors splashed in bright, bold Aztec colors. Tonight you'll find out what happens when chefs trained in haute cuisine indulge their passion for Mexican food. Dishes served at **Cafe Marimba** (2317 Chestnut Street between Scott and Divisadero; 415–776–1506; moderate), are "*musica* for your mouth." From Oaxaca mole and La Paz red snapper tacos, priced $8.00 to $12.00, you'll think you took a left turn off a Baja plaza. If the fog has just chased you indoors, the effect of bold color and exotic aromas is even more uplifting.

Sweet Heat (3324 Steiner Street between Chestnut and Lombard; 415–474–9191; inexpensive) has the best veggie burritos and fish tacos. They make a delicious nonfat cilantro-yogurt dipping sauce to go with chicken wings. Swing by **Andalé Taqueria** (2150 Chestnut Street between Steiner and Pierce; 415–749–0506; inexpensive) for dinner and a pitcher of sangria on the sidewalk patio warmed by an adobe fireplace. Rotisserie-grilled chicken accounts for the popularity of their chicken tacos and burritos. Ever taste a spinach tortilla wrapped around mango salsa and grilled snapper? Designer burritos are wholesome and hearty at **World Wrapps** (2257 Chestnut Street between Pierce and Scott; 415–563–9727; inexpensive).

❧❧❧

Obie award-winning premieres have made the **Magic Theatre** (Fort Mason Center, Building D; 415–441–3687) an international destination for avid playgoers. Sam Shepard (*Fools for Love, Cruising Paradise*), whose work earned him a Pulitzer Prize, Michael McClure, and up-and-coming playwrights find an appreciative audience. Magic Theatre's five-play season begins in October and extends until June or July.

On exceptionally fine evenings, forgo the taxi ride and walk along the shoreline back to the inn. If you are lucky, a full moon will light your way.

DAY TWO: MORNING

Breakfast

There's plenty of time to enjoy a good breakfast before casting off. **Bechelli's Coffee Shop** (2346 Chestnut Street between Scott and Divisadero; 415–346–1801; inexpensive) opens at 7:00 A.M. While Bechelli's photo gallery evokes the golden age of film, the U-shaped counter of this Deco diner has an authentic old-time feel. Waffles, omelets, or eggs-over-easy are all served with neighborly small talk. **Judy's Cafe** (2268 Chestnut between Pierce and Scott; 415–922–4588; moderate), another option for Sunday brunch, opens at 7:45 A.M.

❧❧❧

Head over to Fort Mason for your cruise. Stop at **Greens Restaurant take–out counter** because you need to bring lunch on board. Also purchase beverages. The nature cruises board behind Building A. **Oceanic Expeditions** provides expert naturalists and comfortable 50-foot cruisers with open observation decks. The bounty of the Bay Area supplies the rest. **Farallon Islands** is the largest seabird rookery in the eastern Pacific south of Alaska. Best of all, the islands are located 27 miles west of the Golden Gate Bridge. Between May and November, **Farallon Islands Nature Cruises** take you to see dolphins, sea lions, seals, and seabirds. Humpback whales also use the Farallons as a summer feeding ground. Between November and March, **Whale Watching Cruises** follow a scenic route up the coast. Most sightings of gray whales occur between Bolinas and Point Reyes. The morning hours of a clear, windless day are ideal to avoid the ocean's whitecaps. Spouts from a whale's blowhole can rise as high as 15 feet.

ITINERARY 22
One day

EDEN ON THE EDGE

THE PRESIDIO

*N*o city in the world can boast such bounty. Dense residential neighborhoods border a full 1,480 acres of forest, meadows, dunes, and ocean bluffs. Not only city dwellers but red-tailed hawks, golden eagles, and woodpeckers have room to breathe.

When the National Park Service took over the Presidio in 1995, a home was created for endangered native wildflowers and bird species. Magnanimous enough to fulfill many obligations, the national park preserves the past of what was once a military Valhalla. If you listen closely, you hear reveille at dawn, taps at night, and the Stars and Stripes flapping in a steady breeze. And if in the evening you stroll down Lover's Lane, a well-traveled byway formerly used by soldiers rendezvousing with their sweethearts, you may hear the echo of two centuries of footsteps.

Practical Notes: Want to learn about early aviation history at Crissy Field or retrace Juan Bautista de Anza's 1776 route as you explore the west side of the Presidio? The Park Service has a variety of ranger-led activities appealing to many interests. In one walk, you hear the stories of the men memorialized on street signs. If the antics of Freddie Funston don't thrill you, maybe the architecture will. Call ahead for a copy of the quarterly calendar of events. The **Presidio Visitor Information Center** (Building 102; 415–561–4323), open every day from 10:00 A.M. to 5:00 P.M., is on the west side of Montgomery Street on the Main Post. The **Presidio Museum** (Funston at Lincoln; 415–561–4331), located in the Civil War–era Post Hospital, is open Wednesday to Sunday. Or visit the park service Web site (http://www.nps.gov/goga) and click "Park Events." Another coming event, in a year or so, the Presidio will open a B&B in an officer's residence.

MORNING

Romance at a Glance

♥ *Hike Presidio trails, including Lover's Lane.*

♥ *Shop or browse Sacramento Street's exclusive stores.*

♥ *Lunch al fresco on the terrace at Tuba Garden.*

♥ *Learn about the Presidio's military history at the Presidio Museum.*

The Presidio's trails and roads have been open to hikers and bikers for a long time. Many residents know the trails by heart, so they know where to look for wildflowers in spring and what hilltops have the most inspiring vistas of bay and ocean. Now the nineteenth-century architecture can be enjoyed as well. The historic military buildings, considered the finest this side of West Point, will be leased out. Newer construction, like the Wherry Housing built in 1953 after architectural standards declined, will be torn down and returned to open space.

The Army left behind a record of two centuries of wars, campaigns, and skirmishes. Whatever loss the Army suffered, the burden is great for the new custodians. The National Park Service not only has 800 buildings on its hands but also a Burger King, bowling alley, gym, golf course, theater, and pet cemetery.

It's nice to think, when you take a look at the National Cemetery at the Presidio, that war has become obsolete. The Presidio was established during a period of intense empire-building. This windswept bluff became the farthest-flung military post of the Spanish Empire. The location proved disastrous for the adobe fort. Wind and storms knocked the walls down. After the Army planted trees, the base became livable. The red brick barracks housing the **Visitor Information Center** (Building 102, Montgomery between Lincoln and Moraga; 415–561–4323) were the first permanent housing for enlisted men, built in the Georgian style between 1895 and 1897. Pick up a map to show you where Lover's Lane begins. It makes a 2-mile loop, connecting with the Ecology Trail.

Lover's Lane is just beyond Tennessee Hollow. A marker explains that the First Tennessee Volunteer regiment camped in this hollow before shipping out to the Spanish–American War in the Philippines. Lover's Lane crosses a brick footbridge and goes up a gentle grade. The Sixth Army Engineers, in drawing a map, didn't scratch out its name and substitute the name of a military hero. Were there real lovers involved?

Perhaps like the Russian captain and the señorita (see sidebar, page 180) you'll find this path romantic. The row of eucalyptus trees didn't shield lovers along this beautiful 200-year-old byway. On an 1868 map, it is part of the old Spanish Trail between the Presidio and Mission Dolores. How long the Indians may have used it is anyone's guess. Russian ships often visited the Presidio. In 1816 a botanist aboard the Russian square-rigged *Rurik* explored the dunes (undistracted by beautiful daughters) and named eighty-two Bay Area species of wildflowers. Check with a park ranger (415–561–4323) for when the bloom is at its height. Around the first of April, the wildflowers take over. Of the surviving fifty-four species in the Presidio are cow clover, giant vetch, beach strawberry, yarrow, coyote brush, yerba buena, mock heather, blue violet, California lilac, and yellow bush lupine.

At the high point of **Lover's Lane** go through the pedestrian gate at Pacific and Presidio. Look at the north side of the steep 3200 block of Pacific, which seems to be a single house: long, narrow, and clad in brown shingles. It is not one but a group of compatible houses abutting one another and the Presidio wall. The most famous architects at the turn of the century had a hand in the design: Bruce Porter, Willis Polk, Ernest Coxhead, and Bernard

In 1790 Russian Captain Rezanov met and fell in love with the Spanish commandant's daughter. The Russian settlers at Fort Ross had sent him down to the Presidio for supplies. Spanish hospitality was extended to the captain, who was introduced to the youngest daughter. Consuela pledged her love and watched Rezanov depart with the promise to return and wed her. She never saw him again and passed the rest of her life in solitude. No one had brought word to the Presidio that the captain had fallen from his horse and died.

Maybeck. The homeowners along Pacific Avenue had a long-standing agreement by which the Army trimmed the cypress trees so their view of the bay was not compromised. You'll notice their stunted appearance. It's unlikely the National Park Service will provide the same service. They argue that pruning the top weakens the trees, causing heavy horizontal limbs. Beyond the Presidio wall is the affluent neighborhood of Presidio Heights. The homes are delightful and the shopping area, a few blocks down Presidio Avenue, possesses an old-world élan that invites browsing after lunch.

Lunch

You can tell a lot about the neighborhood by the kind of stores and restaurants that line Sacramento Street. **Tuba Garden** (3634 Sacramento Street between Locust and Spruce; 415–921–8822; moderate) serves a lunch or brunch al fresco on a terrace overlooking a European garden. Entrees range from $9.00 to $12.00. If the fog moves you inside, a hand-painted mural and fresh flowers maintain a country estate ambience. In addition to brunch, you can order salads or the daily grilled fish special. Tuba Garden serves a refreshing cinnamon-scented iced tea. The **Magic Flute** (3673 Sacramento Street; 415–922–1225) across the street also serves al fresco lunch (until 2:30 P.M.) and dinner.

AFTERNOON

Now that you know how the residents lunch, you can satisfy your curiosity about what they buy. The **Art Collective** (3654 Sacramento Street between Locust and Spruce; 415–474–9999) is a good stop for oil paintings, watercolors, other mixed-media prints, and sculpture. **Interior Perspectives Antiques** (3461 Sacramento Street between Walnut and Laurel; 415–292–5962) offers a similar selection. If you have a pampered pooch or puss at home, stop at **Ken Grooms'** (3429 Sacramento Street between Walnut and Laurel; 415–673–7708). They have faux Waterford crystal water bowls in case you dare not arrive home empty-handed. A trio of shops near Baker Street offers another look at how Presidio Heights residents decorate. Whimsical, unique, elegant, yes—frivolous, no. You'll find functional goods at **American Pie** (3101 Sacramento Street at Baker; 415–929–8025), **Virginia Breier** (3091 Sacramento Street at Baker; 415–929–7173), and **Sue Fisher King** (3067 Sacramento Street between Baker and Broderick; 415–922–7276). If they won't do, try **Forrest Jones** (3274 Sacramento Street at Presidio; 415–567–2483), which brings you back to Presidio Avenue. An armful of shopping bags may slow your progress down Ecology Trail. Leave the oil paintings, fireplace screen, and damask duvet cover with the respective merchants. You can always pick them up tomorrow. Turn the corner, pass the crumbling sandstone column engraved with the military eagle, and reenter the canopy of Monterey cypress.

Lover's Lane is also part of the Ecology Trail loop. Bear to the left and follow the trail to **El Polin Springs.** In a circle of willow trees, one so old its trunk heaves out of the ground, is a little park with picnic tables. In its center is a cobbled reservoir, fed by two small streams. A marker reads: EL POLIN SPRINGS. From the spring in this clump of willow trees, the early Spanish garrison attained its water supply.

All maidens who drink from this spring during the full of the moon will be assured of many children and eternal bliss.

—Ohlone Indian legend about El Polin Springs

General Mariano Vallejo, writing in 1876, attributed the large families of the garrison to the water of El Polin. "The families of Miramontes, Martinez, Sanchez, Soto, Briones, several times had twins." On the subject of eternal bliss, he didn't declare himself. Being this close to a source of eternal bliss may inspire you to clasp someone's hand and whisper something that draws a smile.

Where the picnic tables are now, Indians used to camp. The existence and peculiar qualities of El Polin were known to the Indians from a remote period and its name came from their language. The miracle is that it still exists. Guidebooks generally overlook it. If the National Park Service receives the money it needs, this spring will be drinkable again. Lobos Creek, the city's only remaining stream, will be restored as a naturally flowing stream.

From El Polin you are about half a mile from the Main Post and parade ground. Stroll past Pershing Hall to the Officer's Club. If it is open, ask to see the murals and the wall from the previous building incorporated into the club. It was part of the headquarters of the Presidio in 1776 when Captain Juan Bautista de Anza occupied it. Take Funston down to the Presidio Museum. The row of Italianate Victorian officers' cottages were built in 1862 during the Civil War. That war transformed the Presidio into a major military base.

The wars that kept the Presidio bustling are no more. But the **Presidio Museum** (Lincoln Boulevard and Funston) gives you a peek into the past. A city guide conducts tours every

Saturday at 2:00 P.M. Ed, a rare breed, points out what you don't see. The most popular item on display is the contents of an Army surgeon's black leather bag. The neatness with which the surgeon's tools are arrayed and labeled belie their gruesome utility. "We had to take out the saws because they frightened the schoolkids," said Ed. If he hadn't said that we might not have noticed the tension between that display case and the enlistment posters for the Spanish-American War on the wall, showing a dashing Teddy Roosevelt–type Rough Rider.

Unlike most military installations, the Presidio participated in the life of San Francisco. Photos show the entire base as windswept and barren in 1880 as it was in 1780. The Army planted trees to halt erosion and provide windbreaks. Now more than 400,000 trees cover the former base. An elaborate, flamboyant diorama of the 1915 Pan Pacific Exhibition with the fabled Jeweled Tower is one of the museum treasures. It is a small-scale model of the entire fair that extended along the bayshore at Crissy Field.

Leave by the back door to visit the earthquake cabins. The Army built these structures by the thousands to house San Franciscans left homeless by the 1906 earthquake and fire. The photos record images of city parks temporarily serving as refugee camps and a wagon hauling a cabin to a new site in the Richmond.

After you leave the Museum, follow Lincoln Boulevard west (it turns into Crissy Field) to reach the **Pet Cemetery.** This makes a wonderful place to stop. Directly ahead is the historic Coast Guard Station, now leased by the Gorbachev Foundation, a think tank on global peace set up by the former Soviet president. The flat area between you and the bay was wetlands filled in for the 1915 Panama Pacific Exhibition. Soon after, it was the city's first airfield. Again if funds are forthcoming, the maintenance buildings and the Doyle Drive overpass will be removed and the wetlands restored to their natural state. This trade of concrete for cordgrass marsh and dunes will cheer not just city dwellers but also the spirits of the Ohlone Indians.

ITINERARY 23
Two days and one night

INTO THE WOODS

GOLDEN GATE BRIDGE TO OCEAN BEACH

*F*orced indoors because of a blizzard? A grueling CPA exam? Sixty-hour workweeks? Perhaps this is not the time to "paint the town." If your body is screeching for fresh air, go with your lover to the viewing platform of the Coastal Trail. You will be awed by the constant dueling of land and sea. The breeze off the Pacific will rally you. The light, sky, seagulls, freighters, and unbroken openness will return a smile to your lips. Before you lies Marin Headlands, to the west the Pacific Ocean, to the east Golden Gate Bridge. Lush green Lincoln Park fills the view to the south.

Your reaction gives wordless tribute to generations of far-sighted San Franciscans. Gazing at all this land, none of it privately owned, seems incongruous in a city where property is so precious people forgo front yards and endure homes limited to 25-foot lots. All the more reason, residents say glowingly, that the outdoors deeply satisfy. As you embark on this itinerary and break out of the habits of an indoor lifestyle, anticipate a few heady side effects. You may detect in yourselves a sudden surge of well-being . . . a fresh rosy complexion . . . the urge to run barefoot in the sand . . . and, most startling, an outbreak of lighthearted gaiety. Succumb completely and you may never be the same.

Practical Notes: I would like you to succumb to all of it in style, perhaps while dressed in the

Romance at a Glance

♥ *Enjoy a picture-perfect view from your room at Seal Rock Inn (415–752–8000).*

♥ *Walk the bridge and coastal bluffs.*

♥ *Lunch at the Palace of the Legion of Honor Cafe.*

♥ *Enjoy sunset cocktails and dining at Cliff House (415–386–3330).*

♥ *Stroll Ocean Beach to Fort Funston's hang-glider area.*

San Francisco Fog Jacket, available from the **TravelSmith mail order catalog** (800–950–1600; http://www.travelsmith.com). You could buy it and put a note inside about how you'd like to see your lover in that jacket—slouching against a rail of the Golden Gate Bridge and gazing at you with that look. TravelSmith holds the formula for how to suit up for not a walk but an outdoor adventure. Ask about their Berkeley store, a 30-minute drive east of San Francisco. Accoutrements on the trail? Walking stick, binoculars, a Great Dane? Mrs. Wiggles' Rocket Juice? However you equip yourselves for the occasion, pack a map of the **Golden Gate National Recreation Area** (GGNRA; 415–556–0865). You need a Historical Trail Guide produced by the National Park Service that shows the Coastal Trail.

The rest is in the hands of Mother Nature. If fog completely blankets the shoreline, wait until it lifts. From Bridge to Cliff House, the trail weaves a gentle route: mostly level or downhill. Switch directions if you want more of a workout. Plan on a 6-mile day with an hour for lunch. On Monday when the museum and museum cafe are closed, pack a lunch and open your spread at one of the many view spots along the trail. Gauge your time so you are seated at Phineas T. Barnacle at sundown.

DAY ONE: MORNING

Deposit bags and car at the **Seal Rock Inn** (545 Point Lobos Avenue at Forty-eighth; 415–752–8000; $86–$112). When you make a reservation, ask for a room on the top floor facing the Forty-eighth Avenue side across the street from Sutro Heights Park. The rooms at Seal Rock Inn are modest in all ways but location. The rooms are furnished in outdated motel chic: swag lamps, walnut headboards, shower stalls, Formica counters. But open the drapes and feast your eyes on the view. When the skies clear after a winter rain, when wildflowers bloom, when Indian summer lulls the landscape, this is the perfect place to be.

Don lightweight hiking boots, fleece-lined anoraks, and fanny packs, and hop a cab to the Golden Gate Bridge. The plan today is to walk across the Golden Gate Bridge to the Marin viewpoint and back. You pick up the Coastal Trail, visiting gun emplacements, then descend a log staircase on the face of a great sand dune. After enjoying Baker Beach, you'll pass through a side gate into Sea Cliff and follow Sea Cliff Avenue to China Beach. You will lunch at the Legion of Honor Cafe in Lincoln Park. The Coastal Trail leads to Lands End and Point Lobos, your ultimate destination for a spectacular sunset.

Begin at the **Golden Gate Bridge Plaza.** Lock arms for the windy walk across the bridge. You may feel like laundry whipped about on a clothesline. Just hold onto your cap or sun visor around the towers. I've lost at least five over the years. Stop mid-span and let it sink in where you are. Parisians love the Eiffel Tower, San Franciscans the Golden Gate Bridge. To the west lies the Pacific Ocean and to the east the bay, the fabled inland sea that eluded European explorers. To a sailor on lookout, the 1.2-mile opening appeared as a continuous coast because Angel Island and Alcatraz fill in the gap between the two points. Besides that, the fog, ever the efficient gatekeeper, barred the opening.

Though nasty to walk through, the fog is a master trickster, covering the roadway so the towers seem to hover. Walking the bridge puts you in the middle of the action. Facing west, you see Lands End on the south and Point Bonita on the north. When yachts throng the water, and tankers and container ships come and go, watch how the sailors tack deftly around them.

One hour brings you to Marin and back again, with time for photos. Check out the glass roundhouse that is home to the **Golden Gate Bridge Visitor/Gift Center** (415–923–2331) for maps, books, or cards. The bridge claims the title of most-photographed structure in the world. Built to enhance the beauty of the location, the bridge was designed with Art Deco lights, towers, industrial orange paint, and, best of all, sidewalks.

Access to the **Coastal Trail** is under the bridge. You are embarking on an outdoor experience you won't soon forget. This trail is unmatched for its vistas, its wind-sculpted Monterey cypress, and its military relics. Most of the **Coastal Defense Batteries** date from the turn of the century. The abandoned batteries are slowly being reclaimed by the bluffs. Look for gun slits among the tangled foliage. Peer through a rusted door or metal grating. These miniature fortresses hid the bunk rooms and eating areas. Can you imagine sentry duty in a hollow concrete box?

Fort Scott Overlook is a favorite viewing spot in the evening for limousines. The bridge at this angle shows its graceful symmetry. For a while the Coastal Trail follows Lincoln Boulevard, but you are walking in the same direction as traffic along the **Coastal Bluffs;** follow the trail down to **Baker Beach.** It's too treacherous here for swimming, but the beach is fine for a picnic, a sand castle contest, or even nude sunbathing. Drinking water and restroom facilities are available. The Baker Beach Bunkers were built to defend the Golden Gate Bridge from aerial attack during World War II. **Battery Chamberlain,** built in 1902, is open weekends only (415–556–0560). You can enter the thick concrete bunkers and watch the disappearing gun in action. A new trail over Lobos Creek, one of San Francisco's last fresh water sources, leads to the gate into Sea Cliff.

At this point you leave GGNRA and enter the Richmond, a bland district except for Sea Cliff. The streets are lined with English Tudor homes, cliff-hugging chateaux, and turreted stone cottages. The front yards add to the enchantment. Actor Robin Williams sometimes flies a dragon flag from a flagpole in his yard. Sea Cliff Avenue takes you to a sloping drive down to **China Beach** (at the end of Sea Cliff Avenue off El Camino Del Mar). Nuzzled into a cove is a great swimming beach that is often deserted. The Pacific washes ashore into the arms of the gentle cliffs. You may want to linger awhile and listen to the waves, comfortable in a rocky alcove.

When you come up through Sea Cliff, El Camino Del Mar leads into **Lincoln Park** and the GGNRA trailhead for the Coastal Trail, to which you will return after lunch. Lincoln Park is a 270-acre rolling green meadow on the Point Lobos Headlands. Golfers at Lincoln Park Municipal Golf Course have striking views of the bay and bridge.

Whispering world
A sigh of sighs
The ebb and the flow
of the ocean tides.
One breath, one word
may end or may start
a hope in a place of the lover's heart.

—Enya, from "Hope Has a Place"

Lunch

The midday repast is on the lower terrace of the museum. Roam the galleries of the **California Palace of the Legion of Honor** (Thirty-fourth Avenue and Clement; 415–750–3600; closed Monday) and view works by Pieter Brueghel the Elder, Rubens, Rembrandt, and Watteau as well as sculpture by Picasso and Rodin set in a spectacular atrium. On the garden level, poke around the **Museum Store** for unique gifts. This splendid museum has an equally impressive cafe. At the **Legion Cafe** (415–221–2233; moderate), chefs apply a creative hand to the menu. Everything in the case is fresh and colorful: grilled Portobello mushroom sandwiches on focaccia, Mediterranean stuffed vegetables with lemon vinaigrette, Caesar salad, salad Nicoise, and roasted chicken are among the choices. After you place your order at the counter, you can take a table inside or on the terrace. You may want to buy a tin of Legion Cafe biscotti. In a city of many biscotti recipes, this one is a hit.

DAY ONE: AFTERNOON

Retrace your steps to the trailhead. From the platform you can see the same privileged view of the Pacific, Marin, Baker Beach, and the bridge as do Sea Cliff residents. Some mansions are built on sheer rock cliffs. Follow the trail, which descends through an old, still-active landslide. In fair weather the trail provides firm footing. From the north side of Lincoln Park Golf Course, you come down a long, steep staircase. As you go over the cliffs by Lands End, stay on the trail. The windswept view alone would place it in the same annals as the coasts of Ireland or Tasmania now that the sleek apparition of the Golden Gate Bridge has dropped from sight. During low tide you might spy two shipwrecks just beyond a small beach. You end up at the Merrie Way parking lot above Cliff House.

DAY ONE: SUNSET

The Cliff House contains two restaurants, **Upstairs at the Cliff House** and **Seafood & Beverage Co.** and two cocktail lounges, **Ben Butler Room** and **Phineas T. Barnacle,** all with the same address and phone number (1090 Point Lobos; 415–386–3330). Casual and fun with a fireplace and jukebox, the Phineas T. Barnacle has a picture-window sunset view. You can go directly from your hike, or you can call and ask what time the sun begins its dive into the ocean.

DAY ONE: EVENING

Dinner

Have cocktails at the Ben Butler Room, which overlooks Ocean Beach, home of mile-long combers, and Seal Rocks (400 feet offshore), home of pelicans and cormorants. Sea lions haul up nowadays at Pier 39, abandoning their old home on Seal Rocks. The room is thick with atmosphere from decades of couples professing their love. Manager Alan Goldstein says more marriage proposals occur in this room than anywhere else in the city. Request a table at the north end when dining at the **Seafood & Beverage Co.** (415–386–3330; moderate) to have a change of view. Window tables and elevated booths take full advantage of the restaurant's priceless asset—the churning Pacific. A few adventurous items highlight the menu, such as Santa Fe salmon and West Coast bouillabaisse, but the ever-popular stuffed filet of sole outsells them all. Entrees range from $15 to $20.

Filet of sole is probably the only menu item left over from previous cliff houses. This austere building contains no hint of the grandeur of its predecessor, an eight-story chateau with spires and a flag-bedecked tower. Inside the seaside turn-of-the-century palace, elegant dining rooms served stuffed filet of sole, crab cocktails, and shrimp Louis. Dancing and entertainment followed. Lost to fire in 1907, it was the most adored of the three cliff houses. The Sutro family held on to the current Cliff House until 1952, blaming declining fortunes on the two world wars and the Depression. It has survived under the auspices of the GGNRA, which acquired the building in 1977.

Walk on Ocean Beach after dinner, in the sand or on the promenade. Slip a naked toe into the receding surf. If this is a Friday or Saturday you may hear music coming from the upper floor of the **Beach Chalet.** Surf-rock bands and jazz trios perform 10:30 P.M. until closing. On other evenings you may be able to join the **Star Party** at Lands End. The San Francisco Amateur Astronomers (415–566–2357) gather there to watch and learn about the wonders of the night sky. Look through their telescopes and ask about your favorite constellation or astronomical phenomenon. Dress warmly and bring a flashlight. Meet at the USS *San Francisco* Memorial parking lot 5:30 P.M. to 7:00 P.M. on El Camino del Mar, just north of Forty-eighth and Point Lobos Avenues. Reservations are not required but phone for more information and current weather conditions.

DAY TWO: MORNING

The breakfast room at **Seal Rock Inn** (415–386–6518; inexpensive) opens at 6:30 A.M., and tables fill up with hearty eaters. The menu has omelets of Spanish, Greek, Italian, Hawaiian, and Swedish origin. After breakfast, cross the street to **Sutro Heights Park** and enter the drive past what's left of the lion gate.

❦

As Adolph Sutro discovered, this bluff-top site overlooking the Cliff House and ocean beyond is an ideal spot for sunsets and beach views. An engineer who made his fortune in the Nevada Comstock Lode, Adolph Sutro was San Francisco's original romantic. He built a Victorian castle and planted groves of fir, Monterey cypress, and Norfolk Island pine. He shipped classical statuary from Europe, paying more for the shipping than for the statues. Best of all, Sutro opened his home and elaborate gardens to the public. Look in the shrubbery for hidden statues, try to find *Diana and the Stag*. This marble statue proves Sutro's dream home wasn't a fable. You should also go up to his parapet, built so he could fire cannons and listen to the raucous sea lions of Seal Rocks.

Below the parapet, the concrete-faced rock cliffs are finished to look like real rock. Sutro wanted to disguise the use of concrete to reinforce the slope, which, as you witnessed yesterday, is prone to slides. By the 1930s the estate had fallen into disrepair, and the statues and the house had been vandalized. In 1979 a park ranger discovered an urn in the rockwork of the cliff below the parapet. After checking the family vault at the columbarium, it was discovered that Adolph Sutro's ashes were missing. His daughter may have been carrying out her father's wish to be buried within earshot of his beloved sea lions on his coast. A descendant claimed the urn before the story could be proven.

Walk down to **Cliff House.** Visit the National Park Service Visitors Information Center on the lower level. Adolph Sutro built a steam railroad along California Street to take San Franciscans out to Cliff House, through the dunes and wasteland of the Outside Lands, to benefit from the sea air. Go into the **Camera Obscura,** an invention of Leonardo da Vinci. You look down onto a giant screen in the center of a tiny room. Projected onto the parabolic surface is Seal Rocks and Ocean Beach picked up by the camera rotating on top.

Use caution in exploring the ruins next door, as the steps and walkways can be slippery. The pools and staircases date not from antiquity, as they seem, but from 1886. **Sutro Baths** was a massive glass-enclosed spa resembling the baths of Imperial Rome. Six saltwater swimming

pools heated to different temperatures lay beneath a colored glass roof. San Franciscans streamed to the baths, taking the train out for a nickel. Bathers swung on trapezes, shot down slides, performed swan dives from springboards. Tropical palms lined the walkways; restaurants served 1,000 at a seating. Galleries displayed sculptures, paintings, and artifacts from Aztec, Mexican, Egyptian, Syrian, Chinese, and Japanese cultures. In 1966 the site was sold to land developers who began demolition to erect high-rise apartments. A fire finished the job.

The apartments were never built. As you walk out to the promontory above **Point Lobos,** nothing mars the view. The ocean is especially fierce in late winter and throughout the spring. As a storm approaches, the sky roils in harmony with the waves. This westernmost tip of San Francisco was named by the Spanish after the sea lions, whom they called *lobos marinos,* or sea wolves.

Save late morning for a long walk on **Ocean Beach,** a great strolling beach, stretching more than 6 miles from the Cliff House to a point south of Fort Funston (415–239–2366). At 2 miles you can leave the beach to visit the San Francisco Zoo or continue to Fort Funston. Look for a trail just as the cliffs begin; it will lead you to the top of the cliffs.

Lunch

Walk back and have lunch overlooking the Pacific at the **Beach Chalet Brewery & Restaurant** (1000 Great Highway between Fulton and Lincoln; 415–386–8439). The Beach

Chalet—a 1925 Willis Polk–designed lodge and restaurant with WPA murals and mosaics—was a hit the moment it reopened. On the first floor is a model of Golden Gate Park and frescoes depicting San Franciscans at leisure in the 1930s. Upstairs, tables run alongside a bank of windows filled with sea, sky, and spinning seagulls. This magnificent vista isn't matched by the food. But choose something to complement the Chalet's 12 house brews and you'll be happy. Moroccan couscous, oysters on the half shell, lightly battered fried calamari with shaved fennel or a smoky grilled pizzetta topped with roasted peppers, artichokes, mozzarella, and a basil puree all go well with the five-brew sampler. Popular brews include Beach Blanket Blonde (a light-bodied ale with a crisp finish) and Playland Pale Ale (from the Playland amusement park that sat near the beach).

FOR MORE ROMANCE

The **San Francisco Zoo** (415–753–7165) puts on the sexiest tour in town in honor of Valentine's Day. Held weekends in February, the tour features descriptive narratives about animal mating behavior. The $30 charge includes champagne and truffles and an opportunity to purchase a limited edition commemorative Sex Tour t-shirt.

Another encore for this itinerary is a wildly romantic place you can visit year round: **Point Bonita Lighthouse.** Cross the Golden Gate Bridge and exit at Alexander Avenue; take the first left toward Marin Headlands, where a sign welcomes you to Golden Gate National Recreation Area. Conzelman Road winds for 4 miles to the Point Bonita parking lot. Rising on a volcanic spit where Marin Headlands meets the ocean, the Point Bonita beacon lies at the far side of a wooden footbridge. Below you the waters of the Pacific churn spectacularly. The glistening Fresnel lens inside the lighthouse "is like a jewel," says the park ranger. "It will last forever." Visitors are also welcome to Point Bonita on monthly full-moon tours. Since these tend to fill up quickly, call two months in advance. The Point Bonita lighthouse trail is open from 12:30 to 3:30 P.M. Saturday and Sunday. Make reservations for the full-moon tour through the Marin Headlands Visitors Center (415–331–1540).

ITINERARY 24
Two days and one night

OASIS FOR LOVERS
GOLDEN GATE PARK

*M*erlin, visiting the nineteenth century in the guise of John McLaren, climbed the crest of a sand dune—the wind clutching his garments, the sand stinging his eyes—and had a vision. He would transform the "outside lands" of San Francisco into a glorious oasis. Bending to his task, he planted barley, then lupine, then trees. People mocked his efforts: ". . . a dreary waste of shifting sand hills . . . a fog resting on it heavy enough to give asthma to a sea lion." But eventually Monterey cypress, pine, and blue gum took root. McLaren's rhododendrons miraculously bloomed.

People then flocked to the park for country outings; on a spring morning, carriages jammed the panhandle. Golden Gate Park became so popular that a resort area, Haight Ashbury, sprang up at its eastern boundary and became one of San Francisco's most interesting neighborhoods. The Victorian houses here are reminders of a time when a couple's home was their castle. If they wanted a turret or a filigree arch, they could order it from a mail-order catalog.

In the 1890s interest in exercise boomed. Tennis was the *in* sport, which accounts for the twenty-one courts in the park. Bicycle rental shops also sprouted on the park's periphery and the roadway now called John F. Kennedy Drive was paved so ladies and gents could ride their bikes. Well into its second magical century, Golden Gate Park is still best enjoyed by bike. In this itinerary you and your love can cycle through McLaren's legacy of waterfalls, lakes, gardens, meadows, and groves and share a turn-of-the-century resort experience.

Romance at a Glance

♥ *Sleep in a four-poster at the Victorian Stanyan Park Hotel (415–751–1000).*

♥ *Hike a wild woodland trail through Sutro Forest.*

♥ *See a laser light-and-music show.*

♥ *Dine on sensual Middle-Eastern cuisine at YaYa (415–566–6966).*

♥ *Rent bikes and explore Golden Gate Park from top to bottom.*

Practical Notes: Most days of the year the weather is perfect for biking. From late January to early November, you'll get weather forecasts that call for sunny, breezy days high in the 60s. Take that as a packing guide. Another prerequisite: a street map of San Francisco. Reserve a room at **Stanyan Park Hotel** (750 Stanyan Street at Waller; 415–751–1000; $99–$245) across from the park. Better yet, make it a suite with a bay window. Neighborhood restaurants generally close on Monday.

DAY ONE: MORNING

Stanyan Park Hotel was built in 1905 as demand for accommodations grew. The Victorian decor and four-poster beds maintain the ambience of bygone resort days. Each of the six suites has a bay window and fireplace. Wear sturdy shoes and layers, for the weather and terrain are changeable. A cobblestone staircase, a woodland path strewn with eucalyptus leaves and cones, and a rocky plateau await you. Pick up a map from guest services at the hotel. If you want any provisions for your morning walk, stop at **Real Foods** (1001 Stanyan Street at Carl; 415–564–1117). They carry organic fruit and a complete line of baked goods. Check the deli case for *samosas*, which are fried pastries filled with vegetables or meat.

Mount the stone staircase at Farnsworth Lane (off Willard), where the city noise is muffled by the enclosure of hillside homes and trees. The entrance into Sutro Forest is at the end of **Edgewood Avenue,** one of the few city streets paved in red brick. When the University of

California medical school moved from Berkeley in the 1910s, the faculty built their homes here, replicating the redwood-shingle Craftsman bungalows across the bay.

This entire hill, a gift to the city from Adolph Sutro's daughter, Dr. Emma Merritt, was barren when her father bought it. A native of Bavaria, Sutro missed the tree-covered hills of his homeland. By buying saplings and having youths plant them, he established the annual Arbor Day. What stands before you is the result—**Sutro Forest.**

The trail narrows and climbs steeply into the wild woodlands a few yards from the entrance. If you meet a bear at the next junction, grab hands and flee. (Actually, no bears are here anymore, but it's wild enough to make you expect them to appear.) Otherwise, follow the ridge around to the left. Through the canopy, you can spot the twin spires of Saint Ignatius Church.

When the trail leads across a rocky outcrop, stop for a moment. Below you lies **Ishi's camp.** California's last Native Indian was found in 1910 cowering in a corral, his health sadly deteriorated. Stanley and Theodora Kroeber, residents of Edgewood Avenue, brought him into the twentieth century. He was captivated by the cable cars, which he rode on every outing. He worked part-time as a janitor at the medical school. Theodora recounted the last four years of his life spent under their guardianship in *Ishi, The Last of His Tribe.* In mild weather, Ishi liked to live at this campsite.

Did the heavily scented air comfort him? Moisture from the fog releases into the air the salutary oil locked in eucalyptus leaves. The trail ends at Johnstone Drive, where a modern encampment, the home of the University of California's Medical School chancellor, sits in a thick grove, a circular drive the only hint of its presence. The main staircase is flanked by massive boulders, and the roof mimics the texture and color of pine bark. Compare the chancellor's home to the student barracks along Johnstone.

Cross Clarendon Avenue to Dellbrook Avenue (to the right) and walk uphill at La Avanzada. You may not see your destination, for the base of **Sutro Tower** rises in the city's heaviest fog belt. Just as fog drip-feeds the forest, it keeps these streets perpetually wet. Built in 1968 on the site of Sutro Castle, this tower, still the highest structure in San Francisco, is

A self-made millionaire who at one time owned one-twelfth of San Francisco, Adolph Sutro called his Monterey pine and eucalyptus forest "the children of my old age, which will live on long after I am laid to rest."

obsolete now that a cable has been laid. But who could imagine the San Francisco skyline without it? The fog often severs the top from its base. Designed with rigging that makes it look like a corsair, the top seems to sail on a white sea like the Ancient Mariner's lost ship.

Circle the city reservoir and take the road down from the silent sea of fog. Turn right on Linbrook and bear left at Mountain Spring. The home at number 32–34 has a brick arch. Beyond the entryway you'll see a rustic villa. The stable serves as a garage for the owner's BMW. Otherwise, it could be a way station in the Pyrenees. Turn left at Twin Peaks Avenue and watch on your left for the wooden staircase to **Tank Hill.** Don't let the unromantic name deter you. Lovers who gather here on balmy nights know its secret places. Let Twin Peaks enjoy its fame; Tank Hill is the true valentine. Find a comfortable rock and enjoy the sights. To the left are Sutro's "children," trees now over a hundred years old. On the right a barren hilltop is named on city maps as "future park." Downtown, the Bay Bridge, and the Mission District form a handsome symmetry. Up here today, Marin and Mount Tamalpais are hidden behind a sheet of fog.

Lunch

A second set of stairs cut into the left slope lead down to Belgrade. Walk down Cole Street to have lunch with the neighbors. A great place to explore, Cole Valley is where **Tassajara and Just Desserts Bakery** (1000 Cole Street at Parnassus; 415–664–8947) was started by Zen

Buddhists. A tiny French bistro, **Zazie** (941 Cole Street between Parnassus and Carl; 415–564–5332; moderate), serves an exceptional lunch until 2:30 P.M. Some of our favorites are Provençal fish soup, roasted trout, pasta, and *petit pain* sandwiches. Entrees range from $5.00 to $10.00. **Bambino** (945 Cole Street; 415–731–1343) is next-door if you want pizza, pasta, and minestrone. Burritos are running neck–to–neck with pizza in popularity. I'm not surprised that a tacqueria replaced the creperie. **La Coqueta** (86 Carl Street at Cole; 415–566–1274) sells burritos as fast as the staff can make them.

DAY ONE: AFTERNOON

After lunch follow Frederick to Ashbury. Don't pass **Ashbury Market** (205 Frederick Street at Ashbury; 415–566–3134) without taking note. Residents all over the city trek out here to stock up on French, Italian, and Californian wines. Turn right at Ashbury and look for the columns flanking Piedmont Street. Walk up Piedmont noticing the 1850 farmhouse at number 11. The brown shingle at 1526 Masonic was built in 1910 by Bernard Maybeck. Follow Masonic uphill and turn right onto Upper Terrace. The street spirals to the summit, giving sweeping views of the bay at each successive curve. Mount Olympus, as this park is locally known, is the geographical center of the city. In an earlier decade a monument called *Triumph of Light*, a project of Adolph Sutro, marked the spot. Though Sutro embraced classical art and culture, the name Mount Olympus derives from a crippled milkman. Neighborhood boys nicknamed him, "Old Limpus." You can take a shortcut down the steps from number 330; they lead into Clayton Street and Seventeenth Avenue.

DAY ONE: EVENING

Performed inside the Morrison Planetarium, **Laserium** (Academy of Sciences, Golden Gate Park; 415–750–7138; tickets available through www.ticketweb.com) is a laser visuals and music show held Saturday and Sunday at 5:00 P.M. A 1.5-watt gas laser draws multicolored patterns onto the planetarium dome, while an argon laser slices the air. The phantasm swirls overhead to the music of Pink Floyd and Peter Gabriel, Rimsky-Korsakov and Andreas Vollen-weider, or Enya and Vangelis.

Dinner

Are you curious about fusion cuisine? Look for the crooked windows of Cal-Asian restaurant **The House** (1269 Ninth Avenue at Irving; 415–682–3898) where you'll find winning combinations of classic Western dishes (pork chops, veal chops, baby back ribs) with Eastern flavors. The dining room reflects the hybrid cuisine. The menu includes grilled Chinese chicken salad with sesame-soy vinaigrette, Caesar salad with wok-seared scallops, taro-pork spring rolls, veal chop with fresh shiitake-oyster sauce, and a stellar dish everyone raves about: grilled Chilean sea bass topped with ginger-soy sauce. Desserts are straight from the cuff American: apple crumb pie à la mode and crème brûlée.

Diners and beer connoisseurs have another option: **Golden Gate Park Brewery** (1326 Ninth Avenue at Irving; 415–665–5800). A 50-foot-long, curvilinear blond-wood bar runs against one side of the room, and along the other a continuous upholstered banquette with white-clothed tables. Make your way up to the mezzanine dining area to be above the general commotion. Golden Gate Park serves up traditional beer-friendly dishes, such as fried calamari, steak and potatoes, burgers, short ribs, Caesar salad, and steamed Manila clams. But you can also indulge in serious dining. Try the grilled Niman Schell New York steak with herb butter and grilled fingerling potatoes or the maple-cured pork chop with apple-ginger sauce. For dessert try the Hippie Hill Hoppy ice cream sundae made with faintly malty ice cream drizzled with caramel sauce and peanuts. Entrees range from $8.00 to $19.00.

DAY TWO: MORNING

Greet an emerald world at your bedside window, a porthole to a day of promise. Resist assuming that the park's pleasures depend on the absence of wind and fog. Except for astute choices in clothing, it makes no difference if the park is sunny or stippled with fog.

When you rent bikes at **Park Cyclery** (1865 Haight Street at Stanyan; 415–751–RENT) get a bike lock. **Magic Skates and Bikes** (3038 Fulton Street at Sixth Avenue; 415–668–1117) will rent you in-line skates. The first stop is **McLaren Lodge** (Fell Street at Stanyan; 415–750–5105; hotline, 415–263–0991) for maps, tours, and answers to questions. If you prefer more of an indoor jaunt, purchase the **Golden Gate Park Explorer's Pass** (415–750–7459) at McLaren Lodge or at the M. H. de Young Memorial Museum (415–863–3330), the Asian Art Museum (415–668–8921), or the California Academy of Sciences (415–750–7145), and receive a 25 percent discount on admission to each facility. The lodge is staffed Monday to Friday. On weekends from May to October they lead walking tours from the lodge.

The staff will alert you to seasonal offerings. Stellar events are the park's hallmark. Opera in the Park takes place in Sharon Meadow on the opening weekend of the fall opera season. Alfredo Portilla, the young Mexican tenor in town to sing the role of Pinkerton in *Madame Butterfly,* and American soprano Nicole Foland, known for her "distinctive timbre and sexy, free vibrato," both garnered praise for their performances. Free Shakespeare in the Park is held at Liberty Tree Meadow every September.

You can also find out what's in bloom and mark the location on your map. Dahlias, rhododendrons, roses, cherry blossoms, tulips—you may pedal by and not know what you're missing. Just chain your bikes to a bench or bike rack and take off down the trail to explore on foot.

Two enchanting stops to include on your route are the **Conservatory of Flowers** and the **Japanese Tea Garden.** One is a Victorian confection, a glass palace of tropical pools, ferns, and palms currently undergoing restoration; the other is a meditation of dwarf pines, pagodas, a moon bridge, and a bronze Buddha. The moon bridge is also called the Wishing Bridge. Look into the pool from the peak of the moon bridge. With its reflection, it casts a complete circle. When you see it, toss your coin and make a wish. Stop by the Tea House for a pot of jasmine tea and Japanese cookies. If the bard's love sonnets turn you on, the **Shakespeare Garden** contains flowers and plants memorialized in his verses.

Lunch

Since you dined in the Sunset district south of the park last night, have lunch in the
Richmond district, north of the park. The nearest exit is at Eighth Avenue. Restaurants on Balboa
Street cater to Russian émigrés, serving the familiar food of their homeland. **Katia's** (600 Fifth
Avenue at Balboa; 415–668–9292) wears the guise of a Russian tearoom but is a full-fledged
restaurant, where the home-style food has a light California influence. We ordered smoked salmon
and *pozharski*, which is a savory cake of herbed, minced chicken. We wrapped up blinis, borscht, and
housemade dill pickles to go. **Cinderella Restaurant and Bakery** (436 Balboa Street between
Fifth and Sixth; 415–751–9690) has been in business for more than thirty years. Like the émigrés,
you'll love the ravioli stuffed with seasoned beef *(pelmeny)* served in chicken broth, the lamb with
kasha, and the stuffed peppers and cabbage. The soft-crusted house-baked breads have a wonderful
texture. Don't be discouraged by the full tables; the wait is usually not too long.

DAY TWO: AFTERNOON

Reenter the park and head for **Stow Lake,** where boat rentals (415–752–0347) and bike
rentals (415–668–6699) are available. You can tool around the lake in a rowboat, paddleboat, or

motorboat. Some couples bring a picnic aboard (we munched on Katia's dill pickles), for the motorboats poke along at 1 or 2 miles per hour. You can bike around Stow Lake, then cross over a stone bridge to the island. A path parallels the cascading **Huntington Falls** and climbs to the 428-foot summit of **Strawberry Hill.** The neighborhoods surround the park and the bridge, and the Marin Headlands fill up the wider view. As you head toward Ocean Beach on your bikes, you may want to visit Spreckels Lake and the Buffalo Paddock. A canvas of color surrounds the base of the North Dutch Windmill in early spring. The Queen Wilhelmina Tulip Garden is planted with bulbs from the Netherlands. If you've come this far, you may as well go all the way and get your feet wet in the Pacific.

Heading back into the park from Ocean Beach, pick up the **bicycle trail** off Martin Luther King Jr. Drive. It skirts the polo field and Lindley Meadow. A pleasant way to end the afternoon is at **Strybing Arboretum.** Its paths lead through redwood groves, a fragrant garden, and a desert landscape.

FOR MORE ROMANCE

If you are feeling how I think you're feeling, you may want to bike over to **Sunset Sauna** (1214 Twentieth Avenue at Lincoln; 415–753–2559), pedaling down Martin Luther King Jr. Drive to Nineteenth Avenue. You can park your bikes in the backyard, rent towels, and bask in a Finnish sauna. In a cocoon of warmth, you'll sum up the past two days: enchanting.

THE COUNTRYSIDE

ROMANCING THE REDWOODS

TAMALPAIS TO MUIR WOODS

*E*ntrepreneurs, or capitalists as they were called before the turn of the century, targeted "Mount Tam" as prime money-making territory. San Franciscans fled the fog-bound city, alighting in this Marin County paradise. They rode the "crookedest railroad in the world" to Mount Tam's East Peak and descended to partake of refreshments at Mountain Home Inn. The wealthier among them established homes on the sunny eastern slopes above the village of Mill Valley. The area achieved park status in the 1930s virtually unchanged.

You too can exchange urban bustle for mountain calm. Ten trails converge at the Mountain Home Inn's doorstep. You'll walk along a ridge that drops down to a beach town, lunch on barbecued oysters sizzling from the grill, and drive to the mountain's East Peak at dusk for spectacular views of the entire Bay Area. You'll wander among the only stand of old-growth coastal redwoods not to fall to the ax—a world of shade, filtered sunlight, and perpetual dewdrops. The name Tamalpais, taken from the Tamal tribe, immortalizes the Indians who once lived at its feet. In the spirit of these former guardians, undertake this itinerary with gratitude that their lands have been preserved.

Practical Notes: The coastal fog that helps redwoods survive California's long, dry summers also shrouds the sights. Fog disappears during spring and fall, making this a great time to visit Mount Tamalpais. Wildflowers bloom from late January to April. Bring a jacket for cool or wet weather and pack good footwear. Trails are rocky and slippery when wet. While hiking stay on the trail, not only because poison oak can ruin a vacation but trampled plants and soil ruin the woods. Redwood trees are especially vulnerable because their roots are only 6 feet deep. They depend on support from their lateral roots, which radiate 150 feet from the trunk. Shops in Mill Valley are open daily.

DAY ONE: MORNING

Historic hangout for poets, lovers, and hikers, **Mountain Home Inn** (810 Panoramic Highway, Mill Valley; 415–381–9000; $130–$259) is fifteen minutes from the Golden Gate Bridge. Take California State Highway 101 north to the Stinson Beach/Highway 1 exit. Ask for a room with a balcony to savor the view of San Francisco Bay, the Tiburon peninsula, and the East Bay Ridge. Other options among the ten rooms include canopy beds, fireplaces, and Jacuzzi bathtubs.

The **Matt Davis Trail** down to Stinson Beach is an easy 3.7 miles through an earthly paradise. Pick up a trail map at Pantoll Park Headquarters (801 Panoramic Highway; 415–388–2070), 2.5 miles from Mountain Home Inn. Forty miles of hiking trails crisscross Mount Tamalpais State Park's 6,200 acres. Not endless subdivisions but 250 miles of trails are contiguous with its boundaries, expanding the trail system into 20,000 acres of watershed lands. The Mount Tamalpais ridge cuts across the southern portion of Marin County, rising steeply from the ocean as you see on the Matt Davis trail and rolling gently to the bay. Bordering the trail of the chaparral ridge are native trees and shrubs such as star thorn, manzanita, oak, and madrone. Along with the forest, rolling grasslands, and stunning ocean views, the ridge provides

An Indian legend explains that the god of the sun came to earth to be with a lovely Indian maiden. He lingered with her many hours, thus creating the night. When he was forced to return to the sky, he turned his beloved into a beautiful mountain. She lies on her back, her long hair streaming to the east, forever looking for him, forever open to his caress.

front-row seats at nature's finest show. Lovers will find plenty of places to stop and appreciate the setting.

Lunch

At lunchtime, you'll find typical beach-town fare at the restaurants lining Shoreline Highway, the main road through Stinson Beach. Next to the deck at **Stinson Beach Grill** (3465 Shoreline Highway; 415–868–2002; moderate), cookers are constantly replenished with barbecued oysters or honey-glazed oysters to keep up with the demand. Salads, chowder, linguine pastas, Southwestern specials, and sausage samplers are also offered. You can quench your thirst with beer from microbreweries. Entrees range from $5.00 to $17.00.

DAY ONE: AFTERNOON

Hike the Dipsea Trail to Steep Ravine back to your car at Pantoll Park Headquarters. The route is only 2.8 miles, but you climb uphill for two of those miles. After winter rains, Steep Ravine is a thrilling hike over wooden bridges and up staircases. With cascading water and fern grottos in abundance, you may not mind the climb.

DAY ONE: EVENING

By late winter, when fair days and blue skies return to Mount Tamalpais, it is a San Francisco tradition to drive to East Peak for the 1.1-mile summit walk. Take Panoramic Highway to Southside Road to Ridgecrest Boulevard, following signs to the East Peak. After parking, start the nearly level walk at the **Verna Dunshee Trail** sign. From the 2,571-foot crest, you survey 360 degrees of terrain so pastoral it seems to have been stolen from an artist's easel. To the east is the bay with its many inlets and islands. Behind the East Bay Ridge is Mount Diablo, the highest point in the Bay Area. In perfect conditions, you can make out the snow-capped Sierra Nevada, 200 miles away. This view was the only part of Mount Tam the Native Americans never explored—until their chief went up and returned from the top unharmed.

Indian shamans still consider Mount Tamalpais one of three enchanted peaks in California. They perform special rituals with a crystal on the mountaintop every twelve years. Below the summit, hilltop meadows make great gliding ground for hawks. Marin County lakes sparkle like polished mirrors. Corte Madera Slough narrows on its inland journey. Close by its banks is Larkspur and hidden among the greenery, the Lark Creek Inn.

Dinner

As the country road connecting Mill Valley to Larkspur dips in and out of sunlight, it suddenly widens. Sitting handsomely in the bend is a yellow and white Victorian encircled by redwoods. Since **Lark Creek Inn** (234 Magnolia Avenue at William Street in Larkspur; 415–924–7766; expensive) opened its doors it has earned national acclaim for world-class cuisine. This country retreat was built in 1888 during Larkspur's heyday as a rustic resort. In those days campers pitched tents and settled in for the summer; slot machines and dog races were among the popular activities. A narrow-gauge railroad chugged into the cool recesses of the redwood groves packed with picnickers. Permanent residents arrived after the 1906 earthquake and fire, but this stately home by the creek was abandoned by the 1920s. Chef Brad

Ogden bought the derelict structure, chased out the ghosts, and transformed it into a large and airy restaurant with a sunporch and immense skylight. In 1989 the Lark Creek Inn opened for business. In fair weather, choice seating is on the red brick patio overlooking the creek.

The aromas of wood, stews of lobster and oysters, suckling pig, and roasted chicken will draw you into the main dining room. What emerges from the wood-burning oven are the best produce, meats, poultry, fish, and game in the Bay Area. The restaurant operates five acres of gardens in the Napa Valley and a number of local farmers supply produce to the restaurant. Each plateful is rustic, colorful, and unexpected—Americana with a twist. Roasted chicken and mashed potatoes may sound ordinary, but not if it's oak-roasted free-range chicken. Ogden's chicken and his Yankee pot roast and grilled salmon with corn spoonbread are so popular that they appear on the menu year-round. The winter favorite is Dungeness crab chowder with drop biscuits. Bradley's Caesar salad and California sea bass with citrus mustard sauce are summertime stars. Butterscotch pudding brings back childhood memories. Entrees range from $16 to $30.

 handle

The restaurant will have you humming long before you get to **Sweetwater** (153 Throckmorton Avenue near Miller Street; 415–388–2820; open at 8:30 or 9:00 P.M.), a nightclub off the village square. Marin County has attracted top entertainers as residents. Bob Weir, J. J. Cale, John Lee Hooker, and Jorma Kaukonen all have made neighborly stops at Sweetwater. A few regulars appear on the show schedule. Merle Saunders plays everything from rhythm and blues to New Age. Jenni Muldaur, daughter of Maria Muldaur and backup singer for Eric Clapton, is a lovely vocalist. If the entertainer's name doesn't ring a bell, ask what kind of crowd the music caters to. The Folk-rock band Box Set is popular with the twenty to thirty crowd, while lovers of acoustic music flock to hear Ramblin' Jack Elliott, America's Balladeer of the Road. Afterward, the winding Panoramic Highway will deliver you back to your mountaintop haven at the Mountain Home Inn.

DAY TWO: MORNING

Breakfast

Mountain Home Inn offers a choice morning repast outside on the deck at no extra charge, with the bay a shimmering presence in the distance. The deck extends out from the hillside, putting you at eye level with nature. Hawks tilt, spiral, and glide effortlessly. You can order a full breakfast of huevos rancheros, eggs Benedict, or French toast as well as juice, muffins, fresh fruit, and yogurt.

⌘

One hundred and fifty million years ago the ancestors of the present-day redwood and giant sequoia grew throughout the Northern Hemisphere. These prehistoric remnants are now confined to a narrow strip of land stretching from the Oregon border south to Big Sur. The ocean produces abundant fog in selected areas; one of them is the valley of Muir Woods. Cross the road and hike to **Muir Woods** (415–388–2595), first on the Panoramic Trail and then on the Ocean View Trail.

Follow the narrow ridge trail down into the 240-foot-high redwoods of Muir Woods National Monument. Along the way, if the fog has lifted, pause to admire the sparkling ocean views.

John Muir single-handedly started the conservation movement in California. His writing profoundly affected the public attitude toward the remaining American wilderness. He inspired William Kent and his wife Elizabeth Thatcher Kent to purchase this precious acreage which was threatened by lumbering operations and water impoundment. In 1908 President Theodore Roosevelt proclaimed the woods a national monument. The Ocean View Trail leads to park headquarters, where you can view exhibits and learn more about coastal redwoods.

In the damp climate, *Sequoia sempervirens* thrives, some specimens exceeding 240 feet in height. The redwoods' great size and long life are attributed to their high resistance to fires,

> *The redwoods, once seen, leave a mark or create a vision that stays with you always . . . It's not their unbelievable stature, not the color that seems to shift and vary under your eyes; no, they are not like any other trees we know, they are ambassadors from another time.*
>
> —John Steinbeck

insects, and fungi. The oldest known coastal redwood was 2,200 years old, but the usual life span ranges from 400 years to 800 years. Follow the loop trail around Redwood Creek. When it is swollen by winter rains, silver salmon and steelhead trout leave the ocean and fight their way upstream to spawning beds in Muir Woods. Red alder and western azalea thrive here, as does tanoak because of its high tolerance to shade. California laurels bend and curve as they grow from shade to sunlight. Covering the forest floor are shade-loving flowers. Look for black-tailed deer on the hillsides, and gray squirrels and chipmunks scampering around tree trunks. Pick up Fern Canyon Trail to Lost Trail and back to the Panoramic Trail for a steep 2-mile return to Mountain Home Inn.

DAY TWO: AFTERNOON

Lunch

Check out of the inn and spend the rest of the day in Mill Valley. Begin with lunch at **Piazza D'Angelo** (22 Miller Avenue at Throckmorton Avenue; 415–388–2000; open daily). They layer their pizzas with grilled vegetables and homemade sausage.

∼∞∽

Next, soothe your trail-weary bodies with a soak at a spa. If you sign up for a half-day spa program at **Tea Garden Springs** (38 Miller Avenue; 415–389–7123), lunch is included. Tea Garden is a spa sanctuary laid out according to the Chinese feng shui design. From the plant-filled solarium where tea is served, a stone pathway crosses a rivulet and enters a rotunda painted with a brilliant mural of a mandarin's garden. Ten styles of massage are offered at $65 an hour. Eastern-style massages promise tantalizing results and use exotic techniques. Tui-Na, for example, restores vitality and balance of mind, body, and senses. Reflex points and muscles are stroked with rolling movements gently and firmly over the body. Practitioners use not only their fingers but the back of their wrists, heels, and palms. Acupressure, another technique, focuses on trigger points along meridian channels to unblock energy and increase vitality. Whichever treatment you choose, soak together in the Jacuzzi built for two, soothingly enhanced by relaxing herbs.

Once refreshed and relaxed, browse the shops in Mill Valley. A few surprises are among the expected array of village goods. At **Smith and Hawkins** (35 Corte Madera Avenue, off Throckmorton Avenue; 415–381–1800) it's always springtime. Take a rewarding tour of their famed nursery. Most of the merchandise—teak garden furniture, clothing, and garden supplies—mimics exactly the goods in their nationwide catalog. **WilkesSport** (57 Throckmorton Avenue; 415–381–5183) sells $495 Italian shirts you wouldn't want to wear anywhere near dirt. Wilkes Bashford must fancy himself outfitter for Marin County gentry. Among the shelves and racks you'll find fine tailored clothing, suede jackets, riding pants, and leather boots for men and women. **Lindisima** (11 Throckmorton Avenue; 415–388–7818) carries women's clothing for the sophisticated casual look, such as Mizono's sculptured pants suits and Bonnie Strauss's stretch velvet evening dresses. If you are in the market for silk velvet tops in Renaissance colors, stop at **Mirror Mirror** (53 Throckmorton Avenue; 415–388-1143).

FOR MORE ROMANCE

If you can't leave Marin County without soaking the seventies way in a redwood hot tub, head for **The Center for Massage Therapy** (125 Throckmorton Avenue at Miller; 415–383–8770; open daily from 11:00 A.M. to 10:00 P.M.). Their communal hot tub is under a skylight surrounded by tropical plants. If you opt for a massage ($57 an hour), use of the hot tub and sauna is free. Since this is the nineties, though, bathing suits are required.

ITINERARY 26
Two days and two nights

NOVA ALBION

POINT REYES NATIONAL SEASHORE

*A*s you drive onto this immense peninsula in the sunshine, California landscape seems worthy of the Biblical grandeur given it by early-twentieth-century painters. The long stretches of beach, the high central ridge, the pockets of pine forest, are all rendered in beatific light. You'll no doubt wonder if you've strayed into the promised land. Set aside in a national park, a mere 35 miles north of San Francisco, is one of the wonders of the natural world.

The painters weren't lying. Point Reyes National Seashore blooms with wildflowers in spring, invites hikers to freshwater lakes, and bursts with migratory birds. Whales breech off its point, and herds of elk roam its headland. Orange poppies rustle in crevasses upon a sea wall. Sea lions scuffle in the foam, and terns spike the air with their caws.

Plan to enter this realm of sky and sea on the sunniest days of the year, from March to October. You can satisfy the desire to swim, hike, bike, horseback ride, or sea kayak. This itinerary is a wonderful excuse to start a love affair with summer.

Practical Notes: Call ahead for park maps of Point Reyes National Seashore (415–663–1092) and Tomales Bay State Park (415–669–1140) to plan your trip. If you are bringing or renting mountain bikes, also ask for a bike trail map. The old ranch roads are great for mountain bikes, but if you want to see the park's highlights, consider the distances. The lighthouse, for instance, is 22 miles from park headquarters. If you are visiting from mid-March to July 4, stop at **Audubon Canyon Ranch** (415–868–9244), a wildlife sanctuary and conservation center on Bolinas Lagoon. There are so many wondrous forms of wildlife you may want to hook up with a naturalist. **Point Reyes Field Seminars** (415–663–1200) offers Saturday and Sunday tours that focus on whale migration, birdwatching, and tidepools. Resident artists also offer classes through this organization. Attracted by Point Reyes' rugged coast are artists of the *"en plein air"* school. They are busy at their easels in fine weather. Call for their brochure. The Tomales Bay oyster beds are world famous. **Sea Trek** (415–488–1000) has all-day/all-you-can-eat sea kayaking trips. Ask about their "Take an oyster to lunch" excursion.

Romance at a Glance

♥ *Revitalize your spirits at grand, rustic Point Reyes Seashore Lodge (415–663–9000) and Manka's Inverness Lodge (415–669–1034).*

♥ *Hike to Bass Lake for a swim.*

♥ *Drive to Mount Vision to view Point Reyes in moonlight or starlight.*

♥ *Visit the Point Reyes Lighthouse, Tule Elk Range, and Chimney Rock tidepools.*

♥ *Paddle around the oyster beds of Tomales Bay (Sea Trek, 415–488–1000).*

DAY ONE: MORNING

Take California State Highway 1, which is a twisting, plunging roller-coaster ride, west to the Pacific. If you happen to be passing **Audubon Canyon Ranch** (Highway 1, Stinson Beach; 415–868–9244) on a weekend from mid-March to mid-July, you are in luck. This wildlife sanctuary is the nesting ground of the great blue heron. The largest heron in North America, it stands 4 to 5 feet tall and has a wingspan of nearly 6 feet. The ranch provides a safe habitat where they court, mate, and nest.

In early spring herons nest in the tops of the tall redwood trees in Schwarz Grove. Henderson Overlook offers an exceptionally fine view of the nesting birds. Stop at the ranch's registration desk from 10:00 A.M. to 4:00 P.M. for a free self-guiding trail map. As you exit, you may spot herons and egrets fishing for crustaceans in the shallow water and tidelands of Bolinas Lagoon.

On a warm day, you and your companion may be tempted to go for a swim. **Bass Lake** (Point Reyes National Seashore at the Palomarin Trailhead; 415–663–1092) provides the perfect setting. From Highway 1, turn left 1 mile past Audubon Canyon Ranch onto the Olema-Bolinas Road, then turn right on Mesa Road. One mile beyond the Point Reyes Bird Observatory Park is the parking lot for Palomarin Trailhead. It's an easy 3-mile walk over coastal foothills. In spring and summer the air is charged with the sweet scent of lupine, California poppies, cowslips, and iris. Take a canteen of water and a towel. Bathing suits are optional.

Drive on Highway 1 fifteen minutes north of Bolinas and check into **Point Reyes Seashore Lodge** (10021 Highway 1, Olema; 415–663–9000; $105–$200). Every national park should have a grand rustic lodge, and the honey pine facade of the Point Reyes Seashore Lodge, though recently built, fills the bill. The lobby of this Victorian-style lodge rises in two stories of Douglas fir paneling. Even the rooms boast cathedral ceilings with a view of Mount Wittenberg, two acres of lawn and gardens, and a creek spanned by a footbridge into the woods. Several Point Reyes hiking, biking, and riding trails begin here. Most of the lodge's twenty-one rooms have fireplaces, whirlpool tubs, large armoires, and sitting areas in front of bay windows. Specialty suites have bedroom lofts and European feather beds. You may want to book Casa Olema, a residence next-door to the lodge. Built in 1858, it has a grape arbor, a barbecue and picnic area, and a whirlpool tub. Continental breakfast is included, as is a stable for your horse. When was the last time a hotel offered you that amenity?

Lunch

Next-door to the lodge is the **Olema Farm House Restaurant** (Highway 1 at Sir Francis Drake Boulevard, Olema; 415–663–1264; moderate), one of the town's original buildings built in 1845. Sandwiches and salads start at $5; at the high end, you'll pay $12 for a steak sandwich. The spinach salad is served with feta cheese, sundried tomatoes, and raspberry vinaigrette. The Thai prawn salad is a healthy mix of napa cabbage, bean sprouts, red peppers, watercress, and mushrooms. Oyster chowder is offered on every menu. You are in Point Reyes country, known for two things: oysters and earthquakes. Bring sunglasses and straw hats and sit outside on the deck.

DAY ONE: AFTERNOON

When you turn off California State Highway 1 five minutes north of the restaurant and drive along the Bear Valley entrance road, you cross the San Andreas Fault, which nearly splits the Point Reyes Peninsula from the mainland. The national park rests on the eastern edge of the Pacific plate, while the rest of North America, except Alaska, is borne on the American plate. Here in Olema Valley these two great land masses grind together. This meeting of plates is a rift zone. Neither plate can move freely, so tremendous pressures build up along this junction. On Bear Valley's twenty-minute earthquake walk you see evidence of the earth's movement. In 1906 the ground moved 16 to 18 feet. The quake redirected streams, uprooted trees, and shifted fenceposts.

You can park at various trailheads and walk to the highlights of the park, but before striking out, stop at the **Bear Valley Visitor's Center** (Bear Valley Road, Olema; 415–663–1092), open 8:00 A.M. to 5:00 P.M. on weekends and 9:00 A.M. to 5:00 P.M. on weekdays. You can learn about the park's history, geology, cultural heritage, wildlife, and sea life from the exhibits as well as from the slide show in the auditorium. Point Reyes's outstanding features vary with the season, so ask the ranger to guide you to the most promising trails.

Two other attractions at the Bear Valley headquarters are the stables where Morgan horses are raised and trained for patrol, and Kule Loklo, a fascinating replica of a Miwok village. During the years of Spanish rule, the Miwok Indians of Point Reyes had been taken from their homelands to labor in the Spanish missions. After the Mexican revolution, some survivors of the missions wandered back to Point Reyes, where they lived for many years.

Sir Francis Drake Highway gives you access to the park's most stunning terrain. Drive through the village of Inverness, and about 9 miles from park headquarters, where Drake Highway forks to the left, continue straight on Pierce Point Road. A fine place to see wildlife is the **Tule Elk Range,** where 200 elk roam freely. In fall the elk are in rut, so they joust and bugle for dominance of the herd. The Pierce Ranch Trail heads across 3 miles of rolling hills to Tomales Point. The views are long, endless visions of blue with Tomales Bay to the right and the immense Pacific to the left. Miles of stunning, unspoiled seashore meet the waves. You can explore all of California and nowhere else witness such dramatic beauty. Backtrack along Pierce Point Road, turning right at Sir Francis Drake Highway and turn left for the parking lot for the Estero Trail. October signals the winter arrival of thousands of birds to the Point Reyes Peninsula. Nearly 430 species of birds have been recorded. Drakes Estero cuts into the land creating prime shorebird habitat. Estero Trail provides exceptional viewing of ducks, waders, and the splendid monarchs of the sky, the raptors. Nothing blocks your sight lines of Estero de Limantour, Point Reyes, and an infinity of blue.

If it's beach you crave, you're in luck. Continue on Sir Francis Drake Highway to Drakes Beach. It is partially sheltered and perfect for wading, tanning, beachcombing, surfing, and windsurfing. California poppies bloom in clusters on cliffs. Drakes Beach is where Sir Francis Drake, English adventurer and paramour of Queen Elizabeth I, landed to repair his ship. His officers and crew stayed for five weeks in the summer of 1579. The Miwoks helped out by bringing boiled fish and meal ground from wild roots. Wandering inland, the Englishmen sighted herds of deer and elk. Before sailing away in the *Golden Hind*, Drake named this land Nova Albion, for the area's white cliffs reminded him of those at Dover.

Continue along Sir Francis Drake Highway to the tip of Point Reyes Peninsula. From the parking lot, take a five- to ten-minute walk to the **Point Reyes Lighthouse** (415–669–1534). It is open Thursday to Monday from 10:00 A.M. to 4:30 P.M. The 300-step staircase down to the lighthouse seemingly drops you into the open palm of the Pacific. Sea lions bark at the Sea

These beautiful giants breathe air, have warm blood, and give birth to live young. However, their home is in the depths of the dark ocean, concealed from probing human eyes. As the gray whales migrate along the Pacific Coast, we have a brief chance to view them before they descend again into the blue abyss.

Lion Overlook, and California murres wheel, climb, and dive in the relentless search for food. The rocky shelves below the lighthouse are home for thousands of these native birds with snowy bodies and jet-black heads. The historic lighthouse gives you unlimited ocean views, making it easy to sight spouting gray whales—at least from January through April, when hundreds migrate southward to Baja California and then back to the Bering Sea.

DAY ONE: EVENING

Just as twilight sets in, visit the tidepools at Chimney Rock, 5 miles across the point from the lighthouse (on the road opposite the lighthouse). Many intertidal creatures make their home at this place on the ocean's edge, making a meeting of land and sea just as dramatic as the one you saw below the lighthouse. Crabs, sea stars, green anemones, and chitons are some of the fascinating marine animals you will see in the tidepools. On the way back to the lodge, bear right at the Mount Vision Overlook for a view of Limantour and Drakes Esteros, the sweeping curve of Drakes Beach and Point Reyes Beach. If you time your visit to the full moon, the range of land you visited today may be awash in moonlight tonight. The stars sparkle and soft breezes pick up scents of the forest and sea. Even in the gathering dusk, you can see streams and estuaries cutting through the landscape of folded hills, valleys, and beaches.

Dinner

Tonight dining is casual at the **Station House Cafe** (11180 Highway One, Point Reyes Station; 415–663–1515; moderate). The garden patio is lovely in warm weather. Try the polenta tart, baked in muffin cups with gorgonzola cheese. A dozen oysters will cost you $13. Entrees range from $8.00 for the pasta specials to $17.00 for rack of lamb or a twelve-ounce steak.

⁂

Take a walk around the garden behind the Point Reyes Seashore Lodge before settling in for the night. The owners are proud of their roses and camellias.

DAY TWO: MORNING

Breakfast

By 7:00 A.M., a buffet table is set up in the lodge's Fireside Room by the natural stone fireplace. Whatever your morning ritual, you'll find enough variety on the buffet to satisfy your hunger: fresh fruit, pastries, yogurt, local brie, scones, and bagels. Sliding glass doors open to the fresh scent of morning dew on the grass. Don't linger over farewells—you have a full day ahead on Tomales Bay.

⁂

Begin by moving your luggage to Inverness, a resort village of simple cottages. **Manka's Inverness Lodge** (30 Callender Way at Argyle Street, in Inverness; 415–669–1034; $135–$365) is a 1917 fishing lodge in a pine grove, which the dining-room windows frame perfectly. The Craftsman architectural details add elegance to the rustic interior. The bedrooms could have been transported from a Ralph Lauren showroom: bed posts of rough timber, wicker furniture with deep, paisley print cushions, a carved lamp of a wooden boar, and a faux bear rug covering the floorboards. From the guest rooms' deck you can see through the pine boughs to sunny, silent Tomales Bay.

The San Andreas Fault runs underneath Tomales Bay, which is a firth connected to the sea. Since Inverness is also a shire in northern Scotland on the Moray Firth, this area is well named. To cover the 15-mile length of Tomales Bay, take a sea kayaking tour. **Sea Trek** (415–488–1000) offers full-day paddles from 9:30 A.M. to 4:30 P.M. leaving from Heart's Desire Beach 5 miles north of the lodge on Pierce Point Road or from Marshall, a twenty-five-minute drive to the other side of Tomales Bay (take Highway 1). The meeting place depends on which tour you sign up for. Basic paddling instruction takes a few minutes, then you are off with a guide for the day. The shallow bay is surrounded by mud flats and salt marshes that fill with shorebirds at feeding times. Visit the secluded coves and sandy beaches and watch the birds feeding.

DAY TWO: AFTERNOON

Lunch

Long before Sir Francis Drake sailed past the Marin coast, Indian's lived on the beaches of Point Reyes and searched the rocky shores of Tomales Bay for clams and oysters. Buoys and lines mark the oyster beds on the western shore. Tomales Bay grows some of the nation's most succulent oysters. As you paddle around the oyster beds, your Sea Trek guide lifts a cage out of the water so you can see the mollusks growing. The Take-an-Oyster-to-Lunch trip includes an all-you-can-eat oyster lunch. For what are arguably the most prized oysters around, you paddle to **Hog Island Oyster Company.** A freshwater stream runs beneath Tomales Bay at the very point Hog Island owners raise their oysters. The stream dilutes the salinity of this part of the bay just enough to make the oysters a little bit sweeter. Hence the name Hog Island Sweetwater ("Sweets," as they are commonly called), which is now trademarked. Hog Island oysters are plump, juicy, and subtly briny with a creamy aftertaste. You can also indulge in the fresh pasta salads, sandwiches, and chocolate chip cookies.

Next you paddle over to Hog Island and climb up to the meadow that is usually covered with wildflowers. Trillium sometimes grows as high as 3 feet. You'll spot wild strawberries, several varieties of lilies, wild violets, and monkey flower. After you explore the island, linger in the warm sunshine before you paddle back to Heart's Desire or Marshall.

After turning in your paddles and gear, return to Tomales Bay State Park and stop at the park's headquarters. The 1-mile walk up the Jepson Trail takes you to one of the remaining virgin groves of bishop pines in California. Notice the pine cones of these craggy, grotesquely shaped trees. They are unique in that they hang on to the stem they encircle for fifteen years. The cones open and seeds germinate only after exposure to fire or extreme heat. The nature trail to Indian Beach is a good choice for a walk at dusk. As the sun sets over the Inverness Ridge, it casts a glow around the bay. In the fading light, the bay empties of swimmers and boaters. Peace and quiet return.

DAY TWO: EVENING

Dinner

You don't have to travel far for dinner tonight. **Manka's** Inverness Lodge is one of the best dining rooms in West Marin. Have a seat at one of the three fireside tables. The chef often grills quail, wild boar sausage, or figs on a blazing fire. The menu changes nightly. An evening's appetizer choices might include a creamy risotto with prawns, roasted sweet corn soup, and a green salad with crimson baby beets and ginger cream. Entrees could be roasted salmon, pork chops, Alaskan halibut, or medallions of fallow deer. The setting, like an Adirondack lodge deep in the woods, resonates the right tone for this four-star food.

꿨

As isolated as Inverness is, a lively night scene is down the road in Point Reyes Station, a 1900s railroad town. The heart of the town is along Main Street, where storefronts displaying country antiques, handicrafts, and New Age art share space with saddle shops and feed stores. For live music, start at **Station House Cafe** (11180 Highway 1; 415–663–1515) to listen to a folk guitarist and continue at **Western Saloon** (11201 Highway 1; 415–663–1661) where the music varies from jazz and blues to reggae and country. As the clock creeps toward midnight, return to the lodge and cuddle in your feather bed with the window open to the night sounds of Tomales Bay.

FOR MORE ROMANCE

If you can linger in the area another day, have a beach party. Ask Manka's chef to pack a gourmet picnic and head up the road to **Shell Beach,** the best swimming beach of Tomales Bay, known mainly to locals. Pack the car with beach gear and picnic basket and turn right at Camino del Mar, .3 of a mile from Manka's. Go early on weekends, for parking spots tend to fill up. While the bay is not quite the temperature of Caribbean waters, you'll enjoy swimming out to the raft and sunbathing on it while it gently bobs on the waves.

ITINERARY 27
Three days and two nights

ZIN-FULL DISCOVERIES

BIKING ALONG RUSSIAN RIVER

*S*onoma is a many-splendored thing. It could be the Bay Area's closest equivalent to Camelot. But instead of a trusty steed, you ride a state-of-the-art touring bike. Your quest? The wine-tasting rooms of Russian River.

With a little imagination, this itinerary has all the trappings of an Arthurian romance, and one phone call sets it up. The weekend sounds seductively simple: wine, wheels, and the one you love. The Russian River is your steady companion as it loops south from Geyserville, around the edge of Healdsburg, and west through resort towns to the coast at Jenner. The fields flanking its banks yield world-class wine. Alexander Valley is the best place to fall in love with zinfandel, the lusty red wine California claims as its own. Though you may get mildly tipsy on this trip, Backroads bicycle tours gives you a solid introduction to the basics of safe long-distance cycling.

Practical Notes: One service that makes **Backroads** (1516 Fifth Street, Berkeley; 800–462–2848 or 510–527–1555; $495) so special is that they have custom-designed the perfect bike for touring. You have a choice of upright or drop handlebars and a diamond or mixte (women's) frame. Ask for a gel seat and pedals with toe clips. You also need to purchase padded cycling shorts and gloves. The North Face (800–362–4963) has just come out with a line of biking outfits made of Tekware fabric. Call to inquire about the store nearest you. If you don't want to drive the 70-mile trip from San Francisco to Healdsburg, hop into the Backroads van at either the San Francisco airport or a downtown hotel. You stay at the Victorian **Madrona Manor** (1001 Westside Road in Healdsburg; 800–258–4003 or 707–433–4231, included in the Backroads package) with its most authentic rooms in the main house. (The carriage house was gutted and given a modern interior and hodgepodge decor.)

DAY ONE: AFTERNOON

The grand Madrona Manor is just ninety minutes from San Francisco off the Healdsburg exit of Highway 101. Plan to arrive by 4:30 P.M. Cross over the Dry Creek Bridge and enter the gate. The three-story Victorian mansion and carriage house, set on a secluded knoll above the vineyards, is your home for two nights. A wide, welcoming veranda with tall windows leads into the front parlor. High ceilings and hand-carved woodwork signal craftsmanship of an earlier time. In 1880 John Paxton built the house, Healdsburg's most imposing residence. Every morning he would either ride on horseback or be driven to the depot to catch the train to San Francisco. Every Friday evening when the train came in, his groom met him at the station with a saddled horse.

For most of its 100-year history, Madrona Manor has been empty. Even Paxton's son, who inherited the property, only used the mansion as a weekend retreat. When the current innkeepers first saw it a decade ago, everything but its mansard roof was painted bubble-gum pink. The rooms vary in character, so you may be attracted to the turret rooms or the intimate ones with tiny dormer windows at the top of the house. The nine bedrooms and five common rooms contain antique furniture belonging to the Paxton family.

Romance at a Glance

♥ *Spend two days biking to Russian River wineries (Backroads, 800–462–2848 or 510–527–1555).*

♥ *Stay at Madrona Manor, Healdburg's most impressive Victorian mansion (800–258–4003).*

♥ *Savor Sonoma County farm products in Madrona Manor's dining room.*

DAY ONE: EVENING

Meet your cycling companions on the front porch of the Madrona Manor at 6:00 P.M. for wine and hors d'oeuvres. Guests are seated for dinner in four rooms (formerly the front parlor, family dining room, music room, and billiards room), all of which boast impressive antiques and period wall coverings. You are welcome to dine at your own private table or with the group.

Dinner

Seeing the chef in the garden behind the kitchen picking herbs, tomatoes, and field lettuce is becoming more and more common at country inns. Todd Muir, son of the innkeepers, is a gifted chef who is only a few steps away from his garden and orchards. He also uses a brick oven and smokehouse to create distinctive cuisine. He prepares a four-course menu for the Backroads group. Appetizers may include smoked scallops with onion confit and red-pepper oil or a hearty Tuscan bean soup enhanced with smoked root vegetables, shiitake mushrooms, and a drizzle of truffle oil. One of the entree choices is braised rabbit in port and dried cherries. Muir also specializes in venison, seafood, and vegetable entrees, and he pairs each dish with wine from the area.

⋐◎◎◎⋑

After dessert there is a "route rap," in which Backroads warriors describe the terrain and road hazards (such as double-hitch trucks racing to the crush on narrow roads). After the rap go out for a stroll in the side garden where all the manor's flowers are grown or enjoy the night air from the wicker chairs on the porch.

DAY TWO: MORNING

Breakfast

Guests start filing into the breakfast room of the manor at 8:00 A.M. An hour later you are ready to head down the drive. As the map indicates, you have a choice of riding 16, 26, 38, 44, or 59 miles. Fill up your bicycle basket with the snacks, juice, and water that are provided. You don't pedal lock-step after a leader. You are free to follow whatever length route you wish.

Today's bike ride goes through Dry Creek, Alexander Valley, and Chalk Hill. These different regions yield wines of different character. The tip is to sample the wine varietal for which the region is noted. Hillsides in the Dry Creek region are planted with zinfandel and petite sirah. In the last twenty years, though, cabernet sauvignon, merlot, and sauvignon blanc have been planted in the warmer north, and chardonnay and gewürztraminer are in the south. Alexander Valley follows the Russian River from Cloverdale in the north to Healdsburg where the river turns west. Its complex mosaic of soils and temperate microclimates enables the valley to produce exceptional grapes, both red and white.

Stop at **Mazzocco Vineyards** (1400 Lytton Springs Road; 707–431–8159), a small, family-owned winery known for their cabernet and zinfandel. (The owner, by the way, invented the collapsible golf club). **Sausal Winery** (7370 Highway 128; 707–433–2285) is Alexander Valley's oldest wine-making family. Estate-grown varietals come from 118-year-old vines. When other wineries pulled out their zinfandel vines as the wine's popularity waned, Sausal kept theirs. They make zinfandel based on the age of the vine. Private Reserve is from 85- to 100-year-old vines, and a century zinfandel is made from vines more than a hundred years old. Their zinfandel will cellar five to eight years, but it can be opened when young. **Alexander Valley Vineyards** (8644 Highway 128; 707–433–7209) is located on the original homestead of Cyrus Alexander, founder of the valley and producer of excellent merlot.

That sun beating down on you in the open stretches pleases the wine growers and the grapes. There is enough alternation of light and shadow between redwood stands and creek beds to break up the view. Keep swilling that water you packed with you—it's important to replace fluids while cycling, even though you'll notice the route follows mostly level and gently rolling roads. The landscape is often compared to the Bordeaux region of France. On the other side of the Mayacamus Mountains lies Sonoma Valley, home of another thirty-four wineries and 13,000 acres of vineyards. Keep alert; you may startle a family of quail parading into the shadows of the undergrowth with their pompom heads bobbing like Prussian soldiers in dress uniform.

To savor wines and their distinctive flavors, follow the three S's of tasting: swirl, sniff, and sip. Proceed from whites to reds, sampling light-bodied wines before full-bodied ones. A typical tasting may include all of these wines:

Chardonnay: citrus and floral aromas

Sauvignon Blanc or Fume Blanc: herbaceous/vegetal

Gewurztraminer: uniquely spicy and floral/fruity

Cabernet Sauvignon: berry-like fruity flavor

Riesling: delicate mix of floral/fruity flavors and scents

Merlot: soft and fruity

Zinfandel: spicy and berry-like

Pinot Noir: silky texture and lingering freshness

DAY TWO: AFTERNOON

Lunch

At the next stop, lunch awaits you at **Field Stone Winery and Vineyards** (10075 Highway 128; 707–433–7266). At a shady picnic area under spreading oaks, a bountiful lunch buffet is set up between 1:30 P.M. and 2:30 P.M. The pasta salads, sandwiches, and dips are tasty and prepared with fresh ingredients. How about giving each other a quick shoulder massage before hopping back on your bikes?

◈

Visit the winery's rustic underground cellar and taste its award-winning estate-bottled wines. Chalk Hill is named for its light-colored soil, which isn't actually chalk but white volcanic ash. This area is noticeably warmer and more hilly than neighboring regions; its vineyards are planted at the 200- to 800-foot level. Chardonnay is the primary grape grown in the rocky, well-drained soil. Chalk Hill is the only challenging incline of the day. If 16 miles is enough, you can return to Madrona Manor and spend the rest of the afternoon by the pool. The Backroads shuttle van will whisk you and your bikes back at this or two other points along the route. The two wineries you'll visit this afternoon if you decide to go on are **Rodney Strong Vineyards** (11455 Old Redwood Highway; 707–431–1533), where you can view the working sections of the winery, and **Alderbrook Winery** (2306 Magnolia Drive; 707–433–9154), which has a veranda overlooking the vineyard. On the return trip at 5:00 P.M., you may want to wave at the farm workers drinking beer on the porch and listening to Latin music on boom boxes. It's Saturday night.

DAY TWO: EVENING

Dinner

Back at the Manor for dinner, a good choice of entree at harvest time is Cornish hens stuffed with zinfandel grapes, roasted garlic, and thyme. For dessert several offerings sound tempting. Maybe it's a night for champagne sorbet with chocolate tuille cup and red raspberries. How many miles did you bike today? You may order the pear tart with Poir William ice cream and caramel sauce and not feel a tinge of remorse. Bicyclists at the end of a day's ride tend to get up from dinner with two hands on the table for support. The manor house has no elevator to the upper floors so you may feel every step, but you'll both sleep like babies.

DAY THREE: MORNING

Today is departure day, so you check out of the manor before you bike. Today you can ride 16, 20, 31, or 47 miles. When you leave Madrona Manor, you take off in the opposite direction you took yesterday and spend the day at the Russian River wineries. On Sunday morning traffic is light. You have a well-kept single-lane country road all to yourselves. Lined with oak, eucalyptus, and bay trees, the route follows the course of the Russian River through forests and open vineyards. The terrain is gently rolling with a few short hills. Your blood pounds and your heart races on the uphill, but wind pummels your body on the downhill, flicking away moisture. In the spring yellow mustard blooms between the green rows of the vineyards.

Depending on the weather, grape picking usually begins sometime in August with the gathering of varieties used in making sparkling wines (pinot noir and chardonnay). Picking concludes in October with the harvesting of the hearty red varietals such as cabernet sauvignon. Everywhere you go during harvest, the smell of young wine permeates the air. The frenetic pace of the crush season is over by the weekend before Halloween. Then autumn sets in, bringing a change in color on the vines, from green to red, yellow, and orange. Bikers love this time. Indian summer keeps daytime temperatures warm well into October.

Pull off the road at the view point bluff where the Russian River meanders like a ribbon. Far below, canoes crisscross its surface like water spiders. The road dips like a roller coaster after that, taking you down to the banks of the river. The 31- and 47-mile trip includes a visit to **Korbel Champagne Cellars** (13250 River Road; 707–887–2294). Korbel is so widely distributed you don't need to buy a bottle, but they give a good tour. This is one of the few opportunities to take a tour if you want to know how bottle-fermented champagne is produced. The 130-year-old ivy covered buildings are surrounded by redwoods and a rose garden.

Cyclists patronize Westside Drive for the regularly spaced tasting rooms. On the way back toward Healdsburg stop at **David Bynum Winery** (8075 Westside Road; 707–433–2611), run by a former *San Francisco Chronicle* editor. Taste their merlot. The winery has won more than ninety medals in the past three years. Of all the wineries, their T-shirts are the best. **Rochioli** (6192 Westside Road; 707–433–2305) was planted in the 1930s and has great cabernet.

DAY THREE: AFTERNOON

Lunch

You can't miss the high-rise barns on your right used for drying hops in the 1800s. Lunch is served next to a pond in a grove of fig trees at **Hop Kiln Winery** (6050 Westside Road;

707–433–6491). Inside is a gallery displaying works of local artists and a historic tasting room in the former brewery. **Belvedere Winery** (4035 Westside Road; 707–433–8236) is on down the road on the left. If you bike to all these places, you arrive back at Madrona Manor between 3:30 and 4:30 P.M. Even though you have checked out of your room, you are welcome to use a courtesy room to shower and change into your traveling clothes. Afterward, leave the manor and turn right onto Healdsburg Avenue at Healdsburg Plaza, a small town plaza where country-and-western and folk bands play in the summer. Shops around the square offer handcrafted country items, antiques, modern art, and famous Sonoma County cheeses. Spend an hour at **Vintage Plaza Antiques** (44 Mill Street; 707–433–8409), open daily 10:00 A.M. to 5:00 P.M., and you are certain to find a few treasures.

FOR MORE ROMANCE

Would you like to end the weekend on a blissful note? Take California State Highway 116 to Monte Rio and turn onto Bohemian Highway. Enzyme baths are offered in only one place in the United States. **Osmosis** (209 Bohemian Highway in Freestone; 707–823–8231) offers a spa treatment barely known outside Japan. When you arrive you walk into a bonsai garden to sit and enjoy enzyme tea. Then you slip on a kimono and are escorted to a private room for your bath. You are buried up to your neck in a wooden tub filled with a mixture of fragrant cedar fibers, rice bran, and more than 600 active enzymes. The overwhelmingly sweet, clean smell of cedar banishes every ache from your overworked muscles. The shoji doors part slightly so you can look at the pristine rock garden and hills beyond. The two-and-a-half-hour treatment for $110 includes a seventy-five-minute massage given in an open-air pavilion. Afterward, you'll feel and look like Olympians: nice taut muscles with none of the ache. When you're finished, you can take California State Highway 12 to Highway 101 and be back in San Francisco in an hour and a half.

ITINERARY 28
Three days and two nights

D'VINE

NAPA VALLEY

*D*riving into Napa Valley, assume the state of mind of a connoisseur. This itinerary is a playful chase from one end of the valley to the other for the finer things of life—the gifts of Nature, gentle landscapes, easy comforts, vintage train travel—and wine.

Distilled in a glass of wine is the entire story of Napa Valley. You can comprehend in one sip the quality of the sun on ripening fruit, the chill clamp of evening fog, rain-soaked roots, platoons of trucks running fully loaded at harvest time, juice flowing from presses, and the long slumber in oak. The story culminates the moment the wine is opened; you surrender to its timeless gift.

Practical Notes: Harvest time in Napa draws thrill seekers. Some tours have lines worse than Disneyland. Avoiding California State Highway 29 and sticking to the Silverado Trail keeps you out of bumper-to-bumper traffic. Since the best-known tasting rooms along Highway 29 tend to fill up, try the recommended wineries along the Silverado Trail. You can bicycle to these with a bountiful picnic basket from Maison Fleurie. Make lodging and dinner reservations two months in advance if you plan to come in summer or fall. Call **Napa Valley Visitor's Center** for maps and brochures (707–226–7459). Reserve the couple room at Golden Haven (707–942–6793).

DAY ONE: MORNING

Exit California State Highway 101 at Highway 37. Then take a left onto Highway 12/121, which leads you to the Carneros Highway. On either side of the road lie golden hills supporting a symmetry of trellised vines. You are taking a journey through an old-world region that possesses all the refinements of country living. On my first visit abroad, as a college student in France, I first tasted bordeaux and white burgundy. This road always takes me back to that time. You'll recall the French monarchs who built chateaux in France's winegrowing regions. Several European companies now produce wine in Napa, constructing chateaux on the outskirts of farm towns. With the wine came associated French pleasures: cognac and champagne. The Cognac family of Heriard-Dubreuil, principals in Remy Martin, and Domaine Chandon, whose parent company is Moët & Chandon, both settled in the valley.

The first stop, about an hour north of San Francisco, is **Carneros Alambic Distillery** (1250 Cuttings Wharf Road in Napa; 253–9055; open daily from 10:00 A.M. to 6:00 P.M.). They produce alambic brandy using French-built alambic pot stills and naturally cured French Limousin oak barrels, like those used for centuries in Cognac. Turn right on Cuttings Wharf Road. The distillery is on the left. The visitor center doors open and close with a boom, sucking you out of the sunshine. Footsteps echo on entryway flagstones and bounce into the wooden rafters of the lodge. Against a far wall a stone fireplace burns fresh logs. A

Romance at a Glance

♥ *Indulge in genteel comforts at Christopher's Inn (707–942–5755) and French-country charms at Maison Fleurie (800–788–0369).*

♥ *Tour prestigious cognac and champagne houses.*

♥ *Dine at the four-star Domaine Chandon (800–736–2892).*

♥ *Take a mud bath at Golden Haven (707–942–2944).*

♥ *Dine in vintage Pullman cars (Wine Train, 800–427–4124).*

♥ *Sample the award-winning wines of the Silverado Trail's small wineries.*

♥ *Reserve a tour at di Rosa Perserve (707–226–5991).*

unicorn tapestry covers the stone wall above the mantel. The only missing details are the fox hunters in jodhpurs and red coats, milling about the fire with brandy snifters.

A tour of the distillery expands that stereotype. During its eight- to ten-year transformation into brandy, *eau de viv* (distilled wine) continuously evaporates. Inhaling the vapors seeping from the porous wood in the barrel room jolts the sense of smell. The nostrils tingle from a curious blend of roasted vanilla bean, smoldering caramel, and citrus peels melting on a campfire. This Brandenburg of odors continues at the sniffing counter inside the lodge. Because of the high alcohol content, tasting is prohibited, so your nose merely whiffs and sniffs over the rim of amber-filled glasses. Your nose samples each distilled wine separately: pinot noir, French colombard, muscavet. The final blend, folle blanche, uplifts the nostrils like a perfectly executed pirouette. With one's nostrils in such an agreeable state, the impulse is to spring for a $92 bottle of folle blanche. You are being entertained, after all, by the distillery responsible for the rise of American-made luxury brandies.

Follow California State Highway 12/121 to Highway 29 north through Napa. Turn right at Trancas Street, then left at the Silverado Trail and drive for 12 miles. **Mumm Napa Valley** (8445 Silverado Trail in Rutherford; 707–942–3434) is open daily from 10:00 A.M. to 5:00 P.M. Wine critics call Mumm the best sparkling wine producer in the U.S. since Mumm Cuvée Napa Brut Prestige made its debut in 1986. Champagne is not all they do well—they have a tour to match. Sparkling wine is produced using the age-old French "methode champenoise" process, but it is completely automated. Presses are operated by computer, riddling machines turn the bottles to rid them of yeast, and bottling machines do the rest. Champagne tours leave the visitor center hourly from 11:00 A.M. to 3:00 P.M. Tasting prices range from $3.50 to $6.00, and the outside patio overlooks the vineyards.

DAY ONE: AFTERNOON

Lunch

In Napa even the chefs are connecting with agriculture. In the Culinary Academy's organic garden at the **Wine Spectator Greystone Restaurant** (2555 Main Street in Saint Helena;

707–967–1010; moderate) you often see a white toque bobbing among the rows of mint, basil, rosemary, and chervil. The menu echoes the school's endorsement of a plant-based diet and monounsaturated fats. The vegetable garden (not open to the public) is meant to show students the value of flavorful, unusual plants, and the lucky result for restaurant patrons is the enjoyment of produce brought to the table at their peak. At the cooking station (the restaurant is actually like a huge kitchen), you may see Asian greens such as mizuna, curly cress, chilis every color of the rainbow, and Amish paste, a tomato resembling an elongated pink lantern. Heirloom varieties of tomatoes, bred before the age of hybrids, are making a comeback.

Christian Brothers winery and the famous Greystone Cellars used to be Napa's biggest tourist attraction. Now that it houses the hottest dining destination in the Bay Area, the 125-seat restaurant is hardly ever empty. Small plates of antipasti from the tapas bar may suffice for lunch. Try the deep-fried fresh anchovies with lemons, capers, and Romesco sauce (a Spanish red pepper and almond sauce) and sit on the terrazzo. The changing lunch and dinner menus bring to Napa Valley the culinary riches of the Mediterranean. Italy, Spain, France, Greece, North Africa, and the Middle East take turns receiving the weekly spotlight. Among the starring dishes is monkfish cooked in a tagine with fennel, preserved lemons, cracked green olives, caper berries, and saffron broth. The tagine is served with fresh vegetables and a pyramid of couscous. Or you could share a paella or rotisserie poussin with lemon. There are also eggplant moussaka and mussels steamed in sauvignon blanc with chorizo. Appetizers range from $3.00 to $6.00; entrees from $12.00 to $16.00. The restaurant is closed Tuesday.

⋘⋙

Christopher's Inn, (1010 Foothill Boulevard, Highway 29; 707–942–5755; http://www.chrisInn.com; $140–$295) provides the comforts and perspective on life you'd expect in one of the world's most prestigious wine regions. This inn is the sort of place where, I imagine, a couple spends a weekend, driving up Silverado Trail in a bright red Ferrari. The Inn offers ten rooms with fireplaces. Antique collectors and art collectors, the owners have put together beautiful suites combining museum quality furniture with Laura Ashley fabrics—which you can view ahead

of time on the Internet. Ask for Room 16. It has a Venetian glass-framed mirror and handcarved cherry four poster bed and a Jacuzzi tub for two, and it is the only room with a patio garden.

DAY ONE: EVENING

Dinner

Take Silverado Trail south to Yountville Crossroad to California State Highway 29 to California Drive. Turn right on California Drive to reach **Domaine Chandon** (1 California Drive in Yountville; 800–736–2892 or 707–944–2892; expensive), which serves dinner Wednesday to Sunday from 6:00 to 9:30 P.M. Dom Perignon (1668–1715) was the Benedictine monk who perfected the techniques for creating sparkling champagne. Moët et Chandon is the parent company of Domaine Chandon and owner of the monk's Benedictine abbey. The chef is a native of Champagne, France. During the evening it's a magical experience to enjoy his creations on the patio with a lilting breeze moving over the vineyards and pond. Inside, the arch-roofed dining room glows with candlelight.

The French dishes are light, as you'd expect in California, and are great paired with the superb champagne of Moët et Chandon lineage. Chandon Brut Cuvée Carneros Blanc de Noirs complements seafood. Order a bottle to set a celebratory tone to the evening. Mesquite-grilled salmon is wrapped in pancetta with merlot butter. Venison tournedos are served with merlot-juniper essence. Entrees range from $22 to $35. Try the Valrohna chocolate soufflé with frangelico sabayon.

DAY TWO: MORNING

Breakfast

At whatever time you requested, a picnic-basket breakfast—orange juice, a pot of coffee, scones, muffins, and jam—will arrive at your doorstep; a discreet knock tells you it's been delivered. If your room is the one with French doors that open onto a private patio and garden, you have the best possible place to unload your basket.

The soil that produces award-winning wines and exotic vegetables also yields acres of high-quality mud. Millions of years ago Mount Konocti, 20 miles away, erupted and spewed layers upon layers of the prime ingredient in mud baths—volcanic ash. The eruption also left a fissure on the earth through which groundwater reaches the magma at 4,000 feet and then resurfaces as thermal water. The water rises through old sea beds, adding rich mineral and salt traces. Calistoga, situated in the northernmost end of Napa Valley, is known as the hot springs of the West.

Lovers of pleasure were preceded by seekers of health. Calistoga is still an old-fashioned town with tree-lined streets and quaint buildings dating back to the 1800s when Sam Brannan, a millionaire newspaper publisher from San Francisco, developed it as a resort. A good place to enjoy the down-to-earth pleasures of Calistoga is at **Golden Haven Hot Springs Spa and Resort** (1713 Lake Street, Calistoga; 707–942–6793). They mix thermal water with mud from volcanic ash and peat moss in their traditional mud bath treatments. Don't expect glamour or romantic elegance here; this is a rustic motel and spa for mud lovers who want good value. Another plus: couples can spa à deux, wallowing in the mud together in private rooms. The resort has a mineral water pool and outdoor Jacuzzi.

Ancient Sauna

Wappo Indians settled on the land that is Calistoga 8,000 years ago. They established three villages and built sweat lodges over the escaping steam and bathed in the warm waters. They called this land the Oven Place.

DAY TWO: AFTERNOON

When you come into the vine-covered auberge **Maison Fleurie** (6529 Yount Street in Yountville; 800–788–0369 or 707–944–2056; $150–$225), afternoon tea and sweets may be set up in the main lobby. The vine-covered brick building is more than 100 years old. The guest rooms upstairs have a view of the surrounding vineyards. If your vision of perfection is a Provence farmhouse, you will be charmed by Maison Fleurie. The Old Bakery and Carriage House have six additional rooms with fireplaces and an outdoor spa tub. Included in the price is a buffet breakfast as well as tea service from 4:30 to 6:30 P.M.

DAY TWO: EVENING

Give yourself an extra hour before boarding the Wine Train to visit **Old Town Napa** and the Fuller Park District. The Bank of Napa, a rare example of Classical revival and Art Deco, was built in 1923. After exploring downtown, walk south on Seminary Street a few blocks to the **Fuller Park District** to look at a few historic residences. At 741 Seminary Street is an imposing Queen Anne Victorian built in 1892. Walk down Oak Street to number 1435, which is an 1881 folk-Victorian workmen's cottage of the type that prevailed in all parts of Old Town. The large Victorian at 435 Even Street dates from 1875, and the mystery house at 427 Even Street was moved to this location in 1949.

Dinner

The hoot of a train whistle had been absent in Old Town since 1929. Not anymore. The depot is only a three-minute hop from Historic Downtown Napa. **The Wine Train** (1275 McKinstry Street; 800–427–4124 or 707–253–2111; expensive) parked at the station is painted burgundy, champagne gold, and grape-leaf green. This moveable feast takes you past world-renowned vineyards and wineries on a 36-mile jaunt between Napa and St. Helena. Prices range from $70 to $99 for train fare, dinner, wine, and service. When you step aboard into the exquisitely refurbished Pullman parlor and dining cars, fitted with crystal chandeliers, brass trim, and mahogany paneling, you are back in 1915.

If you board the Murder Mystery Train, there's more truth to that statement than you'd expect. Costumed actors dramatize a scandal of 1915 involving winery owner Charles Krug. So be prepared for a bit of intrigue with your poulet à l'orange and Pouilly-Fuissé. Mull over the clues during dinner.

⸻⸙⸻

Afterward, you retire to the parlor car for brandy and cordials and the final scene of the mystery. To solve the murder you need to pin down the characters' alibis, their access to the murder weapon, their motives, and their ability to kill. When the melodrama ends, it's time to have a drama of your own. The rear door of the parlor car opens onto a private platform. The train's lights cast a spectral tunnel around the tracks. You won't come across a better place to kiss in the valley.

DAY THREE: Morning

After the buffet breakfast take advantage of the Maison's complimentary mountain bikes and your proximity to the tasting rooms along the Silverado Trail. Yountville Crossroad connects to Silverado Trail where a cluster of small wineries are within a few miles of each other: **S. Anderson Vineyards** (1473 Yountville Crossroad; 707–944–8642); **Robert Sinsky** (6320 Silverado Trail; 707–944–9090); **Silverado Vineyards** (6121 Silverado Trail; 707–257–1770);

Stelzner Vineyards (5998 Silverado Trail; 707–252–7272); **Pine Ridge** (5901 Silverado Trail; 707–253–7500); **Stag's Leap Wine Cellars** (5766 Silverado Trail; 707–944–2020); **Chimney Rock Winery** (5350 Silverado Trail; 707–257–2641); and **Clos du Val** (5330 Silverado Trail; 707–259–2200). All of these tasting rooms are open daily from 11:00 A.M. to 4:00 P.M. Dropping your bike and striding up to a tasting bar at 11:00 A.M. sounds decadent, but replenishing one's wine cellar is serious business. From the talk at tasting bars you can learn the merits of different vintages. Winegrowers anticipate the release of some spectacular reds from the 1995 vintage. Because heavy rains that year shortened the growing season, the grapes were smaller and more intensely flavored. One of the wineries is bound to be touting an auspicious release— usually only a few hundred cases—which would make it an excellent purchase. Look for chardonnay at Chimney Rock and merlot at Clos du Val.

Once you leave Clos du Val, you are only 1 mile from Oak Knoll Avenue and the frontage road of California State Highway 29. Ride the frontage road until you reach Yountville. Turn right on California Drive, then take a left at Washington Street, which forks into Yount Street and Maison Fleurie. Then it's time to pack your bags and strap on those watches. When you return home with your purchases and open a bottle of wine, the bouquet will take you back to Napa. It will seem like only yesterday.

FOR MORE ROMANCE

After checking out you may want to stop at **di Rosa Preserve** (5200 Carneros Highway, Highway 12/121, Napa; 707–226–5991), where amazing things are happening. The old Winery Lake vineyards remain, cloaking the hillsides, but Rene di Rosa has moved out of the 100-year-old winery, leaving behind 1,500 pieces of art. His gift, the di Rosa Preserve, is a one-of-a-kind artistic spectacle.

At the lakeside gallery where the tour begins, a sculpture of rusted farm equipment—twisted, welded, and reborn as Carmen Miranda—greets you at the door. Boarding a trolley, you ride up to the galleries in the main house and adjacent buildings. Art is everywhere you turn. Veronica di Rosa's watercolors hang in the bathroom. A nude sculpture reclines on the bed. In the garden, kaleidoscope kites whirl between trees; prophetic words drape a clothesline in a field. The doors of a glass chapel beckon.

If the act of accumulating art was redemptive, Rene di Rosa could lay claim to sainthood. His collection—begun in the era of Beat poets, jazz musicians, and the North Beach art scene— is the story of a lifetime. Themes span the decades: hippies, sex, violence, politics, slogans, and apocalyptic writing that seems dated.

You see paintings, sculpture, assemblage art. There's fairytale kitsch in a 20-foot lock of Rapunzel's hair tumbling from the rafters. There's beauty and poetry in a set of handcrafted carts: one drawn by a Chinese merchant carrying a load of earthquake debris, another drawn by a Father Christmas figure whose cloak shelters tiny sparrows.

Jokes and pranks lurk behind doors and under foot. In di Rosa's study rainwater drips from the rim of a banker's lamp, flooding the desk. On a bronze bust a politician's mouth is stuffed with a shoe. The *Titanic* is sinking into swirling seas painted on a pet sofa. Concealed in a small fountain on the floor is the Loch Ness monster; on a timer it rises up, slaps the water with its jaw, and startles whoever's nearby studying serious art.

In the courtyard, a herd of 47 peacocks creates a ruckus, thinking they are the show. Every few minutes a male cuts loose with an earsplitting cry. They glide their cobalt blue heads and sinewy necks past the windows, tassels swaying like the headresses of Egyptian pharaohs. A male tries to spark the interest of a group of females foraging on the lawn. He erects his plumage, flashing emerald iridescence. They don't even look up—as if not to succumb to a showy bit of color. That's not the case among visitors. Excessive, compulsive, exciting, the di Rosa Preserve is the latest, greatest thing to succumb to in Napa.

ITINERARY 29
Two days and two nights

FLIRTING WITH MOTHER NATURE
THE SANTA CRUZ MOUNTAINS

*T*he foothills of the coastal range, extending south from San Francisco to Monterey peninsula, shelter many hiking parks. One of them is Hidden Villa Ranch. Aside from miles of scenic hiking, it has a hostel, farm, visitor center, and a one-room cabin—off an unmarked trail. It had caught my eye in the *Chronicle*'s travel section. It described the archetypal cabin: so heavenly, so secluded. A love nest with no one but us for miles. Frank Duveneck built the cabin on an isolated slope of the ranch as a surprise for his wife. If you know someone who likes surprises, lead him or her unknowingly to Josephine's Retreat.

Practical Notes: If you are springing a surprise on someone, get directions ahead of time to the cabin. Once settled in, you can be just as cozy at **Josephine's Retreat** (650–949–8648) at $35 a night as at the Palace Hotel. The cabin has a refrigerator and a completely stocked mini-kitchen, including a coffee maker. No room service, though, so stop along the way for food, wine, and other beverages. As far as facilities are concerned, the shower is a four-minute walk from the cabin; the outhouse, with a view of the valley, is a half-minute walk. The cabin is not rented in June, July, or August. Call **Edgewood Park** for a trail map (650–363–4020). The Santa Clara Chapter of California Native Plants Society (650–962–9876) leads wildflower tours at Edgewood Park from March to May at 10:00 A.M. on Sunday. The trails of Midpeninsula Regional Open Space District

(650–691–1200) connect with Hidden Villa, so you can hike 10, 15, or 20 miles if you like. Call for a map. Reservations are required for the two-hour tour of **Filoli** (650–366–4640 or 650–364–2880). **Thomas Fogarty Winery and Vineyards** (650–851–6777) in Woodside is open Thursday to Sunday from 11:00 A.M. to 5:00 P.M. And last, order tickets to a performance of your choice at Villa Montalvo Center for the Arts (408–741–3428; http://www.villamontalvo.org). Brochures are ready by April for the May to October season.

DAY ONE: MORNING

A few miles past the city limits on Highway 280 the landscape opens out into broad hillsides. Farther south on the right, forested foothills mark the beginning of hiking country and the Midpeninsula Open Preserve District's network of trails. Between mountain and road winds a 22-mile reservoir that mirrors the dense green mountains. On such a still surface you can imagine a lone Indian from another time paddling homeward. Exit Highway 280 at Edgewood Road. Follow it east to **Edgewood Park** (650–589–5708 or 650–363–4020), one of the best wildflower viewing areas in the Bay Area. The entrance is 1 mile from the highway; make the first right at the sign that reads: OLD STAGE DAY CAMP. The soil in this park is an inhospitable serpentine that has worn from the rock outcropping. Such soil does not support the imported grasses that, elsewhere, tend to grow quickly in spring, smothering the California wildflowers. For a moderate 2-mile hike, take Sylvan Trail (which has early-spring blooms like Indian Warrior) to Ridgeview Loop. Beginning in March, from the oak tree-lined ridge, meadows roll away in an artist's palette of color. Look for blue-eye grass and red flax, cream cups, and

Romance at a Glance

♥ *Escape to a secluded cabin, Josephine's Retreat (650–949–8648).*

♥ *Visit landscaped gardens, an estate, a country store, and a winery.*

♥ *Hike the Bay Area's premiere wildflower area, Edgewood Park (650–363–4020).*

♥ *Dine at Bella Saratoga (408–741–5115).*

♥ *Attend a musical performance in the garden amphitheater of Villa Montalvo Center for the Arts (408–741–3428).*

owls' clover. The bent boughs of California oak offer welcome canopies of shade from which to view the sights. To the east spreads the bay and the San Mateo Bridge and Dumbarton Bridges; to the west lies the Crystal Springs Reservoir. Hawks crisscross the sky in graceful flight.

Take Edgewood Road west and turn right at Cañada Road. **Filoli** (Cañada Road in Woodside; 650–366–4640 or 650–364–2880; $10) is 1.3 miles down on the left. You can view the sixteen landscaped acres and the forty-three-room mansion Tuesday through Saturday from mid-February to mid-November. One of the few grand houses remaining from the late nineteenth and early twentieth centuries, Filoli was built by gold mine owner and water baron William B. Bourn II. He chose this site because it reminded him of the Killarney Lakes. A mural of the Irish lake district circles the ballroom walls. Bourn also gilded the ballroom with 200 pounds of gold from his own gold mines in Grass Valley.

On Friday and Saturday reservations are not required if you just want to take a self-guided tour of the garden. Lurline Matson Roth, heiress of the Matson Shipping Lines fortune, planted two dawn redwoods after their discovery in China in the late 1940s. The dawn redwood is a relative of the coast and inland redwoods of California but was known only in fossils until the momentous discovery of living trees. Mrs. Roth also planted a beautiful rose garden. A short trail leads into the watershed lands and takes you to an Indian midden. The Costanoan or Coast Indians occupied the watershed lands for thousands of years, living on game, shellfish, acorns, and seeds. To preserve the purity of the drinking water, Bourn prohibited housing in the watershed except for Filoli. Because the area around Filoli wasn't developed, the Indian midden remained undisturbed. A shaman was interred by the watershed trail with over 200 artifacts, from bird whistles to quartz amulets. Before departing Filoli, stop at the carriage house, which has been converted into a tearoom and gift shop.

DAY ONE: AFTERNOON

Lunch

Cañada Road leads south into **Woodside,** a petite village frequented by equestrians from the horse ranches and residents of the country estates. Keeping horses must be a popular sport, judging from the well-maintained network of trails through the hills. They ride on horseback down to **Buck's** (3062 Woodside Road; 650–851–8010; moderate) for lunch. The menu admonishes, "No horses left over 24 hours." Buck's sandwiches and salads are hearty enough for non-equestrians. They also have quiche, chili, and soup. Lunch menu prices range from $5.00 to $9.00. Stop at **Woodside Bakery & Cafe** (3052 Woodside Road; 650–851–0812) to select fruit danish, croissants, fruit bars, scones, or cinnamon raisin bread for breakfast tomorrow morning. You can pick up milk, fruit, and snacks for the trail at **Roberts Market** (3015 Woodside Road; 650–851–1511). While you are at this gourmet country market, don't leave without picking up some of their luxurious produce.

❧❧❧

For a look at a leftover from the community of yesteryear, stop by the **Woodside Store** (Tripp Road and Kings Mountain Road; 650–851–7615). Take Woodside Road west to Kings Mountain Road and turn right. The store is 1.5 miles ahead on the corner of Tripp Road. The old Tripp store was originally the Woodside Family Grocery when it opened at the height of lumbering activity in 1854. Dr. Tripp was a dentist from Massachusetts who was lured west during the gold rush. He decided to become a shopkeeper and forgo the rigors of the gold fields. Tripp also fixed the lumbermen's teeth. You can see blacksmith tools, a large-wheel bike, and farming tools.

Continue on Kings Mountain Road 5 miles to Skyline Boulevard. **Thomas Fogarty Winery and Vineyards** (19501 Skyline Boulevard in Woodside; 650–851–6777) is another 5 miles on the left. On a clear day, you can see San Francisco from the winery grounds. They are open 11:00 A.M. to 5:00 P.M. from Thursday to Sunday. You may want to buy a bottle of their reserve chardonnay or pinot noir to toast the sunset from the deck of Josephine's cabin. Traveling Skyline Boulevard from the winery to Page Mill Road takes you along the crest of the Santa Cruz Mountains. The road is sometimes windy and foggy, but the vistas can be superb. You travel through redwood forests and old cypress groves.

In 1856 Dr. Tripp advertised for a housemaid. He married the applicant, Miss Emmeline Skelton, and built a house for the two of them opposite the Woodside Store, now a county museum.

When you reach Page Mill Road turn left, then right at Moody Road. The road winds through the foothills for twenty minutes to **Josephine's Retreat at Hidden Villa** (26870 Moody Road in Los Altos Hills; 650–949–8648). Drive through the green gate on the right and past the adobe farmstand with the colorful bushels of tomatoes, squash, and peppers. Drive over the wooden bridge past the corral to the parking lot. The cabin is a short four-minute walk from the parking lot. Take the first left after crossing the dry creek bed. Many others before you have succumbed to the allure of cabins. Thoreau placed his on Walden Pond, while Josephine liked to sit outside hers on Sunset Hill. She was a Radcliffe graduate and owner of Hidden Villa along with her husband Frank, a Stanford professor and avid gardener. To the Josephines and Franks of the early twentieth century, nature cosseted humans in a primal love nest. Like visionaries, Bohemians, or naturalists, the Duvenecks lived out a utopian romance among their farmlands, forests, meadows, and ridges.

Frank built this rustic pine cabin, simply furnished with a bed, desk, and kitchen table, as a place conducive to "meditation and inspiration." Judging by the guest book, a more amorous communion takes place in the cabin these days.

As far as inspiration goes, that comes later when you curl up on deck chairs. The quiet is so complete you can almost hear the sun slip toward the horizon.

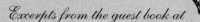

DAY ONE: EVENING

Dinner

Follow Moody Road, which becomes El Monte Road east of Highway 280, to Foothill Expressway. Turn left. Los Altos is a few miles down on the right. Turn right at Main Street, and you'll be in walking distance of two good restaurants. **China Valley Restaurant** (355 State Street between First Street and Second Street; 650–941–9898; moderate) excels at Peking, Hunan, and Szechuan cuisine. You'll hear lots of sizzling hot plates on a busy night. Lovers' Prawns is a dish with two different tastes: prawns sautéed with ginger and garlic, and prawns extra spicy. Entrees range from $7.00 to $11.00. **Skip's Pizza** (299 First Street between State and Main; 650–949–1170; inexpensive) spins their pizza dough by hand and has a wide range of toppings. Save **Draeger's** (342 First Street at San Antonio Road; 650–948–4425) for when you are about to leave town. This gourmet grocer has the most tempting deli case in Los Altos. They have the best selection of imported cheeses, more than 100 varieties, and all the deli food is made in their kitchen. Try the barbecue chicken, wild rice with smoked turkey, Southwest couscous, or Thai salad. Think of what you'd like to have at your picnic tomorrow, arrayed on a checkered blanket in Duveneck Windmill Pasture.

✎

As you explore the streets around Main Street and State Street, you'll see some playful artwork. Jan Meyer of Painted Illusions has painted eight benches and eighteen murals, transforming downtown Los Altos with her whimsical, enchanting images. At 388 Second Street near San Antonio, a mural shows a man proposing to a young woman in a window. He is holding up a ring box with a sparkling diamond. The couple in the mural are genuinely happy. Jan said she waited two years for her son and his girlfriend to announce their engagement. Then she asked them to pose for the mural, which was commissioned by the Diamond Broker.

Spend some time in the deck chairs at Josephine's Retreat before turning in. The stars light up the meadow. Maybe a shooting star will streak the sky as you're watching the heavens.

DAY TWO: MORNING

The ideal way to spend the day is to head out to **Duveneck Windmill Pasture** with a picnic lunch in your backpacks. This moderate two- or three-hour hike begins along Adobe Creek. Take Grapevine Trail up to Ridge Trail, where you can look east to see the entire Silicon Valley.

Lunch

The windmill pasture is a beautiful secluded meadow above the valley floor in the shadow of Black Mountain and Monte Bello Ridge. A windmill remains from former ranch days when cattle freely roamed the hillsides. Spread your blanket on the soft grass and lay out your feast.

                              ৎ৩ৎৡৡৡ

For fast walkers: Hidden Villa trails connect to Monte Bello and Black Mountain, your entry to more than 2,600 acres of the **Midpeninsula Open Space District.** The preserve includes some of the most scenic lands in the Bay Area. Trails cover the entire Stevens Creek watershed, from the 2,800-foot summit of Black Mountain to the grassy slopes of Monte Bello Ridge. A trail map is available from the district office (650–691–1200).

DAY TWO: AFTERNOON

The drive to the small town of **Saratoga** in the foothills of the Santa Cruz Mountains takes about twenty-five minutes. Drive east on Moody Road to Highway 280 to Highway 85 and exit at Saratoga Avenue. Start your tour of the town at the 1904 storefront that serves as the **Saratoga Historical Museum** (20450 Saratoga Los Gatos Road near Oak Street; 408–867–4311). It is open Wednesday to Sunday from 1:00 to 4:00 P.M. Stop here to pick up a free historical walking tour map of the town and see some intriguing exhibits. The Saratoga Chamber of Commerce (408–867–0753) is located next door in an 1864 cottage. Lumbering brought the first settlers. The well-to-do followed, to drink and bathe in the mineral waters that were deemed of such high quality that the town fancied itself the sister resort of Saratoga Springs, New York.

Dinner

Before the performance at Villa Montalvo have an early dinner at **Bella Saratoga** (14503 Big Basin Way at Third Street; 408–741–5115; moderate). They serve California cuisine in the home of an early settler. Lace curtains hang at the windows, the wallpaper is straight from an old Sears catalog, and the chandelier glows as if to welcome home the people who lived here. Entrees include cashew chicken salad, grilled lamb with spinach, and grilled king salmon served with grilled jumbo prawns. Prices range from $10 to $20. For outdoor dining you can choose the porch or the patio. Bella Saratoga opens for dinner at 4:00 P.M.

⌒⌒⌒

Just as Bella Saratoga serves food all over the house, the performing arts center at **Villa Montalvo Center for the Arts** (15400 Montalvo Road at Saratoga Los Gatos Road; 408–741–3428) holds musical and dance performances all over the villa, including outside on the lawn and in the garden amphitheater. Senator James Phelan, also mayor of San Francisco for three terms, built this Italian Renaissance mansion a short .3-mile from town in 1911. He loved the artistic literary life and liked to surround himself with artists and writers. Poets were invited to read their works here at the annual Day in the Hills and compete for prizes. Robinson Jeffers, Joaquin Miller, and Ina Coolbrith read in Montalvo's natural amphitheater and on its terraced lawns. Now the annual music festival is held here. On his death Phelan bequeathed Montalvo as a cultural center. The carriage house was converted into a theater, and waltzes resound through the halls of this fine mansion. An arboretum adjoins the garden; California native plants border the self-guided trails.

Take your seats, perhaps in the garden amphitheater, and as the maestro raises a baton and the music begins, you may drift into reverie. Are your dreams coming true? You have one more night to bed down in your cabin under a halo of starlight. If your weekend in the hills has gone well, why not add a note of your own in the guest book? As you take your leave of Josephine's cabin the next morning, you may be departing with a gold mine of memories.

For More Romance:

If you wish to leave behind the world of distractions, and money is no object, **The Lodge at Skylonda** (16350 Skyline Boulevard, Woodside; 800–851–2222 or 650–851–6625) offers couples remoteness and privacy. Coming through a long wooden gate somewhere in the coastal mountains, you feel as though you stumbled upon the pleasure dome of Kubla Khan. True to its purpose, Skylonda restores mind and body combining the best of the Far East and the twenty-first century with luxury bed linens, garden-fresh cuisine, weight training, aqua-aerobics, Yoga, ta'i chi, massage, and nature outings. On a meadow trail bordered with lupine, forget-me-nots, poppies, and, perhaps a rare wild iris the color of Persian silk, you begin shedding stress. It dissolves completely when you lie, as I did the first afternoon, face down on the floor with Shigayo expertly kneading aching calves and sore feet by standing on them. Whether you're inside or out, as you settle into this solid sixteen-room house of log-and-stone the forest exerts its presence. Exposed logs form the walls in guest rooms and throughout the lodge. The massive timber tresses of the Great Room loom over guests gathered for evening appetizers. The next morning, across the lawn from the deck, a woodpecker hops up and down the trunk of a redwood tree, tapping as musically as with a drumstick. Forest views fill the exercise room windows, where a yoga teacher intones, "stand tall as the redwoods, feel yourselves lengthening."

So much about Skylonda is restful to the senses. Zen-like touches abound in furnishings and decor: bamboo inlaid on the bathroom floor, gardenias scenting the air, a temple gong struck with a padded mallet. The sound is sucked deep into the redwood canyon. Sometime during your stay follow the trail down into the canyon to where La Honda Creek trips over rocks and ledges. Lovely places to linger are the rainbow bridge, bent-tree bench, and meditation point.

Another way to enjoy your stay is to go on the morning hikes. They range from 3-mile strolls to all-morning treks. At Monte Bello Open Space Preserve, the group split into those who wanted the bugle charge up 2,800-foot Black Mountain and those who wanted the nature trail along Stevens Creek. On either hike you set your own pace as red arrows left at the turns loop back to the van. In the afternoons, indulge in the massages of India (Ayurveda), Japan (Shiatsu and Jin Shin Jyutsu), China (T'ui Na), and take the Yoga and ta'i chi classes. If you bring wine from the tasting rooms of Woodside Winery or Thomas Fogarty Winery, the dining room staff will gladly serve you. Choose wines as you would for fine dining. Chef Sue Chapman controls the calories and fat so creatively you still feel you're indulging. As appetizers she may serve smoked salmon and citrus mousse, crustini with a goat cheese and strawberry spread, and an apple and cambenzola spread. Her flavorful salads include Caesar salad with garlic tofu dressing, croutons, and asiago cheese; and baby spinach with lemon vinaigrette. Each evening two entrees are offered: one fish or chicken, the other vegetarian. She pairs roast Alaskan halibut with saffron rice, roasted garlic, tomato and kalamata olives. Another specialty is pine-nut-crusted chicken breast on mashed potatoes with mushroom gravy. Vegetarian entrees are also excellent: stuffed artichoke with ratatouille and couscous; and marinated Portabello mushroom on creamy polenta with zinfandel sauce. Low-fat desserts are more difficult to pull off. One night, though, we had taste-tingling tropical fruit with blackberry sorbet. The secret was that the sorbet was spiced with fresh ginger.

ANNUAL EVENTS

JANUARY	Martin Luther King, Jr., Celebration; call for location; 415–771–6300.
FEBRUARY	Repertory season of the San Francisco Ballet; call for location; 415–865–2000. Chinese New Year Golden Dragon Parade, Chinatown; 415–982–3000. Russian Festival, Sutter and Divisadero Streets; 415–921–7631. San Francisco Orchid Society's Pacific Orchid Exposition, Fort Mason; 415–665–2468. Tribal, Folk, and Textile Art Show, Fort Mason; 415–775–0990
MARCH	Celtic Music and Arts Festival, Fort Mason; 415–392–4400. Saint Patrick's Day Parade, Market Street and Fifth Street; 415–661–2700. Tulipmania, Pier 39; 415–705–5512.
APRIL	Landscape Garden Show, Fort Mason; 415–221–1310. Macy's Easter Flower Show, Stockton Street and O'Farrell; 415–397–3333. Cherry Blossom Festival, Japantown; 415–563–2313. KQED Wine and Food Festival, Concourse Exhibition Center; 415–553–2200. San Francisco International Film Festival, call for locations; 415–992–5000. Opening Day Yachting Season, San Francisco Bay; 415–563–6363. Union/Fillmore Street Easter Celebration, Union Street and Fillmore; 415–441–7055.
MAY	Bay to Breakers, call to register; 415–808–5000; ext. 2222. Carnaval Parade and Festival, Twenty-fourth Street and Mission; 415–826–1401. Cinco de Mayo Parade and Celebration, Twenty-fourth and Mission; 415–826–1401. May through October, SummerStages at Yerba Buena Gardens (Mission Street between Fourth and Third; 415–978–2700). Noontime entertainment offered May through October ranges from music and dance to poetry (12:30 P.M. at center stage in the gardens).

JUNE

Black and White Ball, foot of Market Street; 415–864–6000.
Ethnic Dance Festival, Palace of Fine Arts; 415–474–3914.
Kite-makers Annual Father's Day Festival, Marina Green; 415–974–6900.
Haight Ashbury Street Fair, between Masonic and Stanyan; 415–661–8025.
Stern Grove Midsummer Music Festival; Stern Grove; 415–252–6252.
Union Street Spring Festival and Arts Fair, Union and Fillmore Streets;
    415–346–4446.

JULY

Comedy Celebration Day, Polo Field, Golden Gate Park; 415–771–7120.
Fourth of July Celebration and Fireworks, along waterfront; 415–777–8498.
Blue and Art on Polk, Polk Street and California; 415–346–4446.
Jazz and All That Art on Fillmore, Fillmore Street and California;
    415–346–4446.
Jewish Film Festival, Castro Theatre; 510–548–0556.
KQED International Beer and Food Festival, Concourse Exhibition Center;
    415–553–2200.

AUGUST

Festival of the Sea, Hyde Street Pier; 415–929–0202.
Golden Gateway to Gems, County Fair Building, Golden Gate Park;
    415–564–4230.
San Francisco Shakespeare Festival, Golden Gate Park; 415–666–2221.

SEPTEMBER

San Francisco 49ers football season, Candlestick Park; 415–468–2249.
San Francisco Opera fall season, call for locations; 415–864–3330.
San Francisco Symphony with conductor Michael Tilson Thomas, Davies
    Symphony Hall; 415–864–6000.
À la Carte, à la Park, Sharon Meadow, Golden Gate Park; 415–383–9378.
Opera in the Park, Sharon Meadow, Golden Gate Park; 415–861–4008.
Pacific States Crafts Fair, Fort Mason; 415–896–5060.
San Francisco Blues Festival, Great Meadow, Fort Mason; 415–826–6837.

OCTOBER

Artists' Open Studios, call for locations; 415–861–9838.
Castro Street Fair, Castro Street and Market; 415–467–3354.
Columbus Day Celebration and Parade, Columbus Avenue; 415–434–1492.
Fleet Week, week of Blue Angels fly-over; 415–705–5500.
Great Halloween Art and Pumpkin Festival, Polk Street and Broadway;
    415–346–4446.
San Francisco Jazz Festival, call for locations; 415–864–5449.
Whole Life Expo, San Francisco Fashion Center; 415–721–2484.

NOVEMBER

Harvest Festival, Concourse Exhibition Center; 707–778–6300.
San Francisco Bay Area Book Festival, Concourse Exhibition Center;
    415–861–2665.
Veterans Day Parade, Downtown to City Hall; 415–467–8218.
A Christmas Carol, Geary Theatre; 415–749–2228.
Christmas Tree Lighting, Ghirardelli Square (415–775–5500) and Pier 39;
    415–981–8030.

DECEMBER

Outdoor Ice Skating, Union Square and Justin Herman Plaza; 415–974–6900.
Celebration of Craftswomen, Fort Mason; 415–361–0700.
Nob Hill Christmas Tree Lighting Ceremony, Huntington Park; 415–474–6227.
Festival of Lights, Union Square; 415–922–0770.
The Messiah, Davies Symphony Hall; 415–431–5400.
The Nutcracker, Opera House; 415–861–1177.
New Year's Eve Block Party, foot of Market Street; 415–864–6000.
A Night in Old Vienna, Davies Symphony Hall; 415–431–5400.

GENERAL INDEX

ROMANTIC RESTAURANTS

French

Bizou ($$), 598 Fourth Street, 128
Cafe Claude ($), 7 Claude Lane, 99
Cafe de la Presse ($), 352 Grant Avenue, 99
Domaine Chandon ($$$), 1 California Drive, Yountville, 241
Élan Vital Restaurant & Wine Bar, 40
Fleur de Lys ($$$), 777 Sutter Street, 100
Zazie ($$), 941 Cole Street, 199

Italian

Alioto's ($$), 8 Fisherman's Wharf, 84
Allegro Ristorante Italiano ($$), 1701 Jones Street, 40
Bella Saratoga, ($$), 14503 Big Basin Way, Saratoga, 254
Cafferata ($$), 700 Columbus Avenue, 48
Firenze by Night Ristorante ($$), 1429 Stockton Street, 50
Pane e Vino ($$), 3011 Steiner Street, 161
Piazza D'Angelo ($$), 22 Miller Avenue, Mill Valley, 213
Tommaso's ($), 1042 Kearny Street, 48
Vicolo's ($), 201 Ivy Street, 134
Vivande Porta Via ($$), 2125 Fillmore Street, 152

Asian

Canton Tea House ($), 1108 Stockton Street, 21
China Valley Restaurant ($), 355 State Street, Los Altos, 252
Far East Cafe ($$), 631 Grant Avenue, 25
Golden Dragon ($), 816 Washington Street, 21
Isobune Sushi ($$), Kintetsu Mall, Japan Center, 148
Izumiya ($), Kinokuniya Building, Japan Center, 150
Japanese Tea Garden ($), Music Concourse, Golden Gate Park, 201
Mifune ($), Kintetsu Building, Japan Center, 148
New Asia ($), 772 Pacific Avenue, 21
Tommy Toy's ($$$), 655 Montgomery Street, 24
YoYo Bistro ($$), Miyako Hotel, 1625 Post Street, 145

German

Suppenküche ($$), 601 Hayes Street, 134

Spanish/Latin American

Andalé Taqueria ($), 2150 Chestnut Street, 174
Cafe Marimba ($$), 2317 Chestnut Street, 173
La Coqueta ($), 86 Carl Street, 199
Sweet Heat ($), 3324 Steiner Street, 173

ROMANTIC LODGINGS

ABOUT THE AUTHOR

Donna Peck has had two decades to appreciate the pleasures of San Francisco. While living in a flat atop Russian Hill, she had a blind date that changed her life. A year-long courtship ensued, in which she experienced the city as a great playground for lovers. She has written about San Francisco for Access Travel Guides (HarperCollins) and for a CD-ROM multimedia travel guide series. Her travel articles have appeared in regional travel magazines and in-flight magazines. Ms. Peck lives with her husband and daughter in a hillside bungalow whose most romantic feature is a picture-window view of the Bay Bridge and downtown San Francisco.